CW00411009

79

EXPERTS IN THE CIVIL COURTS

EXPERTS IN THE CIVIL COURTS

EXPERT WITNESS INSTITUTE

Edited by

SIR LOUIS BLOM-COOPER QC

Bencher of the Middle Temple

OXFORD
UNIVERSITY PRESS

OXFORD
UNIVERSITY PRESS

Great Clarendon Street, Oxford OX2 6DP

Oxford University Press is a department of the University of Oxford.
It furthers the University's objective of excellence in research, scholarship,
and education by publishing worldwide in

Oxford New York

Auckland Cape Town Dar es Salaam Hong Kong Karachi
Kuala Lumpur Madrid Melbourne Mexico City Nairobi
New Delhi Shanghai Taipei Toronto

With offices in

Argentina Austria Brazil Chile Czech Republic France Greece
Guatemala Hungary Italy Japan Poland Portugal Singapore
South Korea Switzerland Thailand Turkey Ukraine Vietnam

Oxford is a registered trade mark of Oxford University Press
in the UK and in certain other countries

Published in the United States
by Oxford University Press Inc., New York

British Library Cataloguing in Publication Data

Data available

Library of Congress Cataloging in Publication Data

Experts in the civil courts / Expert Witness Institute ; edited by Sir Louis
Blom-Cooper.
    p. cm.
  Includes index.
  ISBN-13: 978–0–19–929794–8 (alk. paper)   1. Evidence, Expert—
Great Britain.   2. Evidence, Expert—Great Britain—History.   3. Civil
procedure—Great Britain.   I. Expert Witness Institute.
II. Blom-Cooper, Louis Jacques.
  KD7521.E97 2006
  347.42′067—dc22

                                    2006017233

Typeset by RefineCatch Limited, Bungay, Suffolk
Printed in Great Britain
on acid-free paper by
Biddles Ltd, King's Lynn, Norfolk

ISBN 0–19–929794–0   978–0–19–929794–8

1 3 5 7 9 10 8 6 4 2

FOREWORD

For centuries now—at least five—the courts of this country have allowed opinion evidence to be given on scientific and technological matters which are beyond the knowledge and experience of judges and juries, as an exception to the rule of evidence which excluded hearsay testimony from any witnesses. It was not unusual, in times gone by, when a case related to a particular trade, to have a jury empanelled by men engaged in that trade; such jurors could more readily consider the matters in dispute. That practice was, for reasons unknown, discontinued. It was never adapted to expert evidence generally. Indeed the judges (and in earlier times, juries) have been left to decide the issues litigated by the parties who decide what evidence they need to support their claims and defences, including expert witnesses. Broadly speaking, civil litigation has remained adversarial, with the expert witnesses—at any rate historically—appearing to be as partisan as their lay clients and legal representatives. The sobriquet of 'hired gun' until recently, was not inapt, although efforts have been made over the years, culminating in the Woolf reforms of 1999, to mitigate and, so far as possible, even remove the stigma of partisanship.

Does that problem still exist today? I think the answer must, at any rate to some extent, be yes, because it seems to me to be inevitable. It is inevitable because it is human nature. I am open to persuasion that I am wrong about this, but it does seem to me that there is at least a serious risk that a person who is asked to express an opinion by a party or prospective party to litigation, however honest and however hard he or she tries to be entirely objective, will or may trim his or her opinion to meet the interests of the client, at any rate in the grey areas which experience suggests exist in almost every case. Chapter 11 in this book provides a cautionary note to those who think that the new regime for expert evidence will automatically instil an attitude of independence and impartiality on the part of experts.

That said, it seems to me that much has been done to address both this problem and many of the other problems in this field. There are the express provisions of the Civil Procedure Rules. Thus CPR r 35.3, which is entitled 'Overriding duty to the court' provides:

(1) It is the duty of an expert to help the court on the matters within his expertise.
(2) This duty overrides any obligation to the person from whom he has received instructions or by whom he is paid.

Most recently and, to my mind very importantly, the Civil Justice Council produced in June 2005 the *Protocol for the Instruction of Experts to Give Evidence in Civil Claims* (Appendix 3 to this book) which is based on advice and assistance provided by the voluntary bodies in the business of promoting the administration of justice.

I would refer to two aspects of the Protocol. They both stem from section 4. Paragraphs 4.1 to 4.6 set out the duties of experts in some detail. So far as I can see, they essentially reproduce (or at least stem from) the principles identified by Cresswell J in *The Ikarian Reefer*.[1] I cannot resist referring to that case because it was the last case I did as counsel at the Bar. I represented plaintiff ship-owners who were alleged by underwriters to have deliberately cast the vessel away. In short, it was said that they scuttled her by conniving at her grounding and, when that did not do the trick, by setting her on fire. The trial lasted some 80 days and many experts of every kind were called by both sides. Some of them sought to express opinions which were outside their own expertise—a hazard now well recognized by experts—which was one of the reasons that the judge, Cresswell J, set out what appeared to him to be the principles which expert witnesses should follow. He said this in substance:

The Duties and Responsibilities of Expert Witnesses

The duties and responsibilities of expert witnesses in civil cases include the following:

(1) Expert evidence presented to the court should be, and should be seen to be, the independent product of the expert uninfluenced as to form or content by the exigencies of litigation (*Whitehouse v Jordan*[2]). However, the note in Chapter 11 of strictures on that formula should be borne in mind (see para 11.02 below).
(2) An expert witness should provide independent assistance to the court by way of objective, unbiased opinion in relation to matters within his expertise.
(3) An expert witness should state the facts or assumptions upon which his opinion is based. He should not omit to consider material facts which could detract from his concluded opinion.
(4) An expert witness should make it clear when a particular question or issue falls outside his expertise.

---

[1] [1994] 2 Lloyd's Rep 68.
[2] [1981] 1 WLR 246, 256, per Lord Wilberforce.

(5) If an expert's opinion is not properly researched, because he considers that insufficient data is available, then this must be stated with an indication that the opinion is no more than a provisional one. In cases where an expert witness who has prepared a report could not assert that the report contained the truth, the whole truth and nothing but the truth without some qualification, that qualification should be stated in the report, 9 November 1990, per Staughton LJ. Sir Gerald Gordon's comment, quoted by Sir Louis Blom-Cooper and Roger Clements at para 11.05 below, is a useful reminder that opinions are neither true nor false, but a question of professional judgment.

(6) If, after exchange of reports, an expert witness changes his view on a material matter having read the other side's expert's report or for any other reason, such change of view should be communicated (through legal representatives) to the other side without delay and when appropriate to the court.

(7) Where expert evidence refers to photographs, plans, calculations, analyses, measurements, survey reports, or other similar documents, these must be provided to the opposite party at the same time as the exchange of reports.

The second point to which I would refer in the Protocol is para 4.7, which refers to the court's power under s 51 of the Supreme Court Act 1981 to impose costs orders on experts where their evidence has caused significant expense to be incurred and has been tendered in 'flagrant and reckless disregard' of their duty to the court. Paragraph 4.7 sets this out with direct reference to Peter Smith J's decision in *Phillips v Symes*,[3] which established for the first time that costs orders could be made against experts. There has also been a decision of Jacob J in *Pearce v Ove Arup Partnership Ltd*,[4] which established that the court can refer an expert to his professional association, if he is in breach of his duty to the court, although the disciplinary body may disagree with the judge—not a healthy state of affairs.

By referring to para 4.7 and to those cases, I do not intend to suggest that experts are regularly or frequently in breach of their duty to the court. I only wish to emphasize that in recent years the courts have taken the duties of experts more seriously than perhaps they did in the past, and that there are potential sanctions available for use, if necessary. It is hoped that the provisions of the Protocol, taken individually and together, will instil good practice throughout the system.

I also hope that CPR Part 35, the Practice Directions, the Protocol, and case law will all help to create a culture within the system which will encourage

---

[3] [2004] EWHC 2330, [2005] 1 WLR 2043.
[4] [2001] EWHC 455, ChD.

experts to put their duty to the court above the interests of their client whenever a potential conflict arises. When, as sometimes happens, an expert is asked a question which in his heart he knows should be answered in a particular way, but where he also knows that such an answer may be fatal to his client's case, he will nevertheless answer it in that way.

I have listened to many experts giving oral evidence, both as counsel and as arbitrator or judge. I have sometimes wondered what the expert would say if he had been instructed on the other side, assuming that he was supplied with the same factual material. I have also wondered whether we should have a rule that no expert can give evidence of opinion unless he was unaware on whose behalf he was instructed when he was first asked to express an opinion. I appreciate, however, that that is almost certainly not practicable.

I would like to add two further points. The first is to refer to CPR r 35.10, which provides by para (3) that an expert's report must state the substance of all material instructions, whether written or oral and by para (4) that those instructions are not privileged. That is a considerable change from the time when I was still in practice. I think some of the discussions I had with experts over the years would have been much more circumspect if the rule had been in force then.

The second point is that I sometimes wonder whether the adversarial process is a sensible way of putting expert evidence before the court. Fortunately, one of the most important improvements in recent years is to my mind the requirement in every (or almost every) case that the experts are required to meet in order to identify the real issues between them. I hope that this has reduced the amount of oral evidence required and put an end to the almost endless cross-examination which used to go on. I once had a Korean witness in a shipbuilding arbitration, whom we called Sea Water Lee. On our side we conducted a sweepstake as to how long his cross-examination would last. When his cross-examination had lasted three more days than the most pessimistic forecast, we had another sweep. I shall not identify the cross-examiner. I hope that that could not happen today. Chapter 7 provides a useful guide to experts in questioning each other and in their meetings to iron out the areas of disagreement.

Finally, there is a general point that is often overlooked by litigants and their advisers. Experts should appreciate that there is no property in a witness, including an expert witness. I was involved in a case many years ago in which the question was whether a signed charterparty was a genuine charterparty (as they said), or a document which was not a genuine charterparty that had come into existence in order to defraud the plaintiffs' bank (as we said). Our opponents relied upon a covering letter to the master of the vessel, which they relied upon as showing that it was a genuine charterparty. If the letter was genuine, it went far to show that the charterparty was genuine and intended to be acted upon by the master. The plaintiffs sought the opinion of a handwriting expert who expressed his view as to the genuineness of the letter. The expert was told that his services were no longer required. Some time later, the same expert was consulted by our side. He told us that the letter was not genuine. It then emerged that he had already advised the other side.

Our client was adamant that the expert should be called as a witness. The other side objected, but it was held by the Court of Appeal in *Harmony Shipping Co SA v Saudi Europe Line*[5] that there was no property in a witness, including an expert witness; and that we could call him. We dithered about whether we should ask him in the witness box whether he had always held the same opinion. Although the temptation to embarrass the other side was considerable, we decided not to do so. In the event, it was not necessary to call the witness, because it was conceded that the letter was not genuine. The moral of the story is perhaps that every witness is his or her own person and not the property of either party to the litigation. It did expose the weakness in asserting an expert's independence and impartiality. I remember the case chiefly because it was such fun.

By way of historical postscript to the significance of expert witnesses I recommend the extract from the judgment of Lord Campbell, Lord Chancellor, in the *Tracey Peerage* case:[6]

> There was a witness (Sir Frederick Madden) who undertook to say that it was the handwriting of about the middle of the last century. I do not mean to throw any reflection on Sir Frederick Madden. I dare say he is a very respectable gentleman, and did not mean to give any evidence that was untrue; but really this confirms the opinion I have entertained, that hardly any weight is to be given to the evidence of what are called scientific witnesses; they come with a bias on their minds to support the cause in which they are embarked; and it appears to me that Sir Frederick Madden, if he had been a witness in a cause and had been asked on a different occasion what he thought of this handwriting, would have given a totally different account of it.

I thoroughly recommend this book to experts and lawyers of all kinds. I commend the good sense, practical advice, and instruction contained in it, but I draw particular attention to the parts which I must admit I have enjoyed the most. Chief among them is the story in Chapter 1 of the part played by Judge Learned Hand, both when he was at the New York Bar and on the Bench of the famous US Federal Second Circuit Court of Appeals of the mid-twentieth century (see paras 1.01–1.10). I commend too the words of Sir George Jessel in

---

[5] [1979] 1 WLR 1380.
[6] [1839, 1843] X Clark & Finnelly 190–191.

Thorne v Worthing Skating Rink[7] and, in our times, the judgment of Sir Thomas Bingham MR in *Abbey National Mortgage plc v Key Surveyors Nationwide Ltd*[8] (see para 1.12 below).

While I do not subscribe to every opinion expressed in this work—it would be strange indeed if I did—it contains a wealth of learning and innovation. For example, whether assessors have a valuable role to play in some classes of case, notably shipping collision cases, they are not a panacea for every class of case. As I see it, the expert will continue to play a vital part in the administration of justice.

This book reflects how far the law's approach to expert evidence has developed over the years and contains many ideas for the future. I would add only this. It seems to me that in the future the courts are likely to approach expert evidence in a more inquisitorial and less adversarial way. As Sir Louis Blom-Cooper and Jacob LJ note at para 14.14 below, inquiries under the Inquiries Act 2005 are likely to be essentially inquisitorial in nature and even in form. I have always thought the adversarial system to be less than ideal for the resolution of issues between experts. I expect the courts will in the future use their case management powers to resolve such issues in a more inquisitorial way. It may well be that, as Chief Justice Burger wrote in the extract quoted at the head of Chapter 1 of this book: 'Trials by the adversarial contest must in time go the way of ancient trial by battle and blood'.

The Right Honourable Sir Anthony Clarke
Master of the Rolls

January 2006

---

[7] (1877) 6 Ch D 415.
[8] [1966] 3 All ER 184.

EDITOR'S PROLOGUE

It is not difficult to trace the origins of this book. As soon as the Civil Procedure Rules 1998 (CPR) came into force in April 1999, the Expert Witness Institute (EWI) foresaw that the practitioners in the expert witness system—instructing solicitors, counsel, and expert witnesses—would need to be kept abreast of the case law expounding the cold print of the words of Part 35 and any Practice Directions. EWI, in conjunction with a premier international firm of solicitors, Allen & Overy, published in 2001 a compendium of cases from April 1999 to April 2001. Joanna Day and Louise Le Gat (both assistant solicitors at Allen & Overy) did all the arduous work uncovering the decisions from the courts and analysing their contents, accompanied by astute commentaries. So impressive was the exercise that the Governors of EWI decided that a major book, scholarly but essentially practical, should be produced by the time of the seventh anniversary of the CPR. Since Misses Day and Le Gat felt unable to undertake such a major research and literary exercise, it fell to me to be requested by my fellow Governors at EWI to edit this book with the assistance of notable contributors from among those who have been concerned with this burgeoning aspect of civil litigation.

Much of the present public concern about the quality of service from expert witnesses has focused on the criminal courts, particularly in cases involving the child protection system. The Criminal Procedure Rules as yet do not contain anything explicit about how the overriding objective of a fair trial applies to an expert witness, or about the form in which expert evidence should be introduced, or indeed about the use of the criminal court's case management process to define what is in dispute between experts. But draft rules in existence are consciously modelled on CPR Part 35. The Criminal Procedure Rule Committee is determinedly seeking, as far as possible, an alignment of the two sets of rules, at the same time acknowledging the distinct difference between civil and criminal proceedings. Court management may differ markedly in the criminal jurisdiction, with its higher standard of proof in jury trials, from the civil process of trial by judge alone on a standard of proof on the balance of probabilities.

It was decided that, while the merging of expert evidence in the two jurisdictions remains uncertain, even possibly unattainable, this book eschews any coverage of expert evidence in the criminal courts, although occasional references may be made (see, for example, the end of Chapter 11). That said, much of what perplexes the expert in the civil courtroom applies likewise in the forum of the Crown Court in criminal trials with juries as the fact-finders. As the House of Commons Committee on Science and Technology, in its report of March 2005, *Forensic Science on Trial*, observed, in its inquiry (which focused primarily on the use of forensic evidence by the criminal courts) 'many of the points made are of relevance to the civil courts'. A partnership (if not marriage) between the two areas of expert testimony is not yet to hand. It may come in due course.

Many experts in the field of child protection tend to give evidence in both criminal proceedings against abusing carers of children, as well as in child welfare cases in the family court. In the latter court, they function under a regime tailored to suit the primary objectives of proceedings under the Children Act 1989, which is the paramount interest of the child. That discrete regime is deserving of special treatment. Hence, we made allusion to one or two features that are relevant to civil litigation. In particular, the idea of a single joint expert is derived from the family court practice.

The leitmotif of the Woolf reforms has been to curb the unnecessary delay and expense that permeated the uncontrolled use by litigating parties of expert evidence, and CPR Part 35 was designed to do just that. It did not countenance the essence of the system which allows expert opinion to be admitted in evidence on matters outwith the knowledge and experience of judges. Hence, while this book seeks primarily to expound the provisions of CPR Part 35 and the considerable volume of case law which the new regime has spawned, some consideration has been given to the principles that lie behind the reception of scientific and technological evidence in a forensic process that is ineluctably wedded to the adversarial system of trial. Until such time as the theoretical underpinning to the system is addressed and suitably resolved, the present problems will continue to plague the courts.

The provisions of CPR Part 35 and the relevant Practice Direction are contained in Appendices 1 and 2 below. So too is the long-awaited *Protocol for the Instruction of Experts to Give Evidence in Civil Claims* (June 2005), a long-winded title designed to placate the two factions within the expert witness agencies, the one indicating the primacy of litigious practices, and the other contending that the Protocol should first and foremost be designed to achieve consensus within the rival factions. While the Protocol helpfully fleshes out the bare bones of CPR Part 35, it condescends to nothing beyond the boundaries of the established expert witness scene. It replaces the more adventurous *Code of Guidance on Expert Evidence*, published in December 2001 by an independent working party under the auspices of the Civil Justice Council. That body will need to update its Protocol before too long, when case law will inevitably explore and expand the ambit of CPR Part 35.

The task of producing the book has been lightened by the collaborative efforts of the contributors. If tardiness in delivery of manuscripts is a perennial feature of such books, the experience on this occasion was less severe on the editor than might have been expected. No one was seriously out of time. While contributors produced their essays timeously, the editorial function of ensuring harmony between the contributed chapters proved, predictably, arduous. That task was rendered less irksome, however, through the astonishing assiduity of Mrs Lorraine Bennett. It was she who produced the consistent style through the manuscript which OUP strictly demands from authors and their amanuenses. She well deserves from the editor, contributors, and the staff of EWI our profound and eternal gratitude. The texts of the various chapters were routed through the offices of EWI, with commendable efficiency. Brigid Lohrey, in particular, was masterly in gathering in all the answers to the copy-editor's queries and last-minute corrections from contributors. They too deserve my thanks.

EWI is most grateful to the Master of the Rolls, Sir Anthony Clarke, for his elegant foreword. His willingness to pen a foreword at the outset of his term of office in October 2005 is a mark of the importance he attaches to a serious work on expert evidence.

Catherine Redmond and Jonathan Kingham, commissioning editors at OUP, were helpfulness personified. The exacting standards of legal publishing which OUP sets were fully maintained, to the benefit not just to the publishing house with its distinctive imprimatur, but also to EWI and the authors of the book. Our thanks are also due to Rowena Lennon, OUP's Production Editor. Kathryn Swift performed the essential task of copy-editing with meticulous care and an eagle eye for detail. The excellence of the finished product enhances whatever merits the contents may attract at the hands of reviewers.

Sir Louis Blom-Cooper QC

April 2006

CONTENTS—SUMMARY

CONTENTS

LIST OF CONTRIBUTORS

Sir Louis Blom-Cooper QC

Sir Louis Blom-Cooper QC was called to the Bar by the Middle Temple in July 1952 and practised at the Bar until December 2004. He took silk in 1970 and became a Bencher in 1978. He practised mainly in the field of public law, having been involved as counsel in the emergence of judicial review from 1977. He was a Deputy High Court Judge from 1992 to 1996 and a Judge of Appeal in the Court of Appeal of Jersey and of Guernsey from 1988 to 1996. Sir Louis was chairman of the Expert Witness Institute from 1997 to 2005 in succession to Sir Michael Davies, a retired High Court judge and EWI's first Chairman. Sir Louis has remained a Governor of the EWI. His published works include (co-author with Professor Gavin Drewry) *Final Appeal* (OUP, 1972), a study of the House of Lords in its judicial capacity, and (with Professor Terence Morris) *With Malice Aforethought* (Hart, 2004), a study of the crime and punishment of homicide.

Suzanne Burn

Suzanne Burn BA (Hons), MPhil, LLB, LLM (Advanced Litigation) is a district judge, sitting at Bromley County Court. She has been a member of the Civil Justice Council since 2001 and currently chairs the Serious Injury Committee. After a first career in the civil service, local government, and at the local government ombudsman, Suzanne became a solicitor in 1989. She specialized in serious personal injury claims and other complex litigation. From 1994 to 1999 Suzanne was Secretary to the Law Society's Civil Litigation Committee, leading the Society's work on the Woolf reforms—in particular she drafted the first two pre-action protocols for personal injury and clinical negligence, and was a member of the working party that produced the Code of Guidance on Expert Evidence. From 1999 to 2005 she had a portfolio of roles including sitting as a deputy district judge, acting as a legal assessor to the GMC, as a non-executive Director of the London Ambulance Service, chairing the Clinical Disputes Forum (from 2003), and lecturing and training on civil litigation, including to expert witnesses. Suzanne writes widely on civil litigation including for *Civil Procedure (The White Book)*, *Litigation Practice* (both Sweet & Maxwell), and *Civil Litigation Handbook* (Law Society—for which she is editing the forthcoming second edition). She is also the author of *Successful Use of Expert*

Witnesses (Shaw & Sons, 2005) and co-author of *The Expert Witness in Court* (Shaw & Sons, 1999) and *Healthcare Professionals as Witnesses to the Court* (Greenwich Medical Media, 2000).

Roger Clements

Roger Clements FRCS, FRCOG (ED), FAE was a Consultant in Obstetrics and Gynaecology at North Middlesex Hospital from 1973 to 1994, and Medical Executive Director from 1991 to 1994. He is a Risk Management Consultant with QRM Healthcare Ltd. He is a Member of the Clinical Disputes Forum, a Founding Governor of the Expert Witness Institute, and a Fellow of the Academy of Experts. Roger has prepared over 3,000 medico-legal reports for civil (claimant and defendant) and criminal trials, disciplinary inquiries, and employment tribunal hearings. He has given oral evidence on some 90 occasions in the High Court and county court, in disciplinary inquiries, at the General Medical Council, and in employment tribunals, in the United Kingdom, the Republic of Ireland, and New South Wales. Roger was Founding Editor of Clinical Risk, and has written and edited a number of books including *Safe Practice in Obstetrics and Gynaecology* (Churchill Livingstone, 1994) and *Risk Management and Litigation in Obstetrics and Gynaecology* (RSM/RCOG, 2001). He has contributed to *Powers and Harris: Medical Negligence* (Butterworths) and C Vincent (ed), *Clinical Risk Management: Enhancing Patient Safety* (BMJ Publishing Group).

Penny Cooper

Penny Cooper BSc (Hons), Barrister is Associate Dean at the Inns of Court School of Law and Director of Knowledge Transfer at the City Law School, London. She qualified as a barrister in 1990. During her 11 years at the Bar she became a specialist in child protection law. She now regularly designs and delivers training for professionals. Her specialist topics include expert witnesses and witness preparation.

Penny writes for the *New Law Journal, Counsel,* and *LINK,* the magazine of the Association of Women Solicitors. She has also updated and amended *Reporting to Court—A Handbook for Social Services* (TSO). Her training expertise and materials have been relied on by the DfES in its recent Information Sharing consultation.

Evelyn Ebsworth

Evelyn Ebsworth CBE, PhD, MA, ScD, DCL, FRSC, FRSE has been Professor Emeritus of the University of Durham since 1998; and is a corresponding member at the Academy of Sciences, Gottingen. He was the first Chairman of the Council for the Registration of Forensic Practitioners from 1998 to 2005. He was born in 1933 and educated at Cambridge (BA 1954). He was a Fellow at King's College, 1957–9; a Research Associate, at Princeton University, 1958–9; University Demonstrator at the University of Cambridge, 1959–64, and Lecturer from 1964–7; Fellow of Christ's College, 1959–67, and Tutor, 1963–7. He was Crum Brown Professor of Chemistry at the University of Edinburgh, 1967–90; and was appointed the Dean of Science Faculty, 1985–9. He was President, Dalton Division of Royal Society of Chemistry, 1976–9. His roles have also included Chairman, Scottish Universities' Council on Entrance, 1985–90; Vice-Chancellor and Warden, Durham University, 1990–8; and Chairman, Governors of The Leys School, 2003.

The Rt Hon Lord Justice Jacob

The Rt Hon Lord Justice Jacob read Natural Sciences at Cambridge, then read for the Bar and took an LLB from the LSE. He practised at the Patent Bar from 1967. From 1976 to 1981 he was the Junior Counsel for the Comptroller General of Patents and for government departments in intellectual property. He was made a Queen's Counsel in 1981. His practice often took him abroad (Hong Kong, Singapore, Europe, the United States, Australia). He was appointed to the Bench in 1993. From 1997 to 2001 he was Supervising Chancery Judge for Birmingham, Bristol, and Cardiff. He was appointed a Lord Justice of Appeal with effect from 17 October 2003. He was made Hon Fellow of the LSE in 2005. He is Vice-Treasurer of Gray's Inn. Sir Robin has written extensively on all forms of intellectual property. He is President of the Intellectual Property Institute, Hon President of the United Kingdom branch of the Licensing Executive Society, Hon President of the Association of Law Teachers, and a Founding Governor of the Expert Witness Institute. He often lectures on IP topics both in the United Kingdom and abroad. His practice at the Bar involved working with experts in many fields—scientists or engineers concerned with the technology of a particular patent case, accountants concerned with valuation of patents, and so on. As a judge of the Chancery Division and Judge in charge of the Patent List he continued to hear many IP cases. He now sits on most Court of Appeal IP cases, particularly patent cases.

Kay Linnell

Kay Linnell FCA, MBA, FCI Arb is a qualified chartered accountant, who has worked in practice, industry, government, and insolvency regulation since 1973. She is currently a Forensic Director with Smith & Williamson Ltd, one of the top ten accountancy practices in the United Kingdom, and has given written and oral evidence in civil and criminal courts, at employment and disciplinary tribunals, to tax commissioners, and in arbitrations. She is a Governor of the Expert Witness Institute, Chairman of the Examinations Board of the Chartered Institute of Arbitrators, a Court Assistant in the Worshipful Company of Arbitrators, a Certified Fraud Examiner, and a Member of the Fraud Advisory Panel. She has lectured to various societies and organizations and was a co-author of *Tolley's Accountancy and Litigation Support* (Butterworths, 1998) and sole author of *Tolley's Tax Appeals* (Butterworths, 2001).

His Honour Judge Nic Madge

His Honour Judge Nic Madge is a circuit judge, sitting at Harrow Crown Court. He was a district judge from 1995 to 2004, sitting at West London County Court. Prior to full-time judicial appointment, he was a solicitor and partner at Bindman and Partners, heading their Housing Department. Judge Madge is a member of the Senior Editorial Board of *Civil Procedure (The White Book)* (Sweet & Maxwell). He was a member of the Civil Justice Council from 2003 to 2005 and was Chair of the Civil Justice Council Experts' Committee from 2005. Judge Madge writes regularly on law and procedure, including contributions to *Law Society Gazette, New Law Journal*, and *Legal Action*. He is the author of *The Housing Law Casebook* (Legal Action Group) and joint author of *Defending Possession Proceedings* and *Debt and Housing Emergency Procedure* (both Legal Action Group). He is consulting editor on the *United Kingdom Human Rights Reports*. He was formerly a member of the Law Society's Litigation Committee, the Joint Working Party of the Bar and the Law Society on Civil Procedure (Heilbron/Hodge), and of Lord Woolf's Housing Working Party.

Paul McNeil

Paul McNeil is a Partner at City law firm Field Fisher Waterhouse. He is a graduate of Sheffield University and qualified as a solicitor in 1983. Paul specializes in personal injury and clinical negligence on behalf of claimants and has over 20 years' experience in this field. He has acted for claimants in the Clapham, Southall, Ladbroke Grove, and Potters Bar rail accidents. He was a member of the Medical Negligence/Planning Group for Lord Woolf's *Access to Justice* Reports. He edited and contributed to *The Medical Accidents Handbook* (Wiley, 1998). He contributed a chapter on English product liability law to *International Product Liability* (Campbell & Campbell, 1993). He is a member of the Law Society and AvMA (Action against Medical Accidents) Medical Negligence Panels. He is also a member of APIL (Association of Personal Injury Lawyers).

Klim McPherson

Klim McPherson PhD, FFPH, FMedSci is Visiting Professor of Public Health Epidemiology in the Department of Obstetrics and Gynaecology at the University of Oxford. He has worked on the epidemiology of women's health for over 30 years. He was Professor of Public Health Epidemiology at the London School of Hygiene and Head of the Health Promotion Sciences Unit at the School. He has also worked for the MRC at Bristol University and was a Fellow of Nuffield College and in the Department of Public Health and Primary Care. He has recently sat on the Committee on Safety of Medicines and is Vice-Chair of the National Heart Forum. He currently sits on the Public Health Interventions Advisory Council and a Guideline Development Group of the National Institute for Health and Clinical Excellence (NICE) and is on the Women's Health Expert Advisory Group of the Medicines Commission. He is a Governor of the Health Foundation. Currently his main research interests lie in the prevention of coronary heart disease from a young age, the long-term effects of menopausal treatment, and in determining the optimal treatment for women with menstrual problems. He is a Fellow of New College Oxford.

Brian Thompson

Brian Thompson was Company Secretary of the Expert Witness Institute from 1997 to 2006. He is a Fellow of the Institute of Chartered Secretaries and Administrators and was President of that organization in 1992. A graduate of Cambridge University, he spent some 30 years in the insurance industry in the company market, insurance broking, and Lloyd's of London before establishing his own management consultancy in 1993. His various assignments have included working for the Government Know-How Fund in Slovakia, assisting the National Association of Pension Funds in creating their Voting Issues Service, acting as a non-executive director to a software training company, and as the company secretary to a large family company in Norwich. He contributes regularly to *New Law Journal, Barrister* magazine, and other legal journals on issues relating to expert witnesses. He is a Fellow of the Chartered Insurance Institute and a Fellow of the Institute of Risk Management, in which capacity he was involved as a Governor and sometime Treasurer in the initial establishment of that organization. He is a Freeman of the City of London and Liveryman of the Worshipful Company of Chartered Secretaries and Administrators.

TABLE OF CASES

TABLE OF LEGISLATION

1

HISTORICAL BACKGROUND

Trials by the adversarial contest must in time go the way of the ancient trial by battle and blood.

Chief Justice Warren Burger of the US Supreme Court in a speech to the American Bar Association, Las Vegas, 12 February 1984

Shortly after he was promoted to the US Second Circuit Court of Appeals in **1.01** 1925, that great American jurist, Judge Learned Hand, was confronted with the problem of expert evidence in a patent case,[1] a subject upon which he had expatiated in a seminal article in the *Harvard Law Review* a quarter of a century earlier[2] when, aged 28, he was a practising lawyer. The case concerned a claim for infringement of a patent for electrically welding thin-walled tubing, the kind of tubing that was appropriate for use in bicycle wheels. The defendant to the claim had developed a faster method of welding, the issue in the case being whether that infringed the plaintiff's invention. To arrive at a verdict, the court had scrutinized a wealth of complex electrical, metallurgical, and mechanical evidence.

Judge Learned Hand was wont to rely upon his own resources, as when he drew **1.02** on his early training in geometry. He wrote:

> Since, in the defendant's practice, the pressure is radial to the tube, the greatest pressure will be at the centre of the line of contact . . . Geometrically he is right, since the pressure must vary with the cosine of the angle which the direction of the pressure makes with the tangent of the point of contact.[3]

---

[1] *Elyria Iron Steel Co v Mohegan Tube Co Inc et al* 7 F (2d) 827 (1925).

[2] 'Historical and Practical Considerations Regarding Expert Testimony', 15 Harvard Law Review 40 (1901).

[3] Cited in G Gunther, *Learned Hand: The Man and the Judge* (1994) 312.

How many judges today, recalling their limited scientific knowledge of school days, have likewise found themselves able, at least to master the elements of scientific evidence?

1.03 But, like Judge Learned Hand, in order to probe the mysteries of scientific knowledge—in the instant case, welding—how often have judges had to grapple with the conflicting evidence by the expert witness on each side? Judge Learned Hand concluded that there had been no infringement; the patent produced its weld through a 'single condensed shot' of current, while the defendant instead had achieved his 'culmination of heat' from 'several diffused shots': QED, there was no infringement. A short, modest dissent followed:

> I have not, however, been able to persuade my brothers to my view, and that inability has, very naturally, I think, added to the circumstances. The system which submits such questions to the decision of laymen upon the evidence of partisan experts apparently satisfies the profession. I have said elsewhere what I think of it; it would serve no purpose to repeat. As to this complicated case it seems highly undesirable to spread on the books my reason in detail: they follow in substance the testimony of Waterman and Campbell [experts called for the defendant]. I can only say that the plaintiff has not convinced me, and I suppose that that means that I dissent.[4]

1.04 The reference to 'elsewhere' was to Judge Learned Hand's *Harvard Law Review* article in which he had expressed his hostility to the prevailing Anglo-Saxon system of using partisan experts instead of court-appointed experts. And so, in the welding case, he noted: 'The system which submits such questions to the decision of laymen upon the evidence of partisan experts apparently satisfies the profession'. But, in his view, it was a very poor system.

1.05 In his *Harvard Law Review* article, after expounding the common law's treatment of scientific and technical knowledge beyond the understanding of the court, Judge Learned Hand argued that judges and juries should be aided, in resolving the contending submission of the parties' expert witnesses, by an advisory tribunal of independent, court-appointed experts. His advocacy has fallen on deaf ears among reformers of the adversarial form of trial in the Anglo-Saxon legal systems. But the critical question, how best can the legal process effectively use expert knowledge, wherever it will aid in settling disputes, is as stark in 2006 as it appeared to be in 1925, and for centuries before that. The Woolf reforms (which are covered in the rest of this book) singled out the unacceptable delay in litigation and the cost of experts for urgent reform; it did not confront the dilemma of the mode of adducing expert evidence in the civil jurisdiction, although it sought to get rid of the 'hired gun' that traditionally

---

[4] *Elyria Iron & Steel Co v Mohegan Tube Co* 7 F (2d) 827, 831 (1925), cited in Gunther (n 3 above) 312 and 729, n 82.

characterized litigation, even in recent times. The expert's overriding duty to the court theoretically propounds that role.

Since at least the middle of the sixteenth century, the courts in England **1.06** have allowed experts to give opinion evidence. In strikingly modern language, Saunders J in 1553 in *Buckley v Rice Thomas*[5] wrote:

> If matters arise in our law which concern other sciences or faculties we commonly apply for the aid of that science or faculty, which it concerns. Which is an honourable and commendable thing in our law. For thereby it appears we don't despise all other sciences but our own, but we approve of them and encourage them, as things worthy of commendation.

But how to accommodate evidence that did not qualify as eye-witness testi- **1.07** mony? The common law of England had already developed a rule excluding hearsay evidence. Opinions of witnesses, apart from usurping the function of the court, were hearsay. The judicial device was to establish an exclusionary rule that recognized that experts could give admissible evidence on matters scientific or technical which involved issues beyond the everyday knowledge of judges and juries. What the courts did not stop to consider, let alone develop, was any interference with the basic procedures of litigation, whereby parties conduct their disputes by determining what evidence each side needs to support its case. Experts, once allowed to give admissible evidence, were to be treated no differently from witnesses of fact relevant to the disputed issues. The courts thus retained their Olympian aloofness from the arena; court management of the litigation as a concept did not fully enter the English scene until April 1999.

The practice of leaving the calling of expert witnesses almost entirely to the **1.08** litigating parties was never really suitable, if only because the expert, bringing into the courtroom his professional ethics, could not divest himself of partisanship. There was an essential, internal inconsistency between scientific objectivity and espousal of the cause of the paying client engaged in disputatious litigation. Judge Learned Hand described the common law's exclusionary rule, not inaptly, as 'the foster mother of all absurdities'.[6]

The absurdity lies in the fact that, although witnesses in legal proceedings **1.09** cannot express any opinion, inevitably they interpret what they themselves have seen or heard, according to their everyday experience. Some experts, moreover, are called to give eye-witness testimony. Forensic pathologists who conduct

---

[5] (1554) 1 Plowden 118, 124, 75 ER 182.

[6] This polemical phrase was part of his speech to a medical audience, *Albany Medical Annals in Albany, New York*, which was the source of the *Harvard Law Review* article (n 2 above). The phrase was deleted on a protest from his cousin, Augustus Hand, see G Gunther, *Learned Hand: the Man and the Judge* (1994) 60 (n 251), 688.

autopsies give evidence of what they find in and about the dead body, as well as expressing opinion about the cause of death. In many cases—it is particularly prevalent in fraud trials—forensic accountants have to analyse documentary material, which is providing factual evidence. The difference between that testimony and expert opinion is at best indistinct.

1.10 The exclusionary rule treats the expert as an outsider to the normative process of the legal system. Tal Golan, an American scholar, has vividly described the contemporary forensic scene:

> And such the expert would stay—a freak in the new adversarial world, an incompatible and inharmonious, yet indispensable and influential, figure in the modern adversarial courtroom.[7]

A. Judicial Disapproval

1.11 Long before Judge Learned Hand excoriated the Anglo-Saxon adherence to the expert witness's form of testimony, English judges had denounced the legal procedure for experts as irrational. Thus Sir George Jessel, the outstanding Master of the Rolls, in *Thorne v Worthing Skating Rink*[8] (a patent case) wrote:

> Now, in the present instance I have, as usual, the evidence of experts on the one side, and on the other, and, as usual, the experts do not agree in their opinion. There is no reason why they should. As I have often explained[9] since I have had the honour of a seat on this Bench, the opinion of an expert may be honestly obtained, and it may be quite different from the opinion of another expert also honestly obtained. *But the mode in which evidence is obtained is such as not to give the fair result of scientific opinion to the Court* [italics supplied]. A man may go, and does sometimes, to half a dozen experts . . . He takes their honest opinions: he finds three in his favour and three against him; he says to the three in his favour: 'Will you be kind enough to give evidence?' And he pays the ones against him their fees and leaves them alone; the other side does the same. It may not be three out of six, it may be three out of fifty . . . I am sorry to say the result is that the Court does not get the assistance from the experts which, if they were unbiased and fairly chosen, it would have a right to expect.
>
> Then it is said sometimes, why does not the Court appoint an expert of its own?— a course which is sometimes taken by the Court. It is very difficult to do so in cases of this kind. First of all the Court has to find out an unbiased expert. That is very difficult. The Court does not know how many of these experts have been consulted by the parties, either in the case of this particular patent or of a similar patent. It

---

[7] Tal Golan, *Laws of Men and Laws of Nature: the History of Scientific Expert Testimony in England and America* (2004) 7. Tal Golan is Associate Professor of History of Science at the University of California, San Diego.

[8] (1877) 6 Ch D 415, 416–18, cited as a footnote to *Plimpton v Spiller* (1877) Ch D 412.

[9] See *Abinger v Ashton* (1873) LR 17 Eq 358, 374.

may turn out that a particular expert has been largely employed by the particular solicitor on the one side or the other in the case, and it is so extremely difficult to find out a really unbiased expert and a man who has no preconceived opinion or prejudice, *that I have hitherto abstained from exercising the power which, no doubt, the Court has of selecting an expert to give evidence before the Court* [emphasis supplied]. That being so, it throws the Court on its own limited resources, and they are always limited with respect to subject-matter of the patent, a matter which depends on a very great variety of circumstances; and although the Court does derive, no doubt, a great deal of knowledge from the evidence of experts, yet of course, as we all know, in a subject-matter with which a person is not familiar from long training serious mistakes may be made which will not be made by persons who are so acquainted.

A century later, the same sentiments were being judicially expressed—perhaps, **1.12** more decorously. Sir Thomas Bingham MR (now Lord Bingham of Cornhill, the senior Law Lord) said in *Abbey National Mortgages plc v Key Surveyors Nationwide Ltd*:[10]

We feel bound to say that in our opinion this argument [that the appointment of a court expert only by agreement of the parties, under Rule 40 of the Rules of the Supreme Court (now defunct) was 'pointless', since it only added an opinion whose evidence carries no more weight than any other] ignores the experience of the courts for many years. For whatever reason, and whether consciously or unconsciously, the fact is that expert witnesses instructed on behalf of parties to litigation often tend, if called as witnesses at all, to espouse the cause of those instructing them to a greater or lesser extent, on occasion becoming more partisan than the parties. There must be at least a reasonable chance that an expert appointed by the court, with no axe to grind but a clear obligation to make a careful and objective evaluation, may prove a reliable source of expert opinion. If so, there must be a reasonable chance at least that such an opinion may lead to settlement of a number of valuation issues.

By the mid-nineteenth century, the courts had veered away from a state of **1.13** obeisance towards scientists, to a state of judicial suspicion, even hostility. Thus in 1782 Lord Mansfield, confirming the admissibility of matters of opinion, had resolved that 'in matters of science the reasoning of men of science can only be answered by men of science'.[11] Lord Mansfield's decision has been represented as the onset of judicial acknowledgement of the modern practice of party-called expertise. Thus Professor James Thayer, the Harvard Law School authority on the law of evidence, wrote in 1841:

For a long time experts were thought of in the old way, as being helpers of the court . . . but at least the modern conception came in, which regards the experts as testifying, like their witnesses, directly to the jury.[12]

---

[10] [1996] 3 All ER 184, 191.   [11] *Folkes v Chadd* (1782) 3 Doug 157, 159, 160.
[12] JB Thayer, *Select Cases on Evidence* (1841) 666.

1.14 The only difficulty in the Thayer view is that the method of calling experts as witnesses was not novel in 1782. Whatever may be the true reading of Lord Mansfield's decision, about which there is academic controversy,[13] men of science could, exceptionally, give opinion evidence; the judicial view was an unwillingness to distinguish one science from another. If the proposed witness was acknowledged as an expert on the issues before the court, Lord Mansfield described his opinion, formed on given data, as proper evidence. The judicial pendulum, however, swung in the opposite direction. The view was expressed that scientific testimony which ought to be the most decisive and convincing of them all, is of all the most suspicious and unsatisfactory. But creeping distrust of scientific evidence was not only judicially expressed. The scientific community by the middle of the nineteenth century was itself in turmoil.

B. Scientists in Revolt

1.15 A campaign for reform of expert testimony, mounted by scientists and supported by law reformers, arose out of public scandals in two criminal trials of 1856 and 1859, in addition to other trials of that time. Dr Henry Letheby, a professor of chemistry and toxicology at the London Hospital and the Medical Officer for Health in the City of London, one of the more prolific and technology-minded chemists of his age, wrote a letter to *The Times* saying that the apparent contradiction of science (in the courts), 'the seeming uncertainty of its results, and the conflicting testimony of its alumni, are such as to deprive it of that value which it ought to have in the estimation of the public . . . it is clearly time that something should be done to better this condition of things'.[14]

1.16 If science was ever to become a true ally of the legal system, it must, he concluded, be taken out of the hands of the interested parties and employed methodically as an engine of the State. Dr Letheby brought his concerns in 1859 to the attention of the newly created National Association for the Promotion of Social Science (NAPSS), a collection of lawyers and social scientists engaged in promoting law reform.[15]

1.17 NAPSS had been formed, only two years previous to Dr Letheby's letter, by Lord Brougham, Lord Chancellor in 1830 and himself an ardent law reformer. Dr Letheby met in that forum Robert Angus Smith, a leading sanitary chemist at the Manchester Royal Hospital, who had been a leading witness for the defence in a pollution case in 1857. So disturbed was he by the forensic experience that

---

[13] Golan (n 5 above) 41–5.   [14] *The Times*, 27 August 1859.
[15] The newspapers labelled the title as 'sociohybrid', on which Lord Brougham expostulated to his colleagues must be either Latin or Greek, and not a bastard hybrid.

he vowed never again to appear in a court of law. Instead, he began to lobby for reform of the legal procedures to handle expert testimony. He brought his concerns to NAPSS at its meetings in 1857 and 1859 and followed it up with an opening address to the Royal Society of Arts. He proclaimed that 'because it is repugnant to our feelings to see great questions from nature played with, distorted and hidden for selfish purposes', he objected vigorously to the process. The rest of these evils 'lies in the partisan position men of science had come to occupy in the adversarial courtroom'. His words are worthy of recall:

> The scientific man in that case simply becomes a barrister who knows science. But this is far removed from the idea of a man of science. He ought to be a student of the exact sciences, who loves whatever nature says, in a most disinterested manner. If we allow him or encourage him to become an advocate, we remove him from his sphere; we destroy the very idea of his character; we give him duties which he never was intended to perform . . . we lead men who are educated to the mode of thought to act under the auspices of another . . . We teach them to study impartially and then tell them to practice with partiality. Such a division of the moral nature of man is extremely hurtful, both to the individual and to society.[16]

Tal Golan, commenting on that passage, noted how, if the scientific witness **1.18** attained the moral power to resist the circumstances and temptations that impelled him to turn advocate:

> he would still find himself unable to communicate his knowledge to the judge and the jury. No matter how carefully he arranged his testimony or how well he rehearsed his words at home with scrupulous attention to exact phraseology—in court, under the pressure of cross-examination, he would still find, that the great and the small are confounded together by the extreme skill of the practised examiner.[17]

The scientific community's preferred formula was three-fold. Scientists who **1.19** represented parties should be accorded independent status in relation to members of the Bar; evidence should be in writing, with examination and cross-examination by counsel to follow; *and the* judge *should have an assessor to examine the expert witnesses and advise the judge.* Within the Royal Society of Arts, such reforms were bandied about. Dr Smith[18] had advocated in his address to the Royal Society of Arts the contribution of a scientific tribunal before which 'the true scientist might befittingly and confidently appear', added to which there was support for the French practice of referring cases to officially approved scientists who would then submit their reports in writing.

These utterances—not to say murmurings—from the world of science were **1.20** noted and discussed in legal circles, notably in the National Association for the

---

[16] RA Smith, 'Science in our Courts of Law (1860) 7 Journal of the Society of Arts 135, 136–57.
[17] Golan (n 5 above) 111–12.   [18] Smith (n 16 above) 149.

Promotion of Social Science. The reforms, when they came in the Judicature Acts of 1873 and 1875, were, however, achieved by the side-wind of change in the mode of trial in the civil jurisdiction. The evidential rules relating to expert evidence were left untouched. Partisanship within the adversarial system also remained stubbornly impervious to attempts to eradicate it, because the legal profession so ordained it to be.

1.21   Scientific disquiet about the court's handling of expert evidence had focused inevitably on the perceived inability or incapacity of juries to comprehend the nature of testimony outside their common experience and knowledge. The reforms of civil procedure that emerged during 1873–5 were not intended, however, to make any changes in the system of jury trial; indeed the rules for practice made under these statutes expressly provided that the right to jury trial should not be disturbed. The Rules of the Supreme Court in 1883, that survived in essence until 1933, overhauled the system but did not fundamentally alter the mode of trial by jury. The significant change in relation to expert evidence, however, was as follows.

1.22   The court or judge was accorded an unfettered discretion to order trial with or without a jury only in three situations:

(1) in matters assigned to the Chancery Division;[19]
(2) any matter which before the Judicature Acts could be tried without a jury without consent of the parties—it covered all Chancery actions and all Admiralty actions; and
(3) any matter requiring *any prolonged examination of documents or accounts* or any scientific or local investigation which could not in the opinion of the court conveniently be made with a jury.

In *Jenkins v Bushby*[20] Lindley LJ thought that there was always a power, prior to 1875, in the common law courts to order a trial without a jury, although no authority was cited, and no evidence has been forthcoming to indicate whether expert evidence was heard in cases tried by judge alone. It has been authoritatively estimated, up until the 1870s, that courts of trials were invariably conducted with a jury.

---

[19] Sir Page-Wood, Vice-Chancellor, when chairing the meeting of the Royal Society of Arts in 1860, is reported as having said that 'as a judge he had come to the conclusion that he could set very little value before evidence of opinion given by witnesses brought forward either for a plaintiff or a defendant, and in many cases he had availed himself of the privilege which was accorded to judges of the Chancery Court, of calling in disinterested witnesses in matters of opinion', see Smith (n 16 above) 135, 146, cited by Golan (n 5 above) 117.

[20] [1891] Ch 484, 490.

C. The Modern Mode of Trial

Complaints about the cost and delays in proceedings at common law—shades **1.23** of Woolf—led to the introduction of restrictive legislation in the Administration of Justice (Miscellaneous Provisions) Act 1933, the restrictions on jury trial having been recommended by the Business of the Courts Committee, Interim Report in March 1933. This applied only to the King's Bench Division, and took away any absolute right to jury trial. Jury trial thereafter was to be ordered where there was a charge of fraud, or the case was one of libel, malicious prosecution, seduction or breach of promise of marriage, unless the court was of opinion that the trial required any prolonged examination of documents or accounts or accounts of any scientific or local investigation which could not conveniently be made with a jury.

In short, every civil trial involving expert evidence on scientific matters was **1.24** conducted by a judge sitting alone, probably at least from 1870 onwards, and certainly from 1933 to this day. The furore of the 1860s was thus dissipated by the emerging factor that the judiciary became the decision-maker, for whom the scientific world had dutiful respect for their capacity to understand and adjudicate fairly upon scientific evidence. Even in the consultation process in *Access to Justice* one does not detect anything approaching rumblings from the scientific community about civil court decisions; indeed, it was a deep concern for the handling of expert evidence in the criminal courts that prompted consideration of the establishment of the Council for the Registration of Forensic Practitioners in the late 1990s,[21] alongside the Woolf reforms in the civil jurisdiction which was promoted by other, more immediately pressing concerns, mainly, costs, and delay.

D. Reliability of Experts

There is a tendency today to talk of this as history. But has the new law's **1.25** pronouncement in the Civil Procedure Rules, that an expert has an overriding duty to the court (which no doubt was designed to accord an independent status to the expert witness), really changed the scenery? The assumption that science (particularly forensic science) is itself objective, has been successfully challenged. Saks and his colleagues[22] published a paper in 2003, that documented a large body of research showing how bias was universally present in scientific analysis.

---

[21] See Chapter 2 below.

[22] MJ Saks, DM Risinger, R Rosenthal, and W Thompson, 'Context Effects in Forensic Science: a Review and Application of the Science of Science to Crime Laboratory Practice in the United States' 43(2) Science and Justice 77–90 (2003).

If the expert does not become part of the client's advocacy team, there is always a further danger that the expert is misled by his own beliefs from any evidence that challenges them, and he becomes an advocate for his own opinion. Which is worse? Alternatively, it should be possible to reduce the court's reliance on experts if greater attention were paid to validated measurements, in preference to scientific opinion.[23]

1.26 Courts in England have been left, unassisted legislatively, to determine ad hoc, the relevant expertise and the qualifications for the provision of the expertise. The sufficiency and the relevance of the expert's specialized knowledge and skills have rarely involved any questioning of the particular expert.[24] It has been left to the parties to decide who will give the expert evidence, although since April 1999 the court will decide whether the evidence can be called, and how many experts can be deployed. The quality of the expertise, however, may emerge only as a result of an assault by the opposing advocate, on the basis of specialized knowledge from the opponent's expert. In the United States of America there has been increasingly an insistence upon testing the quality of expertise. Incorporated into the concept of 'knowledge or skills' there has been developed a criteria of soundness. That led to the US Supreme Court justifying the employment of the concept of reliability as a precondition of evidential accountability. Rule 702 of the Federal Rules of Evidence thus provides:

> If scientific, technical, or specialized knowledge will assist the trier of fact to under-stand the evidence to determine a fact in issue, a witness qualified as an expert by knowledge, skill, experience, training or education, may testify thereto in the form of an opinion or otherwise, . . .

1.27 In *Daubert v Merrill Dow Pharmaceuticals*[25] 'knowledge' was held to connote 'more than subjective belief or unsupported speculation'. The term applies to any body of known facts or to any body of ideas inferred from such facts, or accepted as facts on good grounds. Proposed testimony must be supported by appropriate validation on good grounds based on what is known. The *Daubert* principle reflects a long-standing characteristic of US law on expert evidence, that judges will refuse witnesses to give evidence whenever their qualifications are neither relevant nor sufficient. A typical example of the power of refusal is the case of *Bellamy v Payne*.[26] An orthopaedic surgeon was held not to be qualified as an expert witness in a case of professional negligence involving

---

[23] Professor Colin Berry, 8th Sir Michael Davies Lecture, delivered at the AGM of the Expert Witness Institute, 26 April 2005.

[24] A rare instance of (part of) an expert's evidence being held inadmissible, wrongly so, by the Court of Appeal (Criminal Division) in *R v Dudley* [2004] EWCA Crim 3336. The expert was versed in road traffic conditions.

[25] 509 US 579 (1993).   [26] 403 SE 326 (1991).

podiatry (a form of chiropody) because the proffered witness had admitted (1) to keeping up with the contemporary literature *only* on a yearly basis; (2) to have seen only a small number of patients treated by podiatry; and (3) never to have attended a course of lectures given by podiatrists. US law demands great care in examining the basis of allowing experts to give opinion evidence. The effects of *Daubert* have been to exclude aspirant expert witnesses, rather than to admit their opinion evidence. (Questions arise whether the reliability of non-scientific evidence should be treated by the same criteria for evaluating the trustworthiness of forensic science evidence.)

E. Court-Appointed Experts

Historically, there does not appear to have been any legal obstacle to experts   **1.28** being called by the court to give opinion evidence. As early as 1619 in *Alsop v Bowtrell*,[27] a case concerning the legitimacy of a child, physicians testified that it might well be that a woman bore a child 40 weeks and 9 days after her husband's death, and yet it would be his child, because the delay in delivery could be the result of 'ill-usage and lack of strength'. The judges accordingly directed the jury that what the physicians said might be right. As an early example of the court's reception of expert opinion into evidence, it was notable that the witnesses were not stated to have been called by either side. From the meagre report of the case, it appeared that the physicians satisfied the judges as to the reliability of their conclusions before the evidence was put to the jury. The court finally found the physicians' general proposition to be valid, and delivered it as a dictum to the jury to use in its verdict. In the *Worthing Skating Rink* case,[28] Sir George Jessel noted the court's power to call its own expert had not been resorted to simply because the profession likes to keep control of who was to be their witnesses. And there is no evidence that the power has been exercised in modern times, at least not without the agreement of the litigating parties.

By the beginning of the nineteenth century, the exclusionary rule had become   **1.29** well established, and there appeared to be no restriction on experts being called by the parties to litigation, the court (judge and jury) actually taking no part in adducing expert evidence. In *Beckwith v Sydenham*,[29] a marine insurance policy case, Lord Ellenborough, on an objection to opinion evidence being given by eminent surveyors, held: 'As the truth of the facts stated by them was not actually known, that opinion might not amount to much, but still it was admissible evidence'.

---

[27] (1619) Cro Jac 541, 79 ER 464.
[28] *Thorne v Worthing Skating Rink* (1877) 6 Ch D 415.   [29] (1807) 1 Camp 116.

1.30 Given the fact that decision-making was exclusively a matter for the jury in an adversarial form of litigation, the courts were content to leave the adducing of evidence, expert or otherwise, to the disputing parties. But there would have been, nevertheless, no objection to the court being 'advised' or 'guided' by expert testimony, if it chose to seek assistance for judge and jury. With the virtual abolition of the jury in civil cases in 1934, there arose the opportunity for judges, as sole decision-makers, to make use of the assessor system, which became a general statutory power.

1.31 The expert witness system (if it be apt to describe a framework of prescribed rules of court on practice and procedure, supplemented by an uncoordinated crop of judicial decisions, as a system) had not been subjected to any official study or review until it was put under the spotlight by Lord Woolf in his general survey for the Lord Chancellor in the mid-1990s, to modernize the whole range of civil litigation. In his interim report on *Access to Justice*, Lord Woolf said that, apart from issues relating to discovery (the disclosure of documentary material by parties to litigation) the subject of experts provided the greatest concerns of costs and delay to parties taking their disputes to the courts. 'The need to engage experts had become incrementally a source of excessive expense, delay and, in some cases, increased complexity through the excessive or inappropriate use of experts'.[30] Concern was expressed about maintaining experts' independence from the party instructing them, but that was not reflected in the reforms.

F. Lessons from the Family Courts

1.32 Expert evidence in civil litigation had been much influenced—and post-Woolf continues to be influenced—by the experience of the family courts which, at least since the coming into force in October 1991 of the Children Act 1989, are essentially non-adversarial, since the court is concerned with the best interests of the child whose welfare is the court's paramount consideration. As the Court of Appeal said in *Oxfordshire v M*[31] in 1994, citing the precise words of the judge of first instance: 'the game of adversarial litigation had no point when one is trying to deal with fragile and vulnerable people like small children. Any other consideration must come second to reach the right conclusion, if possible'.

1.33 The role of the expert in family cases is to provide 'independent assistance to the court by way of objective, unbiased opinion, in relation to matters within his expertise'. Expert evidence presented to the court must be, and be seen to be,

---

[30] *Access to Justice*, Interim Report (June 1995) ch 23, Experts <http://www.dca.gov.uk/civil/interim/woolf.htm>.

[31] [1994] Fam 151. See also Cazalet J in *Re J (Child Abuse: Expert Evidence)* [1991] FCR 193.

the independent product of the report, uninfluenced by the instructing party.[32] In terms similar to CPR r 35.3, an expert in family proceedings owes an overriding duty to the court that takes precedence over any obligation to the person from whom he has received instructions or by whom he is paid.[33]

Court management, which had not been a prominent feature of civil litigation **1.34** before April 1999, was imposed on family court judges, largely by virtue of s 1(2) of the Children Act 1989. This section provides that delay in the determination of proceedings is likely to prejudice the welfare of the child. Hence, the intervention of the court to ensure expedition became a vital aspect of the procedure. The indicative consequence was that by a rule of court no expert evidence could be adduced without the leave of the court,[34] and the filing of expert evidence is strictly timetabled. Additionally, since no child should be subjected to unnecessary examination, an expert must obtain the leave of the court to carry out an examination for the purposes of any expert report in the proceedings.[35]

The concept of the single joint expert thus owes its origin to the Family Court, **1.35** which has declared a distinct preference for one expert jointly instructed. Where, however, the expert (usually medical) evidence is pivotal to the case, and where the single expert's evidence is by nature not easily challengeable, the court would 'not be slow to decline an application for a second expert'.[36] Where more than one expert is instructed in a particular scientific field, the court will direct that the experts will meet, in order to narrow the areas of disagreement, and to produce jointly a report setting out the areas of agreement and disagreement.

It was not surprising that, pre-Woolf, the judiciary in civil litigation sometimes **1.36** pointed to the practices of the family court as providing a suitable way of adducing expert evidence.[37] But the difference in the nature of the procedures for the two jurisdictions has persisted, highlighting the respective duties and dilemmas of expert witnesses.

---

[32] Children Act Advisory Committee, *Handbook of Best Practice on the Children Act* (June 1997).

[33] Detailed guidance for experts and those instructing them in family cases is now set out in a protocol on best practice, which came into force on 1 November 2003: Appendix C: Code of Guidance for Expert Witnesses in Family Proceedings, the Protocol for Judicial Case Management in Public Law Children Act Cases <http://www.hmcourts-service.gov.uk/docs/protocol-appendix-c.pdf>.

[34] Family Proceedings Rules 1991, SI 1991/1247, r 4.18(3); Family Proceedings Court (Children Act 1989) Rules 1991, SI 1991/1395, r 18(3).

[35] Family Proceedings Rules 1991, r 4.18(1); Family Proceedings Court (Children Act 1989) Rules 1991, r 18(1).

[36] *GW v Oldham Metropolitan Borough Council* [2005] EWCA Civ 1247, [2005] 3 FCR 513.

[37] See, for example, Stuart Smith LJ in *Vernon v Bosley (No 1)* [1997] 1 All ER 577.

G. Back to Woolf

1.37 Under opposition from respondents to the consultation process, to any diminution of the adversarial nature of English litigation, Lord Woolf was weaned away from recommending the imposition of court-appointed experts. But he was keen, nevertheless, to introduce a high degree of control over the use of expert witnesses as part of the overall system of court management in civil proceedings. He reaffirmed the fundamental principle that 'the English way of deciding contentious expert issues was for a judge to decide between two [sic] contrary views'.[38]

1.38 The one innovation of the Woolf reforms has been the concept of the single joint expert. Wherever it was possible to distil the scientific or technological issues on which the court needs to be expertly informed and which do not appear to be contentious, the parties would be encouraged, to the point of insistence, to employ a single joint expert. It was confidently expected that single joint experts would normally be directed to the small claims track and the fast track, and not where the issue was contentious or complex. Additionally, experts could be formally instructed by the parties only with the leave of the court to appoint named experts. Parties would be required to establish that the appropriate expense and expertise was necessary, and the experts would be available to assist the court.

1.39 If Judge Learned Hand's proposal for an advisory tribunal of independent court-appointed experts did not appear to have been noted by Lord Woolf, some slight recognition of the need for direct expert assistance to the judge was accorded. Lord Woolf had recommended in his interim report that the courts should make wider use of their powers to appoint assessors in complex litigation, a power that had been, almost exclusively, exercised in the Admiralty jurisdiction of the High Court.[39] Fears that an assessor system would tend to usurp the role of the judge seemed unfounded. Lord Woolf's recipe was that the function of the assessor—curiously, given the concern about costs, he thought that there should be two, one instructed by each party—would be to 'evaluate' the expert evidence or 'guide' the judge. Assessors would be used only in cases where the complex technical issues were engaged, but Lord Woolf did not seem to contemplate that they would be court-appointed.

---

[38] Access to Justice, Final Report (July 1996) ch 13, Expert Evidence, para 5 <http://www.dca.gov.uk/civil/final/index.htm>.

[39] In *Folkes v Chadd* in 1782, Lord Mansfield in accepting expert evidence from a civil engineer, John Smeaton, had recorded: 'When such questions come before me I always send for some brethren of Trinity House'. Although the case has long served as the *locus classicus* for the rise of partisan expert testimony, the reference to the Trinity House Brethren was the practice in Admiralty cases to the court's use of assessors and not court-appointed experts as witnesses.

Lord Woolf's proposals relating to expert evidence reflect a compromise between **1.40**
a radical reappraisal of the function of opinion evidence on scientific or technological matters beyond the expertise of the judge, and the minor adjustment of
the basic Anglo-Saxon system, so severely criticized by Judge Learned Hand.
Radicalism might be attributed to Lord Woolf, but he was no ascriber to the
English rules on expert evidence being the 'foster mother of all absurdities'.
Part 35 of the CPR largely endorses the Woolf approach—of tinkering with
the established regime of expert testimony rather than an overhaul of a system
under stress.

2

ACCREDITATION: A NOVEL APPROACH[1]

If scientific, technical, or other specialized knowledge will assist the trier of fact to understand the evidence or to determine a fact in issue, a witness qualified as an expert by knowledge, skill, experience, training, or education, may testify thereto in the form of opinion or otherwise.

US Federal Rules of Evidence, r 702

A. Introduction

In Victorian times the understanding of the material world in scientific terms **2.01** was very limited, and courts had to work within those limits. Much of the analysis of evidence had to be based on supposition. Now we understand a great deal more; with proper access to modern science and technology, the work of the courts should be both simpler and more certain. It is in the bringing of science and technology and other skills of the modern world into the courtroom that difficulties may arise: the courts must have both confidence in the expert evidence that is presented to them, and in the competence of the people who present it. The establishment of the Council for the Registration of Forensic Practitioners (CRFP) in 1999 is an attempt to help the courts identify witnesses who are competent in their own sphere of expertise and can indicate their availability to supply reports for the courts and give oral evidence. The impetus for the establishment of the Council came from those who had become worried about the quality of scientific evidence in some high-profile criminal trials. It was quickly perceived that civil proceedings were likewise affected.

---

[1] The author of this chapter is Professor Evelyn Ebsworth, the first Chairman of the Council for the Registration of Forensic Practitioners. The Council's system of registration intended to accredit all those whose forensic work provides the courts with specialist expertise and opinion evidence. Information on the Council's work can be found at <http://www.crfp.org.uk>.

17

B. Origin

2.02　The ideas that led to the establishment of the Council can be found in the Report on Forensic Science from the House of Lords Select Committee on Science and Technology that was published in 1993. A series of high-profile cases where convictions were overturned in the 1980s because of perceived flaws in expert evidence gave rise to widespread concern. There was a general feeling that some system was needed for making sure that standards in forensic science were maintained. Various suggestions were made as to how best to do this. The House of Commons Select Committee on Science and Technology concluded that a statutory body for regulating forensic science was not necessary, because of the limited development of the discipline outside the Forensic Science Service; this view could hardly be sustained today. The Royal Commission on Criminal Justice in 1993 proposed a Forensic Science Advisory Council, but the suggestion of an Advisory Board and a Register for individuals came from the House of Lords.

2.03　While the Government was considering what best to do, the Forensic Science Service consulted widely among organizations involved with forensic science, and called together a meeting of a group of interested parties. A Steering Committee set up a working group in November 1996, whose remit was to examine whether a system of self-regulation could be devised which would ensure and safeguard standards of professional competence and integrity for forensic scientists.

2.04　The Chairman of the group was Lord Lewis of Newnham; the other members were Lord Dainton, Mr Peter Cobb, and Mr Alan Hall. The group was serviced by Mrs Jill Parry, a civil servant seconded from the Home Office, and the Home Office found the money for the Group's work. It consulted very widely, taking oral and written evidence, and reported to the Steering Committee in November 1997.[2] The conclusions were clear. The Report recommended setting up a Register to be managed by a Registration Council. The Register was meant to cover all involved in the forensic process, from crime scene to court; this includes a lot of people who are not strictly forensic scientists, and so the Register was therefore called the Register of Forensic Practitioners. The title has not appealed to everyone, but it has proved impossible to find another that is comprehensive enough to describe the purpose of the proposal. The report set out the broad structure within which the Register might be established and with which the Council might work.

---

[2] *Report of the Forensic Science Working Group*, presented to the Forensic Science Steering Committee, 1 November 1997, Royal Society of Chemistry, ISBN 088404 905 3.0.

C. Starting the Council

In bringing the Council into being, invaluable help was supplied by Jill Parry, **2.05** whose secondment was allowed to continue while the Council got under way. Three others helped in the first year: Dr Bob Bramley, Chief Scientist of the FSS; Mr Ben Gunn, Chief Constable of Cambridgeshire; and Mr Tom Inch, Secretary General of the Royal Society of Chemistry. This group was known as the pre-Board. Over a year, firm proposals were devised for the working of the Council. In the summer of 1999 the first Chief Executive, Mr Alan Kershaw, was appointed; in October 2000 the Register and the Council were formally launched.

D. Principles of Registration

The four principles on which the work of the Council has been based are these: **2.06**

(1) Registration will depend on demonstrated competence against defined standards.
(2) Re-registration will be required every four to five years in order for the registrant to stay on the register.
(3) The Council will aim to be self-funded, on the basis of an annual fee paid by registrants.
(4) Registrants must accept the Council's Code of Conduct and its disciplinary procedures.

Demonstration of competence—the process of assessment

The assessment of competence against defined standards is central to the work **2.07** of CRFP. The standards are related to broad principles that are agreed within the framework of the Council, but the details vary widely from specialty to specialty. In each specialty, the criteria have been developed in working groups of people acknowledged to be experts in that specialty. They have then been discussed extensively within the appropriate community, and modified in response to comments made. Pilot studies were run for all the specialties for which the Register has been opened, even for those (such as science) where standards were already well established.

Though qualifications and references are seen as important, the assessment **2.08** concentrates on the cases that an applicant has handled. Since the volume of work an applicant is likely to have done varies a lot from specialty to specialty, procedures vary as well. The process is deliberately elaborate in order to achieve credibility with both the forensic science community and the courts of law.

When someone applies, they fill in an application form that asks (among other things) for details of qualifications and experience. With it, they complete a case log that is returned to the office with the application form. It lists all cases that the applicant has handled within the past six months—or, if there are more than 50, the last 50 cases. (If there is only one, the assessor can ask for details of earlier work.) The office sends the papers to the lead assessor, who chooses an appropriate specialty assessor. The specialty assessor must be from a different organization, police force, or geographical area, if this is at all possible. The specialty assessor contacts the candidate directly, and asks for details of from two to six cases. After considering these, the specialty assessor reports to the lead assessor. If the recommendation is favourable, registration proceeds. If the specialty assessor is against registration, the lead assessor sends the material to a second specialty assessor. If the second specialty assessor recommends against registration, then CRFP tells the candidate that the application has been rejected. If the second specialty assessor recommends in favour of registration, the lead assessor discusses the case with the two specialty assessors and adjudicates to reach a final recommendation, with the help of a second lead assessor. If the applicant objects to the specialty assessor that has been chosen, a new one will be appointed. There is provision for an appeal against refusal to approve registration.

2.09   The assessors are vital to this process. The specialty assessors are appointed by the Council on recommendations from the lead assessors and the Panel Chairmen, and with the endorsement of their managers if they are in employment. The group of specialty assessors for a particular specialty are drawn from as wide a range of employers, types of work, and geographical areas as possible. They have to attend training sessions; regular meetings of assessors to discuss common problems are held. All the assessors must themselves be registered. In the beginning, this presented a difficulty—one that is common to all new organizations. The determination was not to register anyone without assessment, yet initially there were no registered assessors. This loophole was filled by registering the first group of assessors simultaneously, each of whom was assessed by another applicant assessor.

2.10   Each specialty has a lead assessor. The lead assessors are usually members of the Assessment Panel for their sector; in any case lead assessors keep in touch with the panel chairmen, as well as with the specialty assessors.

2.11   To make sure that applications for registration are dealt with according to the Council's rules, three process verifiers were appointed. These people are academics with an interest in the Council's work, but are not, and would not be registered. They look at sample applications, usually chosen at random, once they have been through the system. They provide a check that is in some sense external to the Council's regime.

Re-registration every four to five years

2.12 Re-registration at regular intervals has been a fundamental element in the principles on which the Council was based, a process at that time relatively unusual in professional bodies. Today it is seen as expected, indeed necessary. Where bodies have run for many years, introducing re-validation can be difficult and contentious; many members of such bodies believed that, once they were registered, they were there for life. The Council decided to ask for re-registration every four years. It is based on much the same process as initial registration: cases handled while the candidate has been registered are considered, just as the case records were considered in the initial application. To make the process easier, those on the register are encouraged to submit a return of the cases they have handled every year, so that at the end of four years there should be little more for the candidate to do.

Council funding

2.13 The original objective was to make sure that CRFP was seen as independent of Government. In the early stages, however, there was no income from registration fees. Without the help and financial support of the Home Office, the Council could never have begun its work. When the Council might become financially independent was determined by two factors: the level of the annual fee and the rate of registration. For the first registrations an annual fee of £125 was decided upon, high enough to give a reasonable prospect of financial independence within three to five years. This fee was not changed in the early years, except for adjustments for inflation; recently it has been increased by rather more than the rate of inflation, but there are no plans for a very substantial increase, which would probably be counter-productive.

2.14 The rate of registration, however, has been slower than hoped for. As a result, financial support from the Home Office remains necessary. The proportion of the Council's income that comes from the Home Office is of course much less than it was in the beginning, but there are matters like the building-up of a reserve fund to deal with potentially very large costs of extended disciplinary hearings that still have to be provided for in financial planning. The Home Office commissioned consultants to support CRFP in preparing a detailed and robust business plan. This proved exceedingly valuable in providing Ministers with reliable information on which to base decisions about future funding. Agreement has now been reached with the Home Office for financial support for the Council that will taper off over the next five years.

Code of conduct and disciplinary procedures

2.15 The Council's Code of Conduct was devised through very broad consultation within the community, and approved by a wide range of representative bodies, including the expanded Steering Committee. It is generally compatible with Codes of Conduct of other groups involved with the forensic process. It includes a clear statement that a witness's duty is to the court and an obligation on anyone on the Register not to give evidence on subjects outside his or her recognized expertise.

E. Management of the Register—Administrative Structures

2.16   The Council for the Registration of Forensic Practitioners is a company limited by guarantee. It meets three times a year, and is responsible for decisions on policy as well as for the proper conduct of the system that reports to it. Its membership is broadly based, and in the original constitution was specified as follows:

> Chairman
> Three nominated members:
>> A judge, nominated by the Department of Constitutional Affairs
>> A representative of the Home Office, appointed by the Home Secretary
>> A representative from the Scottish Office.
> Eight members appointed in consultation with each of the following groups:
>> The Law Society
>> The Bar Council
>> The Association of Chief Police Officers and ACPO (Scotland)
>> The Learned Societies (the Royal Society of Chemistry and the Institute of Biology)
>> The United Kingdom Forensic Science Liaison Group
>> The General Medical Council
>> The Sector Skills Council
>> The Consultative Forum—see below.
> Five ex-officio members: these are the chairmen of the (potentially five) Sector Assessment Panels.
> Three members elected by those on the Register.
> Three co-opted members, chosen from outside the professions involved in the work of the Council and normally described as lay members; one of these to be an eminent scientist, proposed by the President of the Royal Society.

2.17   The various boards and committees working under the authority of the Council are as follows:

(1) *The Executive Board.* This is responsible for detailed management of the Register and of registration. Initially it met more often than the Council did; in the early days meetings were held every month or six weeks, but now

it is not necessary to meet so often. There is provision for 11 members, as
follows:

Chairman

Chief Executive

Sector Assessment Panel Chairmen

Two providers of forensic services (originally one from the private and one
    from the public sector)

A barrister

A representative of the 'Standards' bodies that nominate Council members.

(2) *Sector Assessment Panels.* From the beginning there were three: Incident
Investigation, Medicine and Healthcare, and Science. These panels are the
bodies that oversee the details of the processes of assessment. Their membership is drawn from the expert communities involved in the various
sectors, and members are chosen so as to provide a balance of expertise in
the various aspects of each sector and the different organizations for which
assessors work, and to give an element of geographical diversity and representation. The jobs of the Sector Assessment Panel Chairmen are particularly important: they have a lot to do with the choice of panel members,
they have an important part to play in choosing assessors for specific applications, and they may have to help to make judgments on applications
where assessors disagree. Each specialty is assigned to one of the Sector
Assessment Panels. As the range of specialties that the Council registers
becomes larger, it is possible that the number of panels will increase;
even now there are more specialties than places on the panels. This is partly
why the lead assessors for specialties not represented on a panel are so
important.

When the Council decides to consider registering a new specialty, it
normally sets up a working group that will involve the most appropriate
panel chairman and a number of people with recognized expertise in the
proposed specialty. Where it seems fitting, this will certainly include members of the appropriate professional body, Royal College, or teaching institution. The working group will present a proposal for registration, with
criteria for the specialty assessors; this will go to the Executive Board, and
will usually lead to a pilot study. If the pilot study goes well, a definitive
proposal for opening the Register to this specialty will go to the Executive
Board and to the Council.

There are some specialties where criteria are not yet generally recognized
or agreed by the community involved. Many aspects of computer crime, for
example, are coming before the courts; they may need expert testimony, and
yet the criteria by which an expert may be recognized have not in the past
been generally agreed. In specialties like these, the working groups are
particularly important in helping to define appropriate criteria. The Register

has now been opened to some aspects of computer crime, and the related specialties of photography/imaging and telecommunications analysis will follow over the next year.

(3) *The Disciplinary Committee.*   The members of this body are not members of the Council, or of any other of its committees. They are chosen by the Council, but they act independently in response to cases that are brought under the Council's disciplinary procedures.

(4) *The Consultative Forum.*   The original Steering Committee that set up the Working Group chaired by Lord Lewis continued while the Council was established. It heard at various stages how the process was going, and generally approved of what was done. All the while its membership was expanded to include almost any group with a reasonable interest in the work of the Council, and it provided some sort of external accountability. In the Council's Constitution it was renamed the Consultative Forum. It has now been discontinued in favour of more focused groups discussing particular subjects as necessary.

F. Issues Relating to Membership of Council

2.18   Two rather different but related questions have been raised in connection with membership of Council. The Council has set its face against setting up a very large body: to keep the Council as an effective body it has been impossible to give reserved places on Council to particular interest-groups. Some groups, notably the Forensic Pathologists, asked for a place on Council as of right. This conflicts with the principles on which the Council was constructed. In addition a number of organizations and professional associations representing forensic practitioners could not be accommodated.

G. Three-Year Review

2.19   In the process of setting up the Council, an assurance was given that all the Council's procedures and structures would be reviewed after three years. The point at which the review was to start was diffusely defined, but the three-year review was completed two years ago. It proved so helpful that the Council decided to keep a three-year review as part of its normal procedures: it provides a mechanism for regular and predictable review that should help to avoid over-frequent discussions of fundamental issues.

H. Accountability

The Council is a body that faces two ways, like the Roman God, Janus. Its **2.20** inward face is easy to see: it must be accountable to its registrants. It has set about meeting this obligation in two ways. First, three places on the Council were reserved for registrants (now there are four); this gives them a voice in the Council's decisions. Annual meetings have been held to which all registrants are invited. Despite the growing number of them, fewer and fewer came; although this could be seen as a sign that they were satisfied with what the Council was doing, the Council considered that it must find other ways of consulting registrants.

The external element of accountability is harder both to define and to satisfy. **2.21** The Council was established to be independent of Government, though Government bodies are represented on the Council. The presence of the lay members on the Council gives influence on the Council's policies to people not part of its structure, but this is only a partial solution to the problem. The original Steering Committee had many members who could be seen as users of the Register; when this Committee was expanded and renamed the Consultative Forum, it was hoped, and expected that it would give the Council an element of external accountability. Fewer and fewer of its members, however, came to meetings with the Consultative Forum. This problem was considered in the three-year review, which recommended that the Consultative Forum be given up. In place of the meetings with registrants and with the Consultative Forum, the Council has proposed to hold regular Stakeholders' Conferences; the first is planned for September 2006. More generally the Council is keen to find the most appropriate mechanism by which to make itself accountable. It was always seen as fundamentally inappropriate for the Council to report to the Home Office, or indeed to any arm of Government. It has been suggested that the Council might be formally accountable to some element within the judiciary, and this possibility is being explored.

I. The Council and the Legal System

The reasons why the idea of the Council was first proposed lay in failures within **2.22** the criminal law. Lord Lewis's Working Group considered whether its recommendations should apply only within the criminal courts, or whether the Register should cover both the criminal and the civil codes. The Working Group concluded that in terms of forensic practitioners presenting evidence in court there was no distinction to be drawn between the criminal and the civil jurisdiction. It is as important to be able to recognize competent experts whether they are reporting to either jurisdiction. Many experts find they are asked to give evidence in both jurisdictions—this is particularly true of child abuse cases where experts appear in the criminal courts as well as in the family courts. The Legal Services Commission has shown interest in using registration with CRFP as an important criterion when considering whether to fund particular experts.

J. Difficulties Encountered

2.23 On the whole, the Register has developed smoothly, though registration has been slower than hoped. In the process of establishing CRFP, a number of difficulties have arisen and those that are significant are set out below. Many of them are common to other processes of registration.

Reluctance to register

2.24 Though there was a remarkable level of general enthusiasm for setting up the Register, some forensic practitioners have displayed reluctance to register. Some of this reluctance comes from a suspicion that the Register will not carry weight with the judges; this suspicion is steadily being removed as the Register is seen to be valued within the judicial process. Some of it comes from simple inertia: 'Since the scheme is voluntary, why should I register?' Management pressure, in bodies like the Forensic Science Service, is doing a lot to reduce the significance of this attitude. Some stems from a sense among experienced experts that they need no attestation of their competence beyond their qualifications and even their membership of a professional body. This sense is not appropriate in the modern world. The need for external accountability is generally recognized in public life; even professional bodies are not seen as necessarily external, particularly when they exist partly to look after the interests of their members. Furthermore, someone giving evidence in court is primarily giving a legal service, which is not something that most professional bodies have been set up to deal with. This explains why Lord Lewis's Working Group was keen to set up a Registration Council and not a professional association (even of multiple professionals).

2.25 The Council works closely with appropriate professional bodies in drawing up criteria for registration; members of professional bodies must always be involved in every stage of registration, and the Council has never sought to displace any professional body. On the other hand, even the most distinguished and experienced of experts may fail to take account of new developments; external and regular registration is seen as important in maintaining public confidence in the essential part played by experts in courts.

Misunderstanding of the intentions of CRFP

From the beginning CRFP has been insistent that registration must not be **2.26** compulsory. There are still people who maintain that this is really what the Council wants, and others who believe that it is what the Council should want. The Council certainly does not cover all specialties that might come into evidence in courts. Some very unusual topics are brought into litigation. In these circumstances, experts may be called to give evidence only once in a lifetime. It would not be sensible to look for a mechanism to bring people like this into the Register.

It always falls to the trial judge to determine whether an expert witness is **2.27** qualified to give opinion evidence in the particular case on an identifiable issue. There is developing a feeling within the judiciary that courts should be more rigorous in their estimation of an expert's qualification to supply the evidence which is outwith the knowledge and experience of the court. Unless one or other of the parties to the litigation raises the issue of the expert's competence, it is unlikely, given the present system, that judges of their own motion will refuse to admit the evidence of an expert called by either of the parties. Accreditation will not, nor should it, replace the absolute power of the court to decide on the admissibility of expert testimony. But what the scheme of voluntary accreditation is intended to do (and hopefully will) is to provide the parties and the court with a basis of expert credibility and thus heighten the judicial awareness of the need to examine fully the witness's credibility and reliability to give expert evidence. The accredited expert will, in effect, be proffering a mark of potential acceptability to the court.

Ignorance of the Register in courts

If the Register is to have any value, it must be used in the courts. In the early **2.28** days few judges or lawyers knew of it, or of what it set out to do. There was little point in substantial publicity until there was a substantial number of names on the Register. Now that the Register is substantial, a lot has been done to spread knowledge about CRFP. The Council ran a pilot in the courts in the north-west in which a concerted effort was made to tell everyone involved about the Register. A road-show for judges and lawyers is planned for 2006–7; the Judicial Studies Board is being engaged. The Chief Executive has spoken at Judges' Conferences, and the word is spreading fast. This problem becomes less serious every day.

Incomplete coverage by CRFP

CRFP has only been open for registrations for five years. In that time the **2.29** number of registrants has increased to 2,200 with 500 more in the pipeline; the number of specialties has increased from 2 to 24, with nursing and accountancy and a number of smaller disciplines in the pipeline. Nonetheless, a huge range of specialties is likely to lie outside its compass. This will remain a difficulty, but CRFP will continue to expand the Register.

Registration of people at the beginning of their careers

2.30 Registration is based mainly on looking at casework. To be registered, a candidate must have a body of casework to present. Someone at the beginning of a career has no casework, and so cannot, by definition, be registered. This is a significant difficulty. In general, those who have applied for registration have all had a body of casework to present. The best solution is for a beginner to find someone already on the Register to act as a mentor. This will not allow the beginner to present himself or herself to a court as registered, but it will indicate the person is an aspirant expert, and this indication may suffice to gain acceptability by the court.

Problems with disciplinary procedures

2.31 If it is to be credible, CRFP must have and enforce an effective code of discipline. Matters of discipline may be used for revenge or to damage the reputation of an adversary, or to get information by disclosure that may then be used in proceedings elsewhere. For these and other reasons possibilities such as the use of mediation in the initial stages of a complaint are being explored, to see whether the adversarial element can be confined in some way.

K. Conclusion

2.32 During its short life CRFP has achieved much. It is now well established, and is a stable element in the world of standards and structures in the complicated system of ever-changing forensic activity. It has proved to be an effective body, and in general the community of forensic practitioners has been supportive and helpful. CFRP has been acknowledged by the House of Commons Science and Technology Committee in its report, *Forensic Science on Trial*[3] as an important step towards a quality control system that ensures that those who present themselves as expert witnesses are competent to fulfil that role. The report cites an extract from a letter written by the Prime Minister that 'ensuring high standards of professional competence of those experts called to give evidence is crucial to the credibility of the judicial system and the Register [of CRFP] is a tool that can do much to underpin that credibility'.[4]

---

[3] HC 96–1, 29 March 2005 <http://www.publications.parliament.uk>.
[4] ibid 61, para 134.

3

LITIGANT SOLICITOR/EXPERT RELATIONSHIP

> It was not for the Bench to qualify the expert's opinion. If a person was qualified as an expert, his or her expert opinion came along with him or her.
>
> Tal Golan, *Laws of Men and Laws of Nature* (2004) 259

A. Introduction

Expert witnesses are sometimes not very complimentary about solicitors' abilities to foster good working relationships with experts. Bond Solon, the witness training company, carries out regular surveys of expert witnesses. The following results are drawn from the 2004 survey: **3.01**

- 22 per cent of expert witnesses said they were instructed late and a further 34 per cent only just in time;
- 11 per cent said their instructions were poor and a further 39 per cent only adequate;
- 36 per cent said their fees were paid late or very late; and
- 63 per cent said there were firms of solicitors with whom they would never work again.

This is hardly a vote of confidence in solicitors. And in the author's experience **3.02** (from running seminars and training courses for expert witnesses for several years before being appointed a district judge) experts are also critical of solicitors for a number of other reasons, for example for failing to agree their fees before confirming instructions; sending a disorganized, unpaginated, and unindexed bundle of case papers with the instructions; failing to tell the expert when his report has been disclosed; not liaising over the expert's availability for trial and expecting attendance at short notice; not informing the expert when the case has settled and not providing any feedback on the expert's report or performance.

3.03 Solicitors may likewise have criticisms to make about some experts, but in one of the regular surveys carried out by the Law Society's Civil Litigation Committee of their Woolf Network, a few years after the implementation of the CPR, solicitors reported that most experts were familiar with the CPR and understood their duties to the court. It hardly needs stating, but it is important that solicitors and experts work at establishing an effective relationship if the expert's evidence is to play its full role in the resolution of the dispute, or in the trial process.

B. Anticipating the Court's Approach

Will the court give permission for expert evidence?

3.04 Before instructing an expert, even in the early stages of a dispute, litigants and their solicitors need to bear in mind the court's powers to control and manage expert evidence (these are discussed in detail in Chapter 4). In particular, the court has to give permission for evidence from an expert in a specific discipline before the party can rely on that evidence in the proceedings (see CPR r 35.4). CPR r 32.1 allows the court to exclude evidence that would otherwise be admissible, and CPR r 35.1 provides that expert evidence shall be restricted to that which is reasonably required to resolve the proceedings. The aim of the latter rule is to prevent parties introducing unnecessary expert evidence to bolster their case, as not infrequently occurred prior to CPR implementation.

3.05 The case management judge decides, usually at the stage of allocation to track, whether expert evidence is likely to assist the trial judge to decide matters that are in issue. Permission for expert evidence may be refused if the issues in dispute are mainly factual, and when documents or evidence from witnesses of fact seem likely to be sufficient to resolve those issues, particularly in low value claims where the cost of expert evidence would be disproportionate. On the other hand, expert evidence will usually be necessary in professional negligence proceedings, personal injury claims (at least a medical condition and prognosis report) and in disputes concerning specific technical or scientific matters.

3.06 The *Protocol for the Instruction of Experts to Give Evidence in Civil Claims* (see Appendix 3 below) was approved by the Civil Justice Council in July 2005 and annexed to the CPR from October 2005. The Part 35 Practice Direction was amended to require compliance with the Protocol (see Appendix 2 below). Section 6 of the Protocol reminds those instructing experts that they should consider whether expert evidence is appropriate, taking account of the principles set out in CPR Parts 1 and 35 and, in particular, whether:

(1) the expert evidence is relevant to a matter in dispute;
(2) is reasonably required to resolve the proceedings;
(3) the expert has the expertise, experience, and training appropriate to the case; and
(4) the objectives can be achieved by the appointment of a single joint expert.

Parties may, of course, instruct an expert to give advice at any stage of a dispute, **3.07** but if the court decides that evidence from that discipline is not needed to resolve the proceedings, the party will not be able to rely upon it, and may not necessarily recover the costs of the expert's report on the assessment of costs, even if they 'succeed' in the litigation (see Practice Direction—Protocols, para 4.10). Solicitors need to warn their clients of this risk, to ensure they are prepared to fund the expert's fees in any event if the court later decides expert evidence is not necessary. On the other hand, there may be occasions when the client or the solicitor would prefer to seek initial advice on the strengths and weaknesses of the case from one expert, and then if proceedings are issued at a later stage to instruct a different expert to prepare the report for the court. The first advice will remain privileged (see Chapter 6) (but the costs will not be recoverable) so the discussion with the expert can be as wide-ranging as the party or lawyer wishes and include tactics.

Permission limited to a single joint expert?

Parties and their lawyers also need to try to anticipate whether the court is likely **3.08** to order any expert evidence in the proceedings to be given by a single joint expert (see Chapter 5). This is most likely in small claims and cases allocated to the fast track, particularly for experts reporting merely on liability. It may then make sense for the expert to be selected and instructed jointly pre-action, because otherwise the court may allow an expert unilaterally instructed by one party to later become a single joint expert only if the other parties are given all relevant information about the expert's previous involvement (see the Protocol for the Instruction of Experts, para 17.5). This may mean disclosing the expert's initial instructions and first report, which would otherwise remain privileged.[1]

C. Pre-Action Protocols

It is also prudent for the parties and their lawyers, before selecting or instructing **3.09** any experts, to consider whether any of the pre-action protocols apply to the dispute, and if so what guidance is given about expert evidence.

---

[1] *Carlson v Townsend* [2001] EWCA Civ 511, [2001] 1 WLR 2415.

(1) *Personal injury.* The personal injury claims protocol requires the parties from the outset to cooperate on expert evidence. The claimant has to suggest the names of one or more suitable experts to the defendant, who has a right to object to any of those nominated within 14 days. The claimant then instructs a nominated expert to whom the defendant has raised no objections. This procedure should encourage parties to nominate only experts who are considered to be objective and independent.

(2) *Construction industry.* The construction and engineering disputes protocol requires the claimant to provide the names of any experts on whom it is intended to rely, and on which issues, in the letter of claim, and the defendant to do likewise in the letter of response.

(3) *Professional negligence.* The professional negligence protocol contains similar requirements but also recommends that where the claimant has not obtained expert evidence before sending the letter of claim, the parties should consider appointing an agreed expert.

(4) *Housing disrepair.* In the housing disrepair cases protocol, the provisions with regard to expert evidence are very detailed. Tenants are discouraged from automatically instructing an expert, unless health and safety is at risk, and parties are encouraged to instruct single joint experts where possible, with the expert inspecting the property within 20 days of appointment.

The courts expect parties to comply with the protocols; hence the above guidance should be followed when selecting and instructing any expert.

D. Selecting the Expert

3.10 Experts should always be selected carefully, particularly where their evidence is likely to be influential in the outcome of the case. The most important criteria are:

- expertise and experience in the subject,
- objectivity and independence (see Chapter 11 on this issue),
- understanding of the CPR and of their duty to the court in civil proceedings,
- their ability to write intelligible and persuasive reports to a timetable,
- willingness to deal with questions and experts' discussions efficiently and proportionately,
- that there is no conflict of interest (see below), and
- in higher value claims, to be able to give *oral* evidence competently.

Section 7 of the Protocol for the Instruction of Experts advises that the above should be established before the expert is either formally instructed or the court's permission to appoint a named expert is sought.

Qualifications and seniority in the specific area of expertise may be important **3.11** when the expert evidence is very much opinion-based, and where there are known to be disagreements between experts working in the same field. But judges are not necessarily impressed by long CVs. It is the expert's knowledge and skill in his field and ability to apply it to the issues in the case that are important. Solicitors should keep a database of experts whom the firm has instructed, which avoids defamatory comments about their performance.

Other sources of potential experts might include colleagues who do similar **3.12** work in other firms, counsel's chambers, reliable registers, and directories (for example, professional bodies expert witness sections, the experts' organizations). Obtaining an expert from an agency or directory is not without risk, as the solicitor and client will be relying upon the selection and vetting criteria of the particular organization. Directories may accept entries purely by application and payment of the required fee, although some require references from solicitors. Agencies are most likely to be useful when an expert is required in a low-value claim, particularly in a different part of the country from the solicitor's firm. There are many medico-legal agencies providing expert witness services for personal injury claims. The Civil Justice Council is working on standardized recoverable fees for these types of reports, partly to avoid disputes over agency charges. If an expert in a very specialized field is required, careful research may be necessary through the technical journals, universities, and via the internet.

E. Ensuring Expert Independence

Solicitors should be very wary of accepting clients' recommendations for **3.13** experts, especially if the person concerned has already been instructed by the client in the case, or has an ongoing business relationship with him. Clients may not be sufficiently aware of the importance of CPR r 35.3 (that the expert's first duty is to the court), and that a 'partisan' expert may be a liability in the longer term.[2] An employee or close colleague of a party is also generally unlikely to be able to demonstrate sufficient independence when the expert witness in question was a tax barrister from the same chambers as the allegedly negligent defendant.[3] Occasionally the courts have allowed reports from employees.[4] For

---

[2] *SPE International v Professional Preparation Contractors (UK) Ltd* [2002] EWHC 881 and *Hussein v William Hill Group* [2004] EWHC 208.

[3] *Liverpool RC Archdiocesan Trustees Inc v Goldberg (No 2)* The Times, 10 August 2001. This decision has been doubted.

[4] *Field v Leeds City Council* (2000) 17 EG 165 (a housing disrepair claim where the local authority wished to rely upon a report from an employed surveyor); *Admiral Management Services v Para-Protect Europe Ltd* The Times, 26 March 2002 (where the expert was an employed IT specialist).

the same reason, in personal injury claims an independent healthcare professional is preferable to one who is treating the claimant or acting as a case manager in a complex claim.[5]

F. Information about a Potential Expert Witness

3.14 An expert new to a solicitor's firm, and to the client, should provide a short CV and an outline of his expertise, both in his field and in advising in disputes and litigation.

3.15 There is a ongoing debate concerning the merits of introducing an official accreditation scheme for expert witnesses who practice in the civil field (the Council for the Registration of Forensic Practitioners offers voluntary accreditation, at presently mostly for experts practising especially in criminal cases) (see Chapter 2). The Civil Justice Council and the senior judiciary currently take the view that a compulsory accreditation scheme is unnecessary, would be expensive and difficult to administer. But the experiment of voluntary accreditation is being greatly welcomed.

3.16 The expert should also provide his terms of business, and, on request, references from solicitors or clients, and an anonymized specimen report. Where the expert evidence is likely to be crucial, or the case is particularly sensitive or of high value, the solicitor or client may prefer to meet the expert before confirming his instruction. It is also important for the solicitor and client to check that the potential expert will not have a conflict of interest, by giving the expert the names and addresses of the parties, and of the solicitors, and any other experts already instructed.

G. Selecting a Single Joint Expert

3.17 Both parties and their solicitors must agree the identity of the expert. This means that the parties should avoid nominating experts whose instructions all tend to come from claimants (or defendants). When ordering a report from a single joint expert, the court will usually give the parties a limited time to select the expert (often 14 days) failing which either party may apply to the court. In practice, few such applications are made (see also Chapter 5).

---

[5] See *Wright v Sullivan* [2005] EWCA Civ 656, [2006] 1 WLR 172.

H. Terms of Appointment

The client, solicitor, and expert should agree the basis of the expert's fees, and **3.18** the time for delivery of the advice or report before the expert's instructions are confirmed. Section 7 of the Protocol for the Instruction of Experts summarizes what should be agreed at the outset, including:

(1) the capacity in which the expert is to be appointed (party-appointed expert, single joint expert, or adviser);
(2) the services required, for example, report, attendance at court;
(3) the time for delivery of the report;
(4) the basis of the expert's charges (see below);
(5) if a party is publicly funded whether the charges will be subject to assessment by a costs officer.

Frequently, the contract will be between the solicitor and the expert. The **3.19** solicitor will then be responsible for paying the fees, unless there is a specific agreement to the client (or perhaps an insurer) doing so. For an advice or report in a routine matter, a fixed fee may be agreed. But in most cases it will be preferable for the expert to charge on an hourly rate, possibly providing an estimate of the likely fee for the initial report. Additional work, including answering written questions on the report, and preparing for and attending an experts' discussion, will usually be charged on an hourly basis. Many experts charge on a daily basis for attending court and for cancellation of court appearances within a few weeks or days of the trial. The courts have said that cancellation fees are, in principle, reasonable.[6] Other matters to be agreed include whether prior authority is necessary if the estimated fee is likely to be exceeded, and for any investigations, tests, or other disbursements, when and how the expert is to invoice and be paid, and whether interest will be charged for late payment. A solicitor or client may want an expert to agree to deferred payment of his fees, sometimes to the end of the case, particularly when the solicitor is working under a conditional fee agreement and the client is not able or willing to fund disbursements on an interim basis. This is permissible if the expert is willing (see Protocol for the Instruction of Experts, para 7.7) but the expert may reasonably choose to charge interest in this situation. But contingency fee arrangements for experts are not allowed, as this would contravene the expert's duty to the court, and compromise the expert's independence.[7] The only exception might be when the expert is assisting the solicitor and not

---

[6] *Martin v Holland & Barrett* [2002] 3 Costs LR 530.
[7] See Protocol for the Instruction of Experts, paras 7.6–7.7 and *Davis v Stena Line Ltd* [2005] EWHC 420, [2005] 2 Lloyd's Rep 13.

preparing opinion evidence for the court.[8] If the expert is to be instructed as a single joint expert, the usual arrangement is for the parties to share the fee on an equal basis. Occasionally a case management judge may impose a limit on the recoverable experts' fees when giving permission for expert evidence (see CPR r 35.4(4)). This will usually be on proportionality grounds when the proposed expert evidence is likely to be expensive in relation to the value of the claim.[9] Failure to agree the expert's fees with sufficient precision prior to confirmation of instructions can cause disputes at a later stage, which can be an unwelcome distraction to all concerned.

I. Instructing the Expert

3.20 Section 8 of the Protocol for the Instruction of Experts summarizes the matters that should be included in instructions as follows:

(1) names, addresses, and telephone numbers of parties and other relevant basic information;

(2) the nature and extent of expertise required;

(3) the purpose of the advice or report, the matters to be investigated, the main issues, and the identity of the known parties (the author would suggest the identity of other experts also and whether the expert is instructed by one party or as a single joint expert);

(4) the statements of case (if any), disclosure documents and witness statements relevant to the advice or report (the author suggests that witness statements should only be sent if they are in final form or have been disclosed);

(5) whether proceedings have been started and in which court, or are contemplated;

(6) an outline programme for the expert's work (the author suggests it is essential for the instructor to propose a clear deadline for the receipt of the advice/report with sufficient leeway built in for unavoidable delay and minor amendments);

(7) the dates of any court hearings (particularly the trial and whether the expert might need to attend) and the claim number and track to which the case has been allocated (additionally whether the court has given permission for the type of expert evidence sought).

3.21 An expert new to expert witness work in civil claims might also sensibly be sent copies of CPR Part 35 and the Practice Direction and the Protocol with the

---

[8] *R (on the application of Factortame and Others) v Secretary of State for Transport (No 2)* [2002] EWCA Civ 932, [2003] QB 381.

[9] *Kranidiotes v Paschali* [2001] EWCA Civ 357, [2001] CP Rep 81.

instructions, or the website addresses where they can be located, with strong encouragement to download and study them. The expert should also be given specific instructions for the case. These will vary greatly from case to case, but as a minimum they should include a summary of the undisputed facts, a brief explanation of the matters in dispute that are relevant to the expert's work, and any specific issues or questions that the expert is invited to address. Any materials and documents sent to the expert should be clearly listed, either in the letter of instruction, or separately as an index to the bundle or file. Only documents relevant to the expert's work need be sent, plus statements of case, disclosed witness statements, and related experts' reports. Single joint experts should be provided with exactly the same materials as an expert instructed by one party.

The court has the power under CPR r 35.9 to direct that a party provides **3.22** information to a party that an expert needs, and an expert has the power to apply to the court for directions, under CPR r 35.14—this might include that a party disclose documents or other materials to him. Neither power appears to be used very much, but that might be because adequate disclosure is usually made to experts. An expert is under a duty to summarize his instructions, written and oral in his report (see CPR r 35.10(3)). The letter of instruction is not privileged against disclosure (as it was pre-CPR), but the court will order disclosure of the letter and any documents sent to the expert only if the expert's summary of the instructions in his report is incomplete or inaccurate (see CPR r 35.10(4)). This means that those instructing experts need to be very careful in the letter of instruction to avoid trying to lead the expert towards a particular opinion, or expressing views on weaknesses, or referring to tactics.

The interpretation of CPR r 35.10(4) has caused difficulty, particularly in con- **3.23** junction with CPR r 31.14 which states that a party may apply to inspect a document mentioned in an expert's report (among other documents). In the early years after the implementation of the CPR, the courts seemed prepared to order disclosure of *any* documents sent to an expert or referred to in his report.[10] But in 2003 the Court of Appeal gave clear guidance in *Lucas v Barking Havering and Redbridge Hospitals NHS Trust*,[11] a clinical negligence claim. The claimant disclosed with the particulars of claim two medical reports, one of which referred to a report on liability and the other to the claimant's witness statement, neither of which had been disclosed at that time. The defendant applied for their disclosure under CPR r 31.14: the claimant resisted disclosure, relying upon

---

[10] *Bank of Credit and Commerce International SA (In Liquidation) v Ali (No 3)* [1999] 4 All ER 83, *Morris v Bank of India*, 15 November 2001, unreported, ChD, and *Taylor v Bolton Health Authority*, 14 January 2000, unreported, QBD.
[11] [2003] EWCA Civ 1102, [2004] 1 WLR 220.

CPR r 35.10(4). The Court of Appeal concluded that CPR r 31.14 could not have been intended to change the law on privilege, so that privileged documents referred to in an expert's report (such as non-disclosed experts' reports) did not lose their privilege by being mentioned, and the court could order their disclosure only if there was evidence that the expert's summary of his instructions was incomplete or misleading, which was not the case in *Lucas*. The Court of Appeal also sought to draw a distinction between material and non-material documents sent to experts with their instructions. The former are documents that the expert needs to prepare his report, the latter are background documents, and other undisclosed experts' reports would usually fall into the latter category. As the law of privilege continues to be under review by the courts, those instructing experts should still consider carefully which documents an expert really needs to see, and if the decision is taken to send other documents or reports, whether to list them separately as background documents or if appropriate describe them as drafts.

J. Experts' Acceptance of Instructions

3.24   The Protocol for the Instruction of Experts advises experts to seek clarification of unclear instructions (para 8.2), to confirm whether they accept the instructions without delay (para 9.1), to explain if they cannot assist because the work falls outside their expertise, or they cannot comply with the timetable, or have a conflict of interest (such as previous instructions for another party or a professional or personal relationship with one of the parties), or cannot comply with any court orders (para 9.1). An expert may quite properly question whether the issues within his expertise have been correctly identified, or the questions he is being asked to address have been correctly framed, and should as soon as possible identify gaps in information or documents which the party may be able to fill.

K. Instruction of Single Joint Experts

3.25   Parties should try to agree joint instructions to a single joint expert, and the documents they should receive, but they may give separate instructions which should explain the areas of disagreement and which should be copied to the other party.[12] The expert should give seven days' notice to a party before beginning work, when the instructions are late, and should make it clear in the report if it has been prepared without one party's instructions (or having disregarded

---

[12]   CPR r 35.8, Protocol, paras 17.7–17.8, and *Yorke v Katra* [2002] EWCA Civ 867.

them if they arrived very late) (see Protocol, para 17.10). Single joint experts also need to be told the arrangements for invoicing and paying their fees (Protocol, para 17.9).

L. Amending or Adding to Instructions

It is preferable if all the expert's instructions are in one letter. If supplementary **3.26** instructions are unavoidable, the instructor should ensure there is a clear audit trail of instructions on the file, in case there are queries or orders for disclosure later, and the expert must summarize both the original and additional instructions in the report. Oral instructions are to be avoided because of the risk of misunderstanding and inaccurate recording. In more complex or long-running cases additional materials may need to be sent to the expert as evidence is disclosed, including documents obtained from other parties and other experts' reports. Again, a careful note must be kept of what the expert has seen.

M. Keeping the Expert Informed

In July 2005 the Part 35 Practice Direction was amended to require those **3.27** instructing experts to send to experts copies of any court directions or orders that affect them. Paragraph 7.5 of the Protocol for the Instruction of Experts reinforces this. It is particularly important to keep experts informed of changes to the court timetable, especially if it affects the disclosure of their reports, or the timing of written questions or experts' discussion. Experts must also be advised of the trial window or trial date well in advance if the expert is likely to be required to give oral evidence. In large multi-track cases when several experts are instructed, careful coordination of experts (and other witnesses') availability for trial is required, and dates to avoid must be provided before the court lists the case for trial. Many experts appreciate being kept involved in the case until it settles or is tried. In technical cases experts can sometimes advise on documents that should be disclosed by the other party, and help to interpret those that are disclosed. Experts may also helpfully comment upon other experts' reports and assist in drafting written questions for other experts.

N. Changing and Adding Experts

Once the court has decided what expert evidence is reasonably required, and has **3.28** given permission for parties to rely upon reports from particular disciplines, especially if the experts have been named in the directions, it will be difficult to change that expert. This is to discourage the pre-CPR practice of expert-shopping (i.e. commissioning successive reports from different experts until one was obtained that supported the case). Occasionally if a party has made a mistake in the selection or instruction of an expert, or has completely lost confidence in the expert, the court may allow a change but may require the disclosure of any report obtained from the first-named expert as a condition, to avoid the risk that the party is trying to expert-shop.[13] The courts will allow additional experts only infrequently to be instructed later in the proceedings, particularly close to trial where a trial window or date might have to be vacated. The party seeking to adduce the additional expert evidence will have to satisfy the court that it is essential in the interests of justice, and could not have been obtained earlier. Permission is more likely to be granted if an expert has been located who is able to prepare a report quickly, and is available to give evidence on the trial date if necessary.

O. Conclusion

3.29 Selecting and instructing an expert is often a very important step in a case. Clients can only rarely have an input and will have to trust their solicitor. But the CPR give the courts extensive case management powers, so that judges now have control over when expert evidence is to be allowed, from whom, in what form, and at what cost. On occasions, the letter of instruction and materials sent to the expert will be subject to judicial scrutiny, and trial judges, not infrequently, comment adversely upon expert evidence that is partisan or betrays a conflict of interest. Lawyers and expert should, therefore, make every effort to ensure the right expert is instructed effectively and in accordance with the CPR.

---

[13] *Beck v Ministry of Defence* [2003] EWCA Civ 1043, [2005] 1 WLR 2206.

4

COURT MANAGEMENT

Apart from exceptional circumstances, the court takes no initiative at any stage of the proceedings; it has no power or duty to determine what are the issues or questions in a dispute between the parties, save as what may appear from the pleadings or other statements of the parties. The court has no investigative process of its own. It cannot appoint a court expert, nor call for the report of an expert or require experiments or observations to be made, save at the request of a party . . .

> Sir Jack Jacob QC, Master of the Supreme Court 1957–80, in his
> Hamlyn lecture, 'The Fabric of English Civil Justice' (1987) 10–11

A. Pre-Woolf Cases Run by Solicitors

In the years before the implementation of the Woolf reforms lawyers and their **4.01** clients ran litigation. The largely unmanaged, adversarial approach to litigation extended to the use of experts' reports and live expert evidence. If the parties agreed to the calling of expert witnesses, the courts had little or no power to restrict their use.[1]

Although even before 1999, the court had power at, or before, the trial of any **4.02** action to 'order that the number of medical or other witnesses . . . be limited'[2] that power did not extend to excluding expert evidence altogether.[3] In the Court of Appeal, Stephenson LJ said:

> Broadly speaking it is for the parties to decide what witnesses they wish to call and for the judge, before whom the evidence is put, to rule whether it is admissible . . . I cannot find in the rules (and if I did I suspect it would be ultra vires) any general power in a Master, however robust, to take it on himself to decide what evidence is

---

[1] *Access to Justice*, Interim Report (June 1995) 182 <http://www.dca.gov.uk/civil/interim/woolf.htm>.
[2] RSC Ord 38, r 4.
[3] *Sullivan v West Yorkshire Passenger Transport Executive* [1985] 2 All ER 134.

41

necessary for the trial of the action and to take out of the hands of the trial judge and the parties something which, as I understand the procedure, is left to be divided between them . . .[4]

4.03 In *Rawlinson v Westbrook*,[5] Staughton LJ confirmed that, although RSC Ord 38, r 4 allowed the judge to limit the number of experts, it did not extend to excluding such evidence altogether. 'As a result judges and masters were frequently forced to observe the spectacle of litigants like lemmings rushing to their own doom by engaging too many and unnecessary experts'. In that case there had been no need for any expert evidence at all, since both the parties were chartered surveyors who could have given the relevant evidence themselves. Staughton LJ continued:

> But every litigant thought, or at least his solicitor did, that he had to have at least one expert . . . It was high time that the courts were given power to refuse to allow such evidence to be called.

4.04 It was only in the absence of agreement between the parties, or, in personal injury claims, if the substance of expert evidence was not disclosed within 14 weeks of close of pleadings, that the leave of the court was required to call expert witnesses.[6] Even though RSC Ord 38, r 36 provided 'except with leave of the court or where all parties agree, no expert evidence may be adduced at the trial . . . unless the party seeking to adduce the evidence has applied to the court', it was being argued as recently as 1993, albeit unsuccessfully, that the court had no jurisdiction to refuse to give leave. In *Winchester Cigarette Machinery Ltd v Payne*[7] it was argued that the rule 'bound the judge to make an order in [the applicant's] favour at any time up to the commencement of the trial'. In that case the Court of Appeal dismissed an appeal against the refusal to give leave where the summons for leave to call two experts was issued three weeks before the start of a 15-day trial; granting it would inevitably have led to an adjournment. The Court of Appeal held that it was open to a judge to dismiss such a summons 'where a party made his application at the last minute so that there were no longer any directions that could practically be given and which could enable justice to be done'.[8]

4.05 Before 1999, rather than bringing independent opinions to cases, expert witnesses had become 'a very effective weapon in the parties' arsenal of tactics'.[9] Experts were part of their clients' litigation or advocacy team, 'hired guns' who

---

[4] *Sullivan v West Yorkshire Passenger Transport Executive* [1985] 2 All ER 134, 135.
[5] The Times, 25 January 1995.   [6] RSC Ord 38, r 36 and RSC Ord 25, r 8.
[7] The Times, 19 October 1993.
[8] See too *Croft v Jewell* [1993] PIQR P270, CA; cf. *Woodford Ackroyd v Burgess* The Times, 1 February 1999, CA where the issue was the admissibility of a report by someone who was not properly to be characterised as an expert.
[9] *Access to Justice* (n 1 above).

owed no obligation to the court. Some described them as a new breed of litigation hangers-on. Lord Woolf referred to 'a large litigation support industry, generating a multi-million pound fee income . . . among professions such as accountants, architects and others, and new professions . . . such as accident reconstruction and care experts'.[10] They often became partisan advocates for their own opinions, rather than neutral fact-finders or opinion givers. Their partisanship in turn led to polarization, rather than a narrowing of issues. As the Court of Appeal noted in *Abbey National Mortgages plc v Key Surveyors Nationwide Ltd*:[11]

> For whatever reason, and whether consciously or unconsciously, the fact is that expert witnesses instructed on behalf of parties to litigation often tend . . . to espouse the case of those instructing them to a greater or lesser extent, on occasion becoming more partisan than the parties.

4.06 Apart from discovery (now 'disclosure'), the subject of expert witnesses caused Lord Woolf more concern than any other:

> The need to engage experts was a source of excessive expense, delay, and in some cases, increased complexity through the excessive or inappropriate use of experts. Concern was also expressed as to their failure to maintain their independence from the party by whom they had been instructed.[12]

4.07 The concept of proportionality had not at that time entered the legal process. In heavy cases, the fear of experts' costs hampered access to justice for all, except the fabulously wealthy and those persons in receipt of legal aid. Delays were caused not only by the time needed to instruct experts and for them to write their reports, but also because the best experts, those whom the parties were keenest to instruct, were the busiest. Finding gaps in experts' diaries could delay cases for months, even years.

B. CPR Gives Management to the Judge

> [The] new regime contained in the Civil Procedure Rules is designed to ensure that experts no longer serve the exclusive interest of those who retain them, but rather contribute to a just disposal of disputes by making their expertise available to all. The overriding objective requires that the court be provided with all relevant material in the most cost effective and expeditious way.[13]

---

[10] *Access to Justice*, Final Report (July 1996) 137 <http:www.dca.gov.uk/civil/final/woolf.htm>.
[11] [1996] 3 All ER 184, 189, [1996] 1 WLR 1534, 1539. See also GL Davis, 'Current Issues—Expert Evidence: Court Appointed Experts' [2004] 23 CJQ 367 and Peter Smith J in *Phillips v Symes* [2004] EWHC 2330, [2005] 1 WLR 2043, ChD.
[12] *Access to Justice* (n 1 above) 181.
[13] *Mutch v Allen* [2001] EWCA Civ 76, [2001] CP Rep 77, para 24, per Simon Brown LJ.

4.08   The starting point is the overriding objective of enabling the court to deal with cases justly (CPR r 1.1(1)). Dealing with cases justly includes, so far as is practicable, ensuring that the parties are on an equal footing; saving expense; dealing with cases in ways which are proportionate; ensuring that they are dealt with expeditiously and fairly; and allotting an appropriate share of court resources, while taking into account the need to allot resources to other cases (CPR r 1.1.(2)). The parties must help courts to further the overriding objective (CPR r 1.3). More importantly, courts must advance the overriding objective by actively managing cases. This includes encouraging parties to cooperate; identifying the issues at an early stage; deciding promptly which issues need full investigation and trial and accordingly disposing summarily of the others; encouraging the parties to settle; fixing timetables or otherwise controlling the progress of the case; considering whether the likely benefits of taking particular steps justify the cost of taking them; and giving directions to ensure that trials proceed quickly and efficiently (CPR r 1.4).

4.09   The courts' general power to control evidence is contained in CPR r 32.1. That rule allows courts 'to exclude evidence that would otherwise be admissible' (CPR r 32.1(2)). This extent of this power was confirmed in *Grobbelaar v Sun Newspapers*[14] where the court rejected 'the preponderance of academic opinion which took the view that in civil cases there was no discretion in the judge to exclude evidence because its prejudicial effect outweighed its probative value'. The Court of Appeal stated that it could no longer be argued that the court had no jurisdiction to exclude evidence in a civil case.

4.10   When it comes to expert evidence the position is even more restrictive. CPR r 35.4 provides that no expert evidence may be *adduced* without the permission of the court. Parties are still free to *instruct* experts without the court's permission. In general, the only restriction on instructing experts occurs when the consent of the other party is required (for example, where a party wishes to instruct an expert to inspect another party's property, or where a defendant wishes to instruct a medical expert to examine a claimant). There is also a risk that costs will not be recovered. Courts have complete control, however, over the *use* of evidence, including expert evidence, in court.

4.11   The starting point in deciding what expert evidence is to be allowed is CPR r 35.1, which provides that expert evidence shall be restricted to that which is reasonably required to resolve the proceedings. This power to refuse to allow expert evidence does not conflict with Article 6 of the European Convention on Human Rights. The European Court of Human Rights has held that the requirements of a 'fair trial' within the meaning of Article 6 do not include an

---

14   The Times, 12 August 1999.

obligation on the court trying the case to order an expert opinion.[15] It is for the court to judge whether expert evidence would serve any useful purpose. Courts may refuse to give permission for any expert evidence to be called. Alternatively, courts may limit the number of expert witnesses per party, either generally or in a given specialty. Except for cases at the top end of the multi-track, the norm is for a maximum of one expert per specialty. The norm in fast-track cases is for expert evidence to be given in written form without the physical attendance of any expert. Another option is to order that expert evidence may only be given by a single joint expert. CPR r 35.5 provides that expert evidence is to be given in written reports, unless the court directs otherwise.

The particular policy objective underlying CPR r 35.1 is that of reducing the incidence of inappropriate use of experts to bolster cases.[16] The burden rests on the party seeking permission to adduce expert evidence to show that 'it is properly admissible and will genuinely assist the judge in determining the matters which are in issue'.[17] This represents a clear shift from pre-CPR days. In the old days, the question which the parties and their legal advisers asked themselves was 'do we need this expert's evidence to prove our case or disprove our opponent's case?' Now, the question for the parties is, 'if we were in the judge's position, would we reasonably require this expert's evidence to decide the case or an issue in the case?' **4.12**

Parties applying for permission to adduce expert evidence must identify the field in which they wish to rely on expert evidence and, where practicable, a particular expert in that field (CPR r 35.4(2)). Further, they must be able to demonstrate that the proposed expert has relevant expertise in an area in issue in the case; and that he or she is aware of the expert's primary duty to the court when giving expert evidence.[18] **4.13**

In *Mann v Chetty*,[19] Hale LJ in the Court of Appeal, said that when considering what, if any, expert evidence to permit: **4.14**

> . . . the court has to make a judgment on at least three matters: (a) how cogent the proposed expert evidence will be; (b) how helpful it will be in resolving any of the issues in the case; and (c) how much it will cost and the relationship of that cost to the sums at stake.

---

[15] *H v Frances* (1990) 12 EHRR 74, para 60.
[16] *Gumpo v Church of Scientology Religious Education College Inc* [2000] CP Rep 38.
[17] *Clarke v Marlborough Fine Art (London) Ltd (No 3)* [2002] EWHC 11, [2003] CP Rep 30, ChD.
[18] *Field v Leeds City Council* (2000) 17 EG 165.
[19] [2000] EWCA Civ 267, [2001] CP Rep 24, para 17, per Hale LJ. cf. *Rawlinson v Cooper* [2002] EWCA Civ 292, [2002] 1 FLR 1136—appeal allowed where a judge had misunderstood significance of expert's evidence.

4.15 Apart from that case, there has been little guidance as to what 'is reasonably required to resolve the proceedings'. This is hardly surprising, since one of the fundamental principles of the Woolf reforms is flexibility. Apart from cases allocated to small claims or the fast track, there is no 'one-size-fits-all'. What is clear is that, whether or not expert evidence is 'reasonably required' is a decision for the judge responsible for case management, and ultimately the trial judge, and not for the parties or their legal teams. This is made clear by CPR r 35.4.

4.16 Examples of the court's control of expert evidence have arisen where a party has sought permission to instruct a new expert because of loss of confidence in an existing expert. In *Stephen Hill Partnership Ltd v Superglazing Ltd*[20] it was held that courts may give permission to instruct a new expert, if there is good reason for the replacement. In that case, it would have been unfair to force a party to continue to instruct an expert in whom it had lost confidence. On the other hand, in *Ahmed v Stanley A Coleman & Hill*,[21] a claim for professional negligence against solicitors, the defendant's solicitors sent questions to the claimant's expert who had reported on the claimant's injury. The expert answered the questions, unfavourably to the claimant. The claimant sought permission to adduce evidence from a second expert. A district judge refused permission. A circuit judge and the Court of Appeal dismissed appeals. The Court of Appeal stated that it was essential for the operation of the CPR that the authority of judges making case management decisions was not undermined by the Court of Appeal, unless their decisions were clearly wrong, or there had been a serious procedural mishap.

4.17 In *Beck v Ministry of Defence*,[22] a claim for clinical negligence, in which it was alleged that psychiatric treatment exacerbated a condition, the Ministry of Defence instructed an expert psychiatrist, but lost confidence in him because he had insufficient knowledge of the MOD psychiatric referral system. They wanted a new expert, but the claimant refused to be psychiatrically examined. The MOD applied to the court for permission to instruct a new expert. A district judge (and a circuit judge on appeal) granted the application. By the time the case reached the Court of Appeal, the main argument was about disclosure of the first report. Ward LJ said (at para 30):

> Expert shopping is to be discouraged, and a check against possible abuse requires disclosure of the abandoned report as a condition to try again.

---

[20] [2002] All ER (D) 229.   [21] [2002] EWCA Civ 925.
[22] [2003] EWCA Civ 1043, [2005] 1 WLR 2206.

C. Pre-Trial Case Management

Courts must further the overriding objective by actively managing cases (CPR   **4.18**
r 1.4). The form that active case management takes will depend upon the track
to which the claim is allocated. Most case management of claims allocated to the
small claims track (generally claims valued at £5,000 or less, or, where there is a
claim for personal injury for £1,000 or less) or the fast track (generally claims
valued at £5,000 to £15,000) is carried out on paper, without a hearing. Even
where claims are allocated to the multi-track (generally claims valued at over
£15,000), initial case management is often carried out on paper without a
hearing. Where case management issues are more complex and require a hearing, they may be considered at an allocation hearing (CPR r 26.5(4)), a case
management conference (CPR r 29.3), a pre-trial review (CPR r 29.7), or on
application by any party (CPR r 23).

The starting point for directions on expert evidence is normally the allocation   **4.19**
questionnaire, a form which the court serves on all parties when the defendant
files a defence (CPR r 26.3). The completed allocation questionnaire giving
details about the claim and the directions sought must be filed within 14 days.
The allocation questionnaire is then considered by a district judge or master
who either allocates the claim to the appropriate track and makes directions, or
lists an allocation hearing. Parties are encouraged to agree directions.

The types of orders relating to expert evidence which courts commonly make on   **4.20**
allocation are illustrated by the Fast Track Standard Directions contained in the
Appendix to the Practice Direction to CPR Part 28 (see para 4.45 below).

More detailed guidance in relation to claims allocated to the multi-track is given   **4.21**
in the Practice Direction to CPR Part 29. Paragraph 4.8 states that directions
agreed by the parties should, where appropriate, contain provisions about the
use of a single joint expert, or in cases where that is not agreed, the exchange of
expert evidence (including, whether exchange is to be simultaneous or sequen-
tial) and without prejudice discussions between experts. Paragraph 4.10 provides that where the court is to give directions on its own initiative without
holding a case management conference and it is not aware of any steps taken by
the parties other than the exchange of statements of case, its general approach
should be to give directions for a single joint expert on any appropriate issue
unless there is good reason not to do so. Unless para 4.11 (see below) applies,
the court should direct disclosure of experts' reports by way of simultaneous
exchange on those issues where a single joint expert is not allowed. If experts'
reports are not agreed, it should direct a discussion between experts and the
preparation of a statement under CPR r 35.12(3). Paragraph 4.11 provides that
if it appears that expert evidence will be required both on issues of liability and

on the amount of damages, the court may direct that the exchange of those reports that relate to liability should be exchanged simultaneously, but that those relating to the amount of damages should be exchanged sequentially. Guidance on the topics which the court should consider at case management conferences is given by para 5.5. They are likely to include what expert evidence is reasonably required in accordance with CPR r 35.1 and how and when that evidence should be obtained and disclosed, and what arrangements should be made about the putting of questions to experts.

4.22 Courts should not at that stage give permission to use expert evidence unless they can identify each expert by name or field of expertise in the order and state whether the expert's evidence is to be given orally or by the use of a report (para 5.5(1)). The Practice Direction makes it clear that parties who obtain expert evidence before obtaining a direction about it, do so at their own risk as to costs, except where the evidence was obtained in compliance with a pre-action protocol (para 5.5(2)).

4.23 The approach of judges case managing civil claims is very much 'hands on'. They generally insist on justification for the directions sought. In claims allocated to the multi-track, if parties have legal representatives, case management conferences and pre-trial reviews must be attended by representatives who are familiar with the case and who have sufficient authority to deal with any issues that are likely to arise (CPR r 29.3(2)). They must be familiar not only with the content of experts' reports, but also with the practical consequences of such evidence in the litigation. The duty to assist the court means that parties' representatives are expected to adopt a 'cards-on-the-table' approach to all evidence, including that of experts.

D. Proportionality

4.24 The policy of the CPR is that 'litigation should be conducted in a proportionate manner and, where possible, at a proportionate cost'. The aim is that parties should be discouraged from incurring disproportionate costs, as they will not be recoverable unless an indemnity costs order is made.[23]

4.25 The overriding objective of dealing with cases justly includes dealing with cases in 'ways which are proportionate: (i) to the amount of money involved; (ii) to the importance of the case; (iii) to the complexity of the issues; and (iv) to the financial position of each party' (CPR r 1.1(2)(c)). The court's duty of furthering the overriding objective by actively managing cases, includes 'considering

---

[23] *Lownds v Home Office* [2002] EWCA Civ 365, [2002] 1 WLR 2450.

whether the likely benefits of taking a particular step justify the cost of taking it' (CPR r 1.4(2)(h)). Although the concept of proportionality is not specifically mentioned in CPR Part 35, it applies at least as much to experts and their evidence as it does to other aspects of litigation. It was referred to by Lord Woolf CJ in *Daniels v Walker*,[24] the leading case on single joint experts. He said that in a case where there is a modest amount involved, it might be disproportionate to obtain a second expert's report in any circumstances, but that where there is a substantial sum involved, and questions to a single joint expert do not resolve the matter, the parties might obtain their own experts' reports.

There have been few Court of Appeal decisions of principle on the issue of   **4.26** proportionality and expert evidence. A handful of cases, however, give examples of how proportionality operates in practice. In *Mann v Chetty*,[25] Hale LJ said that when considering what, if any, expert evidence to permit, the court has to consider how much the evidence will cost and the relationship of that cost to the sums at stake. When doing this, judges are entitled to take into account the broad ambit of the claimant's likely recovery in the event that the claimant succeeds in the factual allegations. Judges do not always have to take the claimant's claim at face value and simply ask how the proposed costs relate to the claimant's best case.

In *Mann*, a claim for professional negligence against former solicitors instructed   **4.27** in ancillary relief proceedings, the claimant was refused permission to instruct four experts, making eight in all, if the defence instructed their own experts in reply. The defendants said that the 'grand total' cost of the experts would be £33,000, with additional legal costs of around £30,000. The Court of Appeal, not surprisingly, held that, set against the originally pleaded minimum loss of £17,500 which the claimant sought, this would indeed have been disproportionate. The judge had, however, clearly not appreciated that the appellant was now putting his claim at more than £100,000. In those circumstances the Court of Appeal gave permission to adduce the evidence of an accountant, experienced in the valuation of small businesses, to be jointly instructed by the parties.

In *Kranidiotes v Paschali*,[26] there was a dispute involving the value of a shareholding. The amount in issue in the case was at its highest, £78,000 and at its lowest   **4.28** about £15,000. The court directed that an accountant be appointed as a single joint expert. His fees were limited to £10,000. After receiving submissions from the parties, the expert wrote to the court for guidance and quoted a fee of £75,000. Judge Weeks QC, sitting as a deputy High Court judge, terminated

---

[24] [2000] 1 WLR 1382.   [25] [2000] EWCA Civ 267, [2001] CP Rep 24.
[26] [2000] EWCA Civ 357, [2001] CP Rep 81.

the expert's instructions, as the cost was disproportionate, and directed that a cheaper expert be instructed. The Court of Appeal dismissed the defendant's appeal. The judge had exercised his discretion in such a way that the Court of Appeal should not interfere. Aldous LJ said simply: 'the amount of money in issue did not warrant a payment of very substantial costs'.

4.29 *Bandegani v Norwich Union Fire Insurance Society Ltd*[27] was a small claim. The claimant sought the value of a B registered Nissan Cherry car, which he had purchased for £1,500 in September 1996 and which was written off as a result of a collision in February 1997. The claimant said it was still worth £1,500. The defendant insurer said it was only worth £900. Henry LJ questioned, on grounds of proportionality, whether the valuation of the car was a proper matter for the calling, in person, of expert evidence on both sides. He pointed out that 'published guides available in newsagents and used in the trade would give better evidential value for money than the expensive calling of two live experts'. Expertise may be elicited from published sources without the assistance of expert witnesses.[28]

E. Timetables

4.30 The elimination of unnecessary delay and the encouragement of early settlement of those claims which can be settled were both among the principal aims of the Woolf reforms. One of the ways of achieving those aims is the early listing of trials or the early notification of trial windows. 'A central philosophy of the Civil Procedure Rules is that cases must be managed towards the trial window or the trial date'.[29] Trial windows are generally fixed on allocation to track, i.e. soon after the filing of defences. In fast-track cases, trial dates are normally in the region of 30 weeks after notice of allocation is sent out (Part 28 Practice Direction, para 3.12).

4.31 In *Matthews v Tarmac Bricks*,[30] the Court of Appeal stressed that it is essential that parties cooperate both with each other and the court to fix cases for hearing as early as possible, if they want them to be heard on dates which suit their convenience. Where agreement is not possible and the court has to fix a hearing date, the parties must ensure that all relevant material, including the reason for

---

[27] [1999] EWCA Civ 445, [2001] CLY 1550.
[28] See too *Gumpo v Church of Scientology Religious Education College Inc* [2000] CP Rep 38, QBD.
[29] *Calden (Administrator of the Estate of Amanda Calden) v Nunn* [2003] EWCA Civ 200, per Brooke LJ.
[30] The Times, 1 July 1999.

the non-availability of witnesses on particular dates is made available to the court. Doctors who hold themselves out as practising in the medico-legal field must be prepared, so far as practical, to arrange their affairs to meet the commitments of the court. The Part 28 Practice Direction (fast track) states that 'the court will not allow a failure to comply with directions to lead to the postponement of the trial unless the circumstances of the case are exceptional' (para 5.4(1)). The Part 29 Practice Direction (multi-track) contains an almost identical provision (para 7.4(1)). In *Matthews*, the Court of Appeal stated that the court needs to know specifically why any expert is not available for trial, before it will even begin to consider whether the date might be rearranged.

A typical timetable in a claim allocated to the fast track includes exchange of **4.32** experts' reports within 14 weeks after notice of allocation (Part 28 Practice Direction, para 3.12). More time may be allowed in complex multi-track cases, but the emphasis is still on the early exchange of experts' reports. If one party fails to comply with a case management direction (such as exchange of experts' reports), the other party is encouraged to apply for sanctions to be imposed on the defaulting party 'without delay' (Part 29 Practice Direction, para 7.2). Sanctions may include disallowing a defaulting party from relying on expert evidence, the imposition of a stay, orders for costs or payments into court, and, in extreme cases, the striking out of claims or defences (see, for example, CPR rr 3.1 and 3.4).

In view of the importance of solicitors and experts complying with case man- **4.33** agement timetables, the Protocol for the Instruction of Experts emphasizes that solicitors must keep experts informed about the progress of the case. Paragraph 7.5, in particular, states that experts should be informed regularly about deadlines for all matters concerning them. Those instructing experts should promptly send them copies of all court orders and directions which may affect the preparation of their reports or any other matters concerning their obligations. Those instructing experts should also ascertain the availability of experts before trial dates are fixed (para 19.2). In *Rollison v Kimberly Clark*,[31] the Court of Appeal stated that it was unacceptable for a solicitor to instruct an expert shortly before trial, without checking the expert's availability for the trial date. Those instructing experts should also keep experts updated with timetables (including the dates and times experts are to attend) and the location of the court. Experts should be informed immediately if trial dates are vacated (para 19.2).

Notwithstanding these provisions, parties who fail to comply with timetables **4.34** imposed in case management directions may apply for relief from sanctions (CPR r 3.9). *Meredith v Colleys Vacation Services Ltd*[32] is an example of the

---

[31] [2000] CP Rep 85.   [32] [2001] EWCA Civ 1456, [2002] CP Rep 10.

approach of the courts to an application for relief from sanctions in a professional negligence claim against surveyors. The claimant's case was that the property in question was worth £70,000 less as a result of defects not spotted by the defendants. The defendants' case was that the difference in value was between £7,500 and £10,000. Directions given at a case management conference provided for service of experts' reports from a building surveyor and a valuer by a specified date. It was not an 'unless' order. The second defendants experienced difficulties in obtaining instructions because their professional indemnity insurer went into provisional liquidation. The second defendants served a draft of their surveyor's report, but were two-and-a-half weeks late in serving their valuer's report. The valuer's report was served just over a month before trial. The second defendant's solicitors applied for an extension of time, but this was refused. They were debarred from relying on expert valuation evidence. On appeal, the Court of Appeal stated that, on an application for relief from sanctions, the court should consider all the factors specified in CPR r 3.9(1).[33] In *Meredith*, the first instance judge had failed to consider the prejudice to the second defendant if an extension was refused, and had also failed to note that the order was not an 'unless' order. The delay was short and the trial date could be kept. The claimants still had time to deal with the expert's report, even though their own expert was on holiday for two weeks. The availability of an order for costs was an alternative sanction.

4.35 In *RC Residuals Ltd v Linton Fuel Oils Ltd*,[34] the court ordered both parties to serve experts' reports by a particular date. The defendant delayed in sending the claimant's experts, a chemical expert and an accountancy expert, certain material required to complete the reports. The reports were not ready by the date specified and so the claimant failed to serve them. A judge ordered that the claimants' experts' reports be served by 4 pm on a later date, failing which the claimant would be debarred from calling those experts at trial. Each report was completed on the set date. A courier was sent for the chemical expert's report, but he was delayed in traffic so that the report did not arrive at the defendant's solicitors until 4.20 pm. The accountancy expert's report was sent by fax. It was so long that, although the faxing process began at 3.30 pm, the report did not arrive in its entirety at the defendant's solicitors until 4.10 pm. Despite the non-compliance with the order, the claimant and the defendants' experts were able to meet and produce an agreed statement well in time for the trial date. The claimant applied for relief from the sanction imposed for breaching the 'unless' order under CPR r 3.9, but the judge refused the application. He stated that the claimant had a history of breaching court orders, that the

---

[33] *Bansal v Cleema* [2001] CP Rep 6.
[34] [2002] EWCA Civ 911, [2002] 1 WLR 2782.

'only explanation' on the facts before him was that the claimant had left preparation of the experts' reports until the last minute, and that: '. . . that was a mistake. Mistakes have consequences. That's life, and life is tough'.

The claimant appealed, submitting that the judge had not fully considered the **4.36** factors set out in CPR r 3.9(1). The Court of Appeal allowed the appeal. If the judge had considered all the factors set out in CPR r 3.9, there was no doubt that he would have inquired of the claimant as to why he had left preparation of the reports so late, and would have been told of the defendant's part in the delay. The judge had identified the factors weighing against the claimant's application, but had not gone on to consider whether there might have been factors pointing the other way. The court, looking at the whole picture, as it was now able to do, could determine that the claimant's solicitors had, once they realized it was not going to be as simple as they had thought to comply with the time limit, done everything they could to attempt to comply with that limit. In those circumstances, and given that no prejudice had resulted to either of the parties or the trial timetable, the judge should have exercised his discretion to allow the claimant's application.

Expert evidence served late was also admitted in *Jenkins v Grocot*.[35] A care **4.37** expert's report was served four weeks before trial—too late for the other side to commission its own report. Late service was a mistake. Hale J stated that the overriding objective 'to deal with cases justly' includes putting the parties on an equal footing. This will scarcely be the case if one party can spring on the other expert evidence which could not reasonably be foreseen and which the other party has no opportunity to counter. Generally under the CPR it is unjust to exclude relevant evidence. On the particular facts of this case, applying 'the balance of fairness' it was 'narrowly appropriate' to admit the expert evidence. It was not so prejudicial to the claimant that the only fair solution would be to exclude it. On the other hand, in *Calden v Nunn*,[36] a clinical negligence case brought by a husband as administrator, following the death of his wife from breast cancer, the Court of Appeal upheld a designated civil judge's refusal to allow the defendants to call a late additional expert. The defendants had originally rejected the claimant's suggestion that a histopathology expert should be instructed as a single joint expert. Almost two years later, and only months before a second trial window which 'had been delayed far too long', the defendants sought permission to call their own histopathology expert. Judge Grenfell refused permission because he did not believe that the trial window could be maintained if he acceded to the application. The Court of Appeal held that there would be greater unfairness to the claimant in the trial window being lost

---

[35] 30 July 1999, unreported, Lawtel.   [36] [2003] EWCA Civ 200.

than there would be to the defendant in losing the benefit of the histopathology expert at trial.

F. Experts Seeking Directions from the Court

4.38 CPR r 35.14 provides that 'an expert may file a written request for directions to assist him in carrying out his functions as an expert'. This provision gives experts direct access to case management judges to resolve problems which the parties, or their legal advisers, cannot resolve. The CPR do not either prescribe or proscribe the circumstances in which such a request may be made. In practice, it may be made if the parties' instructions or court's directions are unclear, or if a timetable has become unrealistic. The procedure may also be used where additional information is required to prepare a report or if experts are unsure of the propriety of answering questions under CPR r 35.6. This possibility is specifically addressed in the Protocol for the Instruction of Experts (para 16.4) which states:

> If those instructing experts do not apply to the court in respect of questions, but experts still believe that questions are improper or out of time, experts may file written requests with the court for directions to assist in carrying out their functions as expert.

4.39 The power to ask the court for directions was also seen by Peter Smith J[37] as a route for experts who have difficulties as to their evidence in the context of their potential liability for costs. Peter Smith J indicated that in such circumstances, 'the court will be alert to ensure that the expert is given a full opportunity to present his case'.

4.40 A request for directions may be made at any stage, but it should be a last resort, after attempts to resolve any difficulties by contacting those instructing the expert have failed. Indeed, the Protocol for the Instruction of Experts provides that experts should normally discuss such matters with those who instruct them before making any request.

4.41 Paragraph 11.2 of the Protocol states that 'experts' requests to the court for directions should be made by letter containing:

    (a) the title of the claim;
    (b) the claim number of the case;
    (c) the name of the expert;
    (d) full details of why directions are sought; and
    (e) copies of any relevant documentation.

---

[37] *Phillips v Symes* [2004] EWHC 2330, [2005] 1 WLR 2043, ChD.

Unless the court otherwise orders, any proposed request for directions should be **4.42** copied to the party instructing the expert at least seven days before filing any request to the court, and to all other parties at least four days before filing it (CPR r 35.14). CPR r 35.14 provides that experts must, unless the court directs otherwise, provide a copy of any request for directions to the party instructing them at least seven days before filing the request and to all other parties at least four days before filing. The court when giving directions may also direct that a party be served with a copy of the directions.

There have been no cases where the Court of Appeal has commented upon an **4.43** expert's request for directions. It had to consider a judge's response to a request for directions in *Kranidiotes v Paschali*.[38] A single joint expert charged with valuing shares wrote to the court after receiving lengthy submissions from the parties. His task appeared to be considerably more complicated than originally envisaged. He suggested a particular approach and requested instructions from the court as to how he should proceed. The letter resulted in the court dispensing with his services and seeking a cheaper expert. The Court of Appeal declined to interfere in the exercise of the judge's discretion.

G. Conclusion

The shift, from judicial laissez-faire over the employment of expert witnesses by **4.44** litigating parties, to a degree of pre-trial control over the admissibility and extent of expert evidence, has been self-evident. It is too early to assess the overall impact of court management upon the twin defects of the pre-Woolf era—the costs of litigation and the delay in bringing cases to trial. But of the fact that it has clearly reshaped the expert witness system, there can be little doubt. The adversarial system of civil litigation has undergone seismic changes, but the edifice is still standing—some would say, the recent changes have even strengthened it.

Appendix to Part 28 Practice Direction (Fast Track) Fast Track Standard Directions, Expert Evidence

Expert Evidence **4.45**

[No expert evidence being necessary, no party has permission to call or rely on expert evidence].

[On it appearing to the court that expert evidence is necessary on the issue of

[   ]

---

38 [2001] EWCA Civ 357, [2001] CP Rep 81.

and that that evidence should be given by the report of a single expert instructed jointly by the parties, the   shall no later than [   ] inform the court whether or not such an expert has been instructed].

[The expert evidence on the issue of [   ] shall be limited to a single expert jointly instructed by the parties.

If the parties cannot agree by   who that expert is to be and about the payment of his fees either party may apply for further directions.

Unless the parties agree in writing or the court orders otherwise, the fees and expenses of such an expert shall be paid to him [by the parties equally] [   ] and be limited to £   .

[The report of the expert shall be filed at the court no later than   ].

[No party shall be entitled to recover by way of costs from any other party more than £   for the fees or expenses of an expert].

The parties shall exchange reports setting out the substance of any expert evidence on which they intend to rely.

[The exchange shall take place simultaneously no later than   ].

[The   shall serve his report(s) no later than the   and the shall serve his reports no later than the   ].

[The exchange of reports relating to [causation] [   ] shall take place simultaneously no later than   .

The   shall serve his report(s) relating to [damage] [   ] no later than   and the   shall serve his reports relating to it no later than   .

Reports shall be agreed if possible no later than [days after service] [   ].

[If the reports are not agreed within that time there shall be a without prejudice discussion between the relevant experts no later than   to identify the   issues between them and to reach agreement if possible.

The experts shall prepare for the court a statement of the issues on which they agree and on which they disagree with a summary of their reasons, and that statement shall be filed with the court [no later than   ] [with] [no later than the date for filing] [the pre-trial check list].

[Each party has permission to use [   ] as expert witness (es) to give [oral] evidence [in the form of a   report] at the trial in the field of   provided that the substance of the evidence to be given has been disclosed as above and has not been agreed].

[Each party has permission to use in evidence   experts' report(s) [and the court will consider when the claim is listed for trial whether expert oral evidence will be allowed].]

5

SINGLE JOINT EXPERT

Notwithstanding the success of the use of the single joint expert in the Fast Track, the [experts] committee has failed to detect any great enthusiasm for extending the practice up through the Multi-Track. This may perhaps be bound up with attitudes to litigation which are still dictated by pre-1999 notions. If the Fast Track limit should ever be raised, the extended use of the single joint expert may well go unremarked.

Civil Justice Council Annual Report 2004, 15[1]

A. In the Beginning: The Early Evidence

Following the implementation of the Civil Procedure Rules in April 1999, **5.01** which included the novelty of the single joint expert (SJE) in civil litigation, the Lord Chancellor's Department undertook research into how the reforms were working in practice. The first report, entitled *Emerging Findings*, was published in March 2001 and this was followed by *Further Findings* in August 2002. The conclusions were based on information collected by the Court Service on cases heard through the 'Trial Sampler' which all county courts are asked to complete in March and September each year. The data covered, 8,411 cases pre-CPR (March 1994 to September 1997) and 1,979 cases heard post-CPR (September 2000 to September 2001). The analysis showed that post-CPR joint experts were used in 46 per cent of trials involving any experts and this was particularly marked in personal injury cases where the pre-action protocol was a factor. These findings were supported by additional, external evidence.

The *Further Findings* report quoted an article entitled 'Under Scrutiny' which **5.02** appeared in the *Solicitors Journal* in December 2001 which claimed: 'Prior to

---

[1] At <http://www.civiljusticecouncil.gov.uk/164.htm>. The Civil Justice Council has in its report, *Improved Access to Justice—Funding Options and Proportionate Costs* (August 2005) recommended that the limit for fast-track cases be extended from £10,000 to £25,000 and consideration should be given to extending it further to £50,000. The 2005 Report may be found at <http://www.civiljusticecouncil.gov.uk/903.htm>.

the CPR it was relatively rare to appoint a single joint expert to a case, but now such appointments are becoming increasingly common and not just restricted to smaller cases'. The report also referred to a survey of its members conducted by the Expert Witness Institute in late 2001 which indicated that 74 per cent of respondents had acted as a single joint expert and of those, 42 per cent had acted more than 10 times, confirming the trend for the use of single joint experts. A survey conducted by the Law Society Woolf Network in October 2001 asked about the use of single joint experts in the different tracks. The survey found that 82 per cent of respondents felt that the single joint expert was appropriate for the fast track and 52 per cent thought he or she could also be used in multi-track cases. Nevertheless one respondent commented:

> It is considered that joint experts are generally appropriate in fast track cases and generally inappropriate in multi-track cases, although it depends on the nature of the case and the issues involved. In some cases use of a joint expert increased costs as the parties appointed their own expert as well, resulting in three experts in total.

5.03 To find such a level of acceptance for this concept not long after Lord Woolf's review of civil procedure and the implementation of the CPR suggests that there has been a revolution, if only a minor one. In the course of his inquiry Lord Woolf suggested a sea change would be necessary, the reason being his concerns over the issue of unnecessary cost:

> A large litigation support industry, generating a multi-million pound fee income, has grown up among professions, such as accountants, architects and others, and new professions have developed, such as accident reconstruction and care experts. This goes against all principles of proportionality and access to justice. In my view, its most damaging effect is that it has created an ethos of what is acceptable, which in turn filtered down to smaller cases. Many potential litigants do not even start litigation because of the advice they are given about cost, and in my view this is as great a social ill as the actual cost of pursuing litigation.[2]

5.04 Initially, Lord Woolf saw one of the ways of improving the situation was the appointment of court experts and expert assessors. While RSC Ord 40 provided for the appointment of an expert by the court, it could only be done on the application of a party and the power contained in RSC Ord 40 had been rarely used in the past. Nevertheless the climate was changing and Lord Woolf instanced in his Interim Report such an appointment being made by an official referee:

---

[2] *Access to Justice*, Final Report (July 1996) ch 13, para 2 <http://www.dca.gov.uk/civil/final/index.htm>.

In giving reasons for this order, the Official Referee said he saw no just reason for any initial presumption either in favour or against the appointment of a court expert. The question to be asked was '*whether it is likely to assist in the just, expeditious and economical disposal of the action*'. If such an appointment promoted settlement, as it was likely do in a significant proportion of cases, it would advance both expedition and economy.[3]

Moreover, he cited with approval the position in civil law (i.e. European) juris- **5.05** dictions, although he acknowledged that parties were unwilling to take advantage of a court-appointed expert, because it was felt that the expert, and not the judge, would, in practice, decide the case; there would be increased cost in appointing such a court expert in addition to the parties' own experts; and the court expert would have difficulty in handling the matter where more than one acceptable view could be held on a particular issue. While these criticisms had some substance, Lord Woolf felt that the court was perfectly capable of deciding which cases were appropriate for such an appointment and of ensuring that the expert was used effectively.

In the consultation process which followed publication of the Interim Report, **5.06** it became clear that there was still strong resistance to Lord Woolf's proposals on single experts, and he accepted that such experts should, as far as possible, be chosen by agreement between the parties, not imposed by the court:

> Whether appointed by the parties or by the court, he or she would act on instruction from the parties. The appointment of a neutral expert would not necessarily deprive the parties of the right to cross-examine, or even to call their own experts in addition to the neutral expert if that were justified by the scale of the case . . . The consultation process . . . has, at least, revealed a measure of agreement that single experts would be acceptable in certain types of cases or in certain limited circumstances, particularly on issues of quantum.[4]

While Lord Woolf did not see his proposals initiating a 'significant shift towards **5.07** single experts in the short term', he was convinced that the concept had a validity, because:

> A single expert is much more likely to be impartial than a party's expert can be. Appointing a single expert is likely to save time and money, and to increase the prospects of settlement. It may also be an effective way of levelling the playing field between parties of unequal resources.[5]

---

[3] *Access to Justice*, Interim Report (June 1995) ch 23, para 20 <http://www.dca.gov.uk/civil/interim/woolf.htm>.
[4] *Access to Justice*, Final Report (July 1996) ch 13, paras 17, 18.   [5] ibid para 21.

B. The Advent of the Single Joint Expert

5.08 In the event, the shift towards single joint experts was more pronounced legislatively than Lord Woolf envisaged, although he provided the key to achieving this:

> What is needed to initiate such a shift is a clear statement of principle in the rules, coupled with procedures to ensure that parties and procedural judges always consider whether a single expert could be appointed in a particular case (or to deal with a particular issue); and, if this is not considered appropriate, that they indicate why not.[6]

5.09 In drawing up the new rules, the Civil Procedure Rules Committee clearly had Lord Woolf's strictures in mind when considering how the rules relating to the appointment of single experts should be framed. CPR r 35.7 provides that the court shall have power to direct that evidence is to be given by a single joint expert: 'where two or more parties wish to submit expert evidence on particular issues, the court may direct that evidence is given by one expert only'.

5.10 The choice of the expert rests with the parties; only if they are unable to agree who shall be the expert will the court intervene to select either an expert from a list prepared by the parties or to decide who it shall be, in such other way as the court may direct. CPR r 35.8 builds on this foundation by setting out how the single joint expert is to be instructed and paid. Further amplification is provided by the Part 35 Practice Direction, so that if there are a number of different disciplines involved in the resolution of the issue before the court, the leading expert in the dominant discipline is to be identified as the single expert. Experience since April 1999 suggests little need to resort to this.

5.11 As with the introduction of any new concept, it is only to be expected that there will be teething problems and so it was that the courts found themselves saddled with the responsibility for resolving them. In fact the implementation of CPR Part 35 as a whole was itself the catalyst for the generation of a high level of case law at appellate level. The role of the single joint expert was not excluded from this. One reason was that further guidance on the interpretation of CPR Part 35 was not immediately available. It had been envisaged that there would be an expert's protocol: initially the Part 35 Practice Direction in relation to the form and content of the expert's report stated: 'In addition, an expert's report should comply with the requirements of any approved expert's protocol'.[7]

5.12 It was not until December 2001 that the Code of Guidance on Expert Evidence, produced by the working party set up by the Head of Civil Justice, was

---

[6] ibid para 20.   [7] CPR Part 35 Practice Direction, para 1.6.

published, and in the first amendment of CPR Part 35 para 1.6 was dropped from the Practice Direction. So, given the absence of further guidance, it was inevitable that litigating parties and their legal advisers should look to the courts.

C. The View of the Courts

It would be fair to say that most judges in 1999 adopted as a starting point, that **5.13** a single joint expert should be instructed wherever possible. But, in the light of the emerging case law, the courts began to take a more flexible view. Very early on there was a case brought to determine the extent to which it was reasonable to require that the parties in a complex multi-track clinical negligence case should instruct a single joint expert.[8] The district judge had ordered that the parties should jointly instruct a consultant neo-natal paediatrician to report on causation, and should also consider whether any other experts should be jointly instructed. On appeal, Curtis J held that the appointment of a single joint expert was inappropriate, given the complexity and high value of the case. He took the view that in such cases it was preferable for the parties to appoint their own experts to ensure that a full case was presented initially. The decision whether the instruction of a joint expert was justified could be taken subsequently in the light of the issues identified by the experts.

In *Daniels v Walker*[9] an occupational therapist had been appointed as a jointly **5.14** instructed expert, but the defendant was concerned at the extent of the care regime recommended by the expert, and wished to obtain a further care report from another expert. The Court of Appeal agreed that the fact that a party had agreed to the appointment of a joint expert did not prevent the court under the CPR from agreeing that the party might be given permission to obtain a report from another expert. The correct approach in such cases was to regard the joint instruction of an expert as the first step in obtaining expert evidence on a particular issue. In the majority of cases it was hoped that this would not only be the first step, but also the last. Nevertheless, if the reasons were not fanciful, or if there was a part, or indeed, the whole of the expert's report, that the party wished to challenge, then the court had discretion to permit the party to obtain further expert evidence.

The case of *Daniels v Walker* marked a significant development of the concept of **5.15** the single joint expert, not least because Lord Woolf himself gave the court's

---

[8] *S (A Minor) v Birmingham Health Authority* [2001] Lloyd's Rep Med 382, CA.
[9] [2000] 1 WLR 1382.

judgment. (In the early days of the CPR he, in fact, sat on the bench for many of the cases concerned with expert evidence.) Accordingly, he sought to amplify the bare bones of CPR Part 35 with further guidance, suggesting that:

(1) in the majority of cases, the sensible approach was not to ask the court immediately to permit the dissatisfied party to instruct a second expert;

(2) where only a modest sum was involved, the court was entitled to take a more robust line, since the additional cost involved was disproportionate to the value of the case;

(3) the party concerned should consider whether asking questions of the expert on the report might reasonably resolve the matter; and

(4) the party, or indeed both parties, obtain their own experts' reports. The decision by the court as to what evidence should be admitted should not be taken until there had been an opportunity for the experts to meet.

5.16 While the Court of Appeal allowed a further report to be admitted in that case, it also warned that this would not always be permitted, particularly if 'the claimant would be unduly distressed or anything of that nature, by the additional examination'.

5.17 It was also argued for the appellants that the appeal should be allowed in view of the provisions of the European Convention on Human Rights. Refusal to permit the defendant to instruct a second expert witness, it was suggested, would conflict with Article 6 (requirement of a fair trial) because it amounted to barring either the whole claim of the defendant or an essential part of that claim. However, the Court of Appeal held that Article 6 had no relevance, and it was undesirable if case management issues were made more complex by resorting to arguments about Convention compliance. In giving judgment, Lord Woolf expressed the hope that judges would be robust in resisting such arguments.

5.18 The case of *Daniels v Walker* was quickly followed by a number of cases clarifying CPR r 35.7. In the case of *Oxley v Penwarden*,[10] a clinical negligence case, the judge had directed at the case management conference, that if the parties failed to agree on a single joint expert, the court would itself appoint one. On appeal, the Court of Appeal drew attention to the notes to CPR r 35.7:

> There is no presumption in favour of the appointment of a single joint expert, except in cases allocated to the fast track. The object is to do away with the calling of multiple experts where, given the nature of the issue over which the parties are at odds, that is not justified.

5.19 The Court of Appeal accepted that in difficult or complex cases the parties would be likely to be unable to agree on the appointment of a single joint expert

---

[10] [2001] Lloyd's Rep Med 347.

and the court should allow both sides to appoint its own expert so long as to do so was proportionate and just. It could not be right for the court to impose a single joint expert on the parties, because that may well effectively decide an essential issue in the case without giving them the opportunity to challenge it.

A case where an apparently contrary view was taken is *Takenaka (UK) Ltd v Frankel*.[11] This was a libel case which turned on whether the defendant was the author and publisher of defamatory e-mails. A single joint expert was appointed to analyse the contents of the defendant's laptop computer. In giving judgment, Alliot J commented, 'A judge tries the case upon the evidence, and in this case the expert evidence is of the highest quality in an arcane field in which the judge must be guided by that expert evidence'. He noted that the expert had conducted his investigation in an entirely objective manner, as instructed by both parties and without partisan bias. The judge found his evidence compelling and accordingly accepted it. Significantly, the judge had been reminded by counsel for the defendant that this was a trial by judge alone and not by expert, but while the judge was clearly guided by the expert, he did not allow him to decide the matter for the court. It may well be that the judge was mindful of the actual role of the expert in the case—which was one of investigation, probably inadmissibly, rather than of giving opinion evidence. (The line to be drawn between an expert's factual evidence and opinion is often indistinct.) Another important case, *Field v Leeds City Council* (see para 5.23 below) can be partly explained by the same reasoning. It is where experts are giving opinions, for example in professional negligence cases, it is likely to be felt that single joint experts are not appropriate. **5.20**

Further guidance on CPR r 35.7 was provided by *Pattison v Cosgrove*.[12] The parties to a boundary dispute had jointly instructed an expert to prepare a report, but the defendant was unhappy with the report and sought permission to instruct his own expert. Neuberger J identified the following factors which had to be considered: **5.21**

(1) the nature of the dispute;
(2) the number of issues on which the expert evidence was relevant;
(3) the reasons for requiring the second expert;
(4) the amount at stake or the nature of the issues at stake;
(5) the effect of permitting a second expert report on the conduct of the trial;
(6) the delay that might be caused in the conduct of the proceedings;
(7) any other special features; and
(8) the overall justice to the parties.

---

[11] The Independent, 11 December 2000.
[12] [2001] CP Rep 68, The Times, 13 February 2001.

5.22 In this case the court decided that it was reasonable to allow a second expert, if that was what justice required. In fact, the second expert had been involved as an adviser and was to be called as witness of fact, so the admission of a second expert's report would have little impact on either the conduct of the case or the timetable.

5.23 Lord Woolf had also considered the appropriateness of the appointment of a single joint expert in another case, where the main issue was whether an employee of a defendant local authority was sufficiently independent to act as an expert witness. In *Field v Leeds City Council*[13] it was made clear that there was no presumption that the employee could not act as an expert witness, particularly if he had relevant knowledge of the issues, but it was incumbent upon the employer to demonstrate that the individual was fully aware of, and could comply with, the requirements that the CPR imposed on an expert witness. In giving judgment, Lord Woolf made some more general remarks:

> The ideal way of disposing of issues such as that which arise in this case is for one expert to be appointed by both sides . . . I would hope that procedures will be devised where claimants in cases such as this inform the authority of the expert whom they intend to engage so that the views of the authority can be taken into account. This could lead to single experts being appointed more often than has happened in the past which is ideally to be desired.[14]

D. Choosing the Single Joint Expert

5.24 Lord Woolf's aim to restrict the number of experts used has been reflected in the pre-action protocols. Thus the personal injury pre-action protocol provides that the claimant should nominate several potential experts in a particular field and give the defendant an opportunity to object to any of those nominated, otherwise the claimant can choose from those to whom no objection has been raised. It is the claimant alone who then instructs the expert. The claimant then discloses the expert's report to the defendant, who can ask questions of the expert in writing. But in the case of *Carlson v Townsend*[15] events did not run smoothly. In accordance with paras 3.14 and 3.16 of the pre-action protocol, the claimant provided the defendant with three names of consultant orthopaedic surgeons. The claimant instructed one whom the defendant had no objection to. After receiving the expert's report, however, the claimant instructed another expert who was not on the original list. In the High Court the claimant was ordered to disclose the first expert's report, but on appeal, the Court of Appeal overturned

---

[13] (2000) 17 EG 165.   [14] ibid para 22.
[15] [2001] EWCA Civ 511, [2001] 1 WLR 2415.

this decision. Instructing the second expert without giving the defendant the opportunity to object amounted to a breach of the pre-action protocol, but withholding the report did not; that was privileged. The Court of Appeal interpreted the intention behind paras 3.14 and 3.16 of the pre-action protocol as providing a means whereby defendants could identify at an early stage if the claimant intended to use an expert whom they regarded as partisan. The Court of Appeal also confirmed that the instruction of the expert by the claimant alone was not inconsistent with the CPR. The protocols were guides to good pre-litigation and litigation practice but paras 3.14 and 3.16 did not amount to the instruction of an expert on a joint basis.

E. Changing a Single Joint Expert

An expert's report is usually ordered in small claims or fast-track cases from a single joint expert and also in multi-track claims dealing with technical or quantum issues, partly for proportionality reasons. Changing that expert, therefore, is not regarded as being within the spirit of the rules. Occasionally, however, the court will accede to a change, usually where either or both of the parties have lost confidence in the original appointee. For example, in *Smolen v Solon Co-operative Housing Services Ltd*[16] the claimant objected to the first single joint expert after his report had been disclosed, on the grounds that he had regularly been instructed by the defendant's solicitor. While the court was satisfied that there was no evidence of bias, it was accepted that the claimant had lost confidence in the expert and should therefore be permitted to instruct another expert, although a payment into court on account of the second expert's fees was ordered.

5.25

It is interesting that these developments in civil litigation are mirrored in the Family Division. In *GW v Oldham Metropolitan Borough Council*[17] the Court of Appeal felt that in the critical field of paediatric neuro-radiology the evidence might become pivotal and, by its very nature, not easily receptive to a challenge in the absence of any other expert opinion; accordingly, the court should be slow to decline the parents' application for a second expert. Wall LJ explained that the appeal had been allowed, because first, the court was not a rubber stamp; secondly, the court had been asked by the Bar to give any assistance on an important point of practice in family proceedings; and thirdly, because the case demonstrated that, even where there was highly competent legal representation, an expert whose integrity and experience was not in doubt, and a judge

5.26

---

[16] [2003] EWCA Civ 1240.
[17] [2005] EWCA Civ 1247, [2005] 3 FCR 513, see para 1.36 above.

who was both highly respected and a specialist in the field, a risk of injustice remained.

F. Protocol for the Instruction of Experts

5.27   Some six years on from the implementation of the CPR the approach to the appointment of single joint experts has been set out succinctly by the Protocol for the Instruction of Experts.[18] Paragraph 17.2 states:

> The Civil Procedure Rules encourage the use of joint experts. Wherever possible a joint report should be obtained. Consideration should therefore be given by all parties to the appointment of single joint experts in all cases where the court might direct such an appointment. Single joint experts are the norm in cases allocated to the small claims track and the fast track.

5.28   The Protocol also suggests that at an early stage, before matters become contentious, it would be helpful to consider the appointment of a single joint expert for the purpose of conducting 'examinations, investigations, tests, site inspections, preparation of photographs, plans or other similar expert tasks' to assist in agreeing or narrowing issues. There is a caveat, that experts who have previously advised a party (whether in the same case or otherwise) should only be proposed as a single joint expert if all information about the previous involvement is disclosed. The Protocol also reiterates the position that such appointment does not prevent the parties from instructing their own experts to advise, but also makes it clear that the costs of such expert advisers may not be recoverable.

5.29   The instructions given to the single joint expert are clearly a critical matter. The Protocol for the Instruction of Experts sets out helpful guidance to amplify the requirements of CPR r 35.8. The presumption is that the parties agree on joint instructions, but if that is not possible each party may give separate instructions. They should, in any case, try to agree what documents are to be included with the instructions and what assumptions, if any, should be made by the expert. Where the parties fail to agree on joint instructions, the Protocol requires them to identify the areas of disagreement, and this should be made clear to the expert in the instructions. To avoid confusion it is essential, where separate instructions are issued, that the other instructing parties receive copies. This reflects the provisions of CPR r 35.8(1) and (2) which apply even in small claims cases where the parties cannot agree a joint letter of instruction.[19]

---

[18]   Civil Justice Council, *Protocol for the Instruction of Experts to give evidence in civil claims* (22 June 2005), see Appendix 3 below.
[19]   *York v Katra* [2003] EWCA Civ 867.

CPR r 35.8 provides that the parties instructing a single joint expert are, **5.30** jointly and severally, responsible for paying the expert's fee. The Protocol confirms that a statement to this effect should be included in the terms of appointment of the expert, and for his part the expert is required to send invoices simultaneously to all instructing parties or their solicitors, whichever is the more appropriate. CPR r 35.8(4)(a) also provides that the court can make an order limiting the experts' fees and expenses, and if such an order has been made, a statement to that effect must be included in the terms of appointment. In the case of *Kranidiotes v Paschali*,[20] which concerned the valuation of shares in a company, the judge ordered that the joint expert appointed to undertake the work should 'undertake only such investigations and enquiries as are consistent with an overall fee of £10,000 . . . (or such higher figure as may be agreed between the parties . . .) for the production of the report . . .'. The judge's aim was to adopt a proportionate attitude to the trial. The expert appointed, however, came to the conclusion that a full re-audit of the company's accounts over at least the previous three to four years was likely to cost £75,000. The judge concluded that the best course was to dispense with his (the joint expert's) services and to use a cheaper expert. On appeal, it was argued that the judge had concentrated unnecessarily on questions of proportionality and costs, but the Court of Appeal upheld the judge's decision. The Court of Appeal was satisfied that the judge was required to bear in mind the need for a proportionate approach.

What is the position where the expert does not receive instructions from one or **5.31** more of the parties? The Protocol suggests that a deadline (normally of at least seven days) should be given by the expert to all relevant parties. After that time the expert may begin work, presumably if instructions have been received from the parties or ordered by the court. Should the instructions be received subsequently, but before the expert has signed off the report, the expert should consider whether it is practicable to comply with those instructions without adversely affecting the timetable or compliance with the proportionality principle. Should the expert decide to issue the report without taking account of those instructions received after the deadline, he should advise the parties who may consider applying to the court for directions. The report must, in either case, show clearly that the instructions were not received within the deadline, or at all.[21]

---

[20] [2001] EWCA Civ 357, [2001] CP Rep 81.
[21] Protocol for the Instruction of Experts, para 17.10.

G. The Conduct of the Single Joint Expert

5.32 It is important for an expert instructed as a joint expert to approach the responsibilities of the appointment professionally and objectively. The Protocol for the Instruction of Experts emphasizes 'they should maintain independence, impartiality and transparency at all times'.[22]

5.33 This is, however, not straightforward. A party expert, while owing a duty to the court under CPR r 35.3(2), will have access to all the facilities of the instructing solicitor and will probably have conferences with counsel. The joint expert appointed on behalf of all the litigating parties is denied this support and may well find the position between the opposing views very difficult, particularly as single joint experts often report that they do not receive such detailed and helpful instructions as when they are instructed by one party alone. The Protocol requires the single joint expert to 'keep all instructing parties informed of any material steps they may be taking by, for example, copying all correspondence to those instructing them'.[23] This, to an extent, glosses over the fact that the single joint expert can find the whole position very stressful. Indeed, the Protocol provides that a party instructed expert can later be instructed as a single joint expert only if all the information given to the expert by the first party is copied to the second party.[24]

5.34 In a difficult situation, the single joint expert does have the right to seek directions from the court (CPR r 35.14). Should the expert find this necessary, it is required that prior notice is given to the instructing parties at least seven days before the request is filed to the court. The Protocol sets out how this should be effected:

> Requests to the court for directions should be made by letter, containing:
> (a) the title of the claim;
> (b) the claim number of the case;
> (c) the name of the expert;
> (d) full details of why directions are sought; and
> (e) copies of any relevant documentation.[25]

5.35 This, of course, should be regarded as a last resort solution. Before this stage is reached, there should be a way of resolving the parties' concerns. Ordinarily, a party expert can meet with the instructing solicitors to discuss any problems. In the case of the single joint expert the court has determined that CPR r 35.8 is to be interpreted to the effect that there should be no meeting or conference without all the parties being present.[26] The case concerned a claim for medical

---

[22] ibid para 17.12. See Chapter 11 below on the duty to the court.   [23] ibid para 17.11.
[24] ibid para 17.5.   [25] ibid para 11.2.
[26] *Peet v Mid-Kent Area Healthcare NHS Trust* [2001] EWCA Civ 1703, [2002] 1 WLR 210.

negligence, following the birth of twins, one of whom who suffered from cerebral palsy where the defendant NHS Trust offered to pay 95 per cent of the full liability quantum of damages, and this was accepted. It had been agreed that the expert evidence dealing with quantum should be provided by joint experts in each of the seven relevant disciplines—namely, an educational psychologist, an employment consultant, a nursing specialist, an occupational therapist, a psychotherapist, an architect, and a speech therapist—so much for cutting the costs of litigation! Each of the experts produced a report and the claimants' parents sought to have a conference with the experts without the defendant's solicitor being present. The Queen's Bench Master took the view that this was inappropriate, but he ordered that the application of the defendant's solicitor to be present be refused. He ordered that no conference be held by the claimant with the seven joint experts without the written consent of any party with any joint expert. The matter was appealed because the child's father, acting as the litigant's friend, expressed his deep concern over this in a letter to his solicitors explaining why he felt it essential for he and his wife to discuss the case with the experts. The letter was in fact quoted in the judgment by Lord Woolf:

> A crucial part of such conferences is our ability to express ourselves freely, without fear that any of our comments might be used or taken up by the other side in what is still an adversarial process of deciding the final quantum. The presence of the defendant's solicitor's representative would severely inhibit this. Indeed we would find such a presence intimidating and distressing.[27]

Of course there was no reason why the experts, in carrying out their duties, **5.36** should not themselves seek to meet with the claimant, and Lord Woolf said as much: 'There can be no objection to that, a single expert is properly entitled to interview the parents for the purpose of preparing a satisfactory report.'[28] What was not permissible was 'the idea of one side testing the views of an expert in the absence of the other party'.

H. Cross-Examinination

In the course of the appeal *Peet v Mid-Kent Area Healthcare Trust*, reference was **5.37** made to the *Supreme Court Practice*, vol 1 (2001), that the parties should be able to cross-examine the expert witness, if called to give oral evidence at trial. Lord Woolf suggested that it might be appropriate in some cases, but it should not be the norm:

> The starting point is: unless there is reason for not having a single joint expert, there should be only a single expert. If there is no reason which justifies more

---

[27] ibid para 19.   [28] ibid para 21.

evidence than that from a single joint expert on any particular topic, then again in the normal way the report prepared by the single expert should be the evidence in the case on the issues covered by that expert's report. In the normal way, therefore, there should be no need for that report to be amplified or tested by cross-examination. If it needs amplification, or if it should be subject to cross-examination, the court has a discretion to allow that to happen. The court may permit that to happen either prior to the hearing or at the hearing. But the assumption should be that the single joint expert's report is the evidence. Any amplification or cross-examination should be restricted as far as possible.[29]

5.38 This was quoted with approval by Dyson LJ in *Popek v National Westminster Bank plc*[30] with the additional recommendation that if the single joint expert is 'to be subject to cross-examination, then he or she should know in advance what topics are to be covered, and where fresh material is to be adduced for his or her consideration . . . that this should be done in advance of the hearing'. Shortly afterwards in another case, *Austen v Oxfordshire County Council*[31] the Court of Appeal, while accepting as settled law that there is generally no need to test the evidence of a single joint expert in cross-examination, did agree that in the unusual circumstances of this case cross-examination should be allowed.

5.39 From time to time concern has been expressed that the evidence of the single joint expert, acting independently of the parties, is not subject to the same rigorous testing that the evidence of a party expert may be subjected to. In an adversarial process, the court expects the single joint expert to stand aside of that process. The Protocol for the Instruction of Experts sets out concisely the special position of the single joint expert:

> Single joint experts are Part 35 experts and so have an overriding duty to the court. They are the parties' appointed experts and therefore owe an equal duty to all parties. They should maintain independence, impartiality and transparency at all times.[32]

I. Matrimonial Disputes

5.40 The encouragement which the courts are giving to the appointment of joint experts is not without its problems, as will already have been apparent, and the emphasis on the principle of proportionality does throw up procedural difficulties. This can be seen very clearly from cases in the Family Division. The President's Practice Direction of 25 May 2000 stated:

> The introduction of expert evidence in proceedings is likely to increase costs substantially and consequently the court will use its powers to restrict the unnecessary

---

[29] ibid para 28.   [30] [2002] EWCA Civ 42, [2002] CPLR 370.
[31] [2002] All ER D 97.   [32] Paragraph 17.12.

use of experts. Accordingly, where expert evidence is sought to be relied upon, parties should, if possible, agree upon a single joint expert whom they can jointly instruct.

In November 2002 the Family Division produced a Best Practice Guide[33] which **5.41** set out the procedure to be followed when instructions are given jointly to experts with the specific direction: 'The joint instructions to the SJE should reflect the proportionality principle' (para 7).

The appointment of a single joint expert (particularly in matrimonial cases) **5.42** involves, however, a significant amount of trust, and where that involves a husband and wife who are separating and disputing the division of the matrimonial assets, the very nature of the case suggests that trust will be in short supply. The case of *White v White*[34] redrew the principles upon which the court acts: the House of Lords held that, where the Matrimonial Causes Act 1973 applies, the aim should be to achieve a fair outcome. The implication is that, while there should be no general presumption of an equal division of the matrimonial assets, the principle of equality should be departed from only if there is a good reason to do so. A second important influence is the Welfare Reform and Pensions Act 1999 which provided that a divorced wife should be entitled to a share of her former husband's pension rights.

Until the *White* case, the needs of the parties and any minor children were the **5.43** critical factor in the determination of any award. After the *White* case the court's attention has been moved from assessing the needs of the wife to achieving a fair valuation of the assets of the husband. The dilemma facing the family court is twofold. First, the amounts involved in most cases are substantial and are likely to exceed £15,000, which in civil litigation would automatically mean allocation to the multi-track where the use of a single joint expert is unusual, except in relation to specific issues. The second problem is the requirement to contain costs. Judges have been extremely concerned at the amount of the parties' assets swallowed up in the costs of litigation: in the *White* case costs were initially estimated to amount to some 15 per cent of the assets, but subsequently they were almost double this. Inevitably, the court is inclined to use a single joint expert, particularly when it is necessary to value residential property. But to persuade the parties that this is in their best interests is another matter. If the appointed expert is of such a standing in his profession that his objective

---

[33] Available at <http://www.dca.gov.uk/family/arag/bpjexpert.htm>.

[34] [2000] 2 FLR 981. The issue of a fair outcome in apportioning the matrimonial assets has recently been considered by the House of Lords in *Miller v Miller* and *McFarlane v McFarlane* [2006] UKHL 24 and has established that any settlement should reflect not just the wife's immediate needs, but should also compensate for her losses.

assessment will be accepted by the parties, it is probable that he will expect his fee to reflect his reputation and here he will run into conflict with the court which is seeking to ensure that the expert's fees are proportionate. The case of *Kranidiotes v Paschali*[35] is a good example of the judge intervening to dispense with the services of the first appointed expert to use a cheaper expert.

5.44 While the single joint expert may scrupulously observe his duty to the court to be fair and impartial, the parties lack the opportunity to test the validity of the expert's opinion through cross-examination, so that scope for misunderstanding and dissatisfaction will exist. One solution would be for the court to permit the appointment of party experts and order a meeting of the experts at the outset to narrow the issues and to clarify the range of values. On the face of it, this may appear a more expensive approach, but it could well save time and allay the fears of the parties. The use of experts' discussions was an established feature of procedure in the Family Division even before the advent of the CPR.

J. Weighing the Evidence

5.45 The expert must understand that as an expert witness he must not usurp the role of the judge who weighs all the evidence, documentary and from lay and expert witnesses, both written and oral, in giving judgment. Nevertheless, as evidence from single joint experts is usually in the form of a written report only and on a very technical matter this may be highly persuasive. If the expert evidence contradicts, or is not consistent with other evidence, especially that of lay witnesses who give credible oral evidence on issues of fact that is tested by cross-examination, the judge has to consider which evidence to accept. Thus in an RTA personal injury case the judge preferred the evidence of the lay witnesses, even though the evidence of the single joint expert engineer was logical and consistent, and this was upheld by the Court of Appeal.[36]

5.46 This, of course, applies only to cases that are referred to the court for judgment: many cases involving a single joint expert settle on the basis of the report without going to court. When this happens it might well be argued that the single joint expert has facilitated the outcome. In an earlier case, *Coopers Payen Ltd v Southampton Container Terminal Ltd*[37] where the issue concerned the speed at which a trailer was travelling when the load fell off, the judge at first instance preferred the evidence of the witness of fact, but the Court of Appeal took the view that it would be unusual to disregard the evidence of a single joint expert

---

[35] See para 5.30 above.
[36] *Armstrong and Connor v First York Ltd* [2005] EWCA Civ 277, [2001] 1 WLR 2751.
[37] [2003] EWCA Civ 1223.

on an issue of fact on which no other direct evidence was called: 'subject to the need to evaluate his evidence in the light of his answers in cross-examination, his evidence is likely to prove compelling'. More recently in a case for breach of statutory duty,[38] the judge at first instance said he found the claimant to be a truthful and convincing witness and was inclined to believe him, and proceeded to make certain findings of fact before considering whether any of these findings required alteration in the light of the expert's evidence. When he found in favour of the claimant, the defendant appealed on the grounds that the judge had considered the claimant's credibility in isolation from the expert's evidence and had only considered the expert's evidence to establish whether or not it would cause him to change his mind. The Court of Appeal made it clear that where expert evidence was relevant to the way an accident might have happened, the judge should 'consider it at the time he was reaching his conclusions on the credibility of the witness'. But, although the judge had failed to do this, it did not mean that he had reached the wrong conclusion. In responding to written questions from the claimant, the expert had suggested that there were two possible causes of the accident, but gave no further assistance as to which of the two was the more likely. In the circumstances the issue of the credibility of the lay witnesses became critical and, as the judge at first instance had found the claimant to be convincing, his decision would stand, notwithstanding he had not approached the finding of the facts as he should have done.

K. The Future

In his address to the Annual Conference of the Expert Witness Institute in 1999, Lord Bingham of Cornhill, the senior Law Lord, commented that there was everything to be said for the appointment of a single joint expert when the relevant issues were comparatively uncontroversial or on the periphery of the case. He felt, however, that, where the issues were controversial and central to the case, it would be difficult to see how this procedure could work effectively. Experience confirms his view. **5.47**

Single joint experts are most commonly instructed in small claims, cases allocated to the fast track (including personal injury cases where a medical reporting agency may be used by insurers or solicitors and will usually instruct a GP, an orthopaedic surgeon, or an A&E consultant), straightforward cases with a potential value at the lower end of the multi-track, and for quantum reports in some larger cases, especially the less controversial ones. The objectives are to prevent unnecessarily adversarial conduct and to keep the costs of the expert **5.48**

---

[38] *Jakto Transport Ltd v Derek Hall* [2005] EWCA Civ 1327.

evidence proportionate. The Civil Justice Council is working towards a scheme of fixed or benchmark costs for medical reports in low-value personal injury claims, expected to be introduced in 2006 by consensus with organizations representing the medical experts. Such a step is unlikely to be accepted by some medical practitioners on the basis that the value of the case does not necessarily reflect the complexity of the issues and consequently the amount of work involved in providing an acceptable report. Medical experts who disagree with the simplistic approach may well decline to accept instructions. Whatever the rights or wrongs of this approach, however, it represents a pragmatic, cost-effective way of achieving settlement of the claim.

5.49 Elsewhere, acceptance of the single joint expert procedure has still to be firmly established. It has led to a practice which may be observed in large commercial cases of the litigating parties appointing, at their own expense, shadow experts to advise them on the report produced by the single joint expert. Far from producing a less expensive solution, it does in fact introduce additional costs for the parties which they will usually not be allowed to recover. Indeed in the Family Division serious concerns have been raised about using single joint experts in matrimonial cases where a wealthy husband might choose to instruct a shadow expert, which his impecunious wife would not be able to do. This would run counter to the basic premise of the CPR that there should, so far as possible, be equality of arms.

5.50 The experts themselves have often found the position of single joint expert far from easy. Isolated between the opposing parties as the expert is, it has been said that while a successful result will find one party disappointed, frequently the outcome is that both parties will find the conclusion unsatisfactory, and the blame for this is laid at the door of the expert.

5.51 From the many requests for assistance from experts to the Expert Witness Institute it is clear that there are instructing solicitors who are still not aware of the proper procedure for instructing a single joint expert. The Protocol for the Instruction of Experts, which is addressed as much to them as to the expert witness, will help, but its predecessor document, the Code of Guidance on Expert Evidence had been in circulation since December 2001, so solicitors should have already come to terms with the new requirements. A complaint often heard from solicitors is that the procedure for appointing a single joint expert is over-formalized and more time-consuming than former practice. For their part, the experts have frequently indicated that, despite the guidance provided by CPR Part 35, they often fail to receive proper instructions. CPR Part 35 does provide that where the parties cannot agree on the instructions they may provide separate instructions, but it would seem that this is still not always observed.

While, therefore, the use of single joint experts has in the first years of CPR Part **5.52** 35 proved to be a mixed blessing, it may well be that, other than in low-value fast-track personal injury claims, the courts will leave the parties to appoint their own experts and order those experts to meet at an early stage. If the court can have an indication at the pre-trial case management stage of what issues are agreed and what matters remain to be resolved, the prospects for a cost-effective, prompt settlement should be much brighter. In the meantime, the position of the single joint expert continues to evolve, with some distinct advantage to litigants, but not without problems—even if of a teething nature.

6

EXPERTS' REPORTS

A pitiable specimen is that poor man of science, pilloried up in the witness box, and pelted by the flippant ignorance of his examiner! What a contrast between the diffident caution of the true knowledge, and the bold assurance, the chuckling confidence, the vainglorious self-satisfaction, and mock triumphant delight of his questioner!

> 'Cornelius O'Dowd upon Men and Women, and Other Things in
> General', Blackwood's Edinburgh Magazine, September 1864,
> cited by Tal Golan, *Laws of Men and Laws of Nature* (2004) 52

A. The Need for Expert Evidence

The function of the court is to decide on fact and to apply the law. Expert **6.01** evidence of opinion frequently involves the process of inferring from the facts to assist in that first function. The difficulty is that the courts have traditionally excluded opinion evidence from the process lest the 'expert' usurp the role of the judge in deciding fact and law. Nevertheless the necessity and its solution is potentially resolved by s 3(1) of the Civil Evidence Act 1972, which states:

> Subject to any rules of Court made in pursuance of this Act, where a person is called as a witness in any civil proceedings, his opinion on any relevant matter on which he is qualified to give expert evidence shall be admissible in evidence.

This is a broad provision permitting otherwise admissible expert evidence as to **6.02** specialist matters not to be denied to the court merely because it trespasses upon the court's function of determining the issue(s) in the case. Necessary constraint, however, is pressed on the court (and the parties) by the Civil Procedure Rules. These give the civil courts the power and indeed duty to exclude or restrict expert evidence which could strictly be admitted under s 3 of the 1972 Act. Thus, expert evidence is not automatically admissible because it fulfils the criteria set out in s 3. It must also be relevant to the matters in issue and be beneficial to the court in arriving at its conclusions. The court must also accept that there exists a recognized field of expertise governed by recognized standards capable of assisting the court in relation to the matters in dispute.[1]

6.03   Since the CPR requires expert reports to be submitted in written form (see CPR r 35.5(1)) it is almost inconceivable, in modern litigation, that an expert could give evidence at trial without providing a written report which had been previously disclosed both to the court and to the other parties.[2] Indeed this is prescribed by CPR r 35.13:

> A party who fails to disclose an expert's report may not use the report at trial or call the expert to give evidence orally unless the court gives permission.

This chapter considers the court rules and procedures necessary to adduce expert evidence (in report form) at the trial.

B. The Nature of Expert Evidence

6.04   Usually experts' evidence is applied to a factual matrix established by the court, based on oral and written testimony, documents, and other source materials. The expert's function is to assist the court on the basis of his scientific, medical, professional, or technical knowledge so as to identify the subject-matter in connection with the dispute and/or to provide an analysis of the facts and/or to establish an appropriate standard of care.[3] In addition, the expert can assist on causation (how the damage was caused) and quantum of damages (the extent to which the loss sounds in damages). It is not the role of the experts to advise on the issue of law which is the sole province of the judge.[4]

6.05   In some cases an expert may properly give evidence as an ordinary witness, involving factual testimony and opinion evidence. A forensic pathologist[5] in a medical case, for example, may have conducted a post-mortem as to which he will be a witness of fact. Moreover, he may also be an 'opinion expert' because he will inform the court as to the likely cause of death and employ his expertise on

---

[1] See *Barings plc (In Liquidation) v Coopers & Lybrand (No 2)* [2001] Lloyd's Rep Bank 85, para 45, per Evans-Lombe J, where he allowed expert evidence to be given in relation to 'managers of investments coordinating the highly technical and specialised business of futures and derivatives trading' (ibid para 46).

[2] Note that in some cases the court will order that the experts' evidence can be given *only* by way of a written report, for example fast-track cases (see CPR r 35.5(2)) or where single joint experts are instructed. See also *Peet v Mid-Kent Healthcare NHS Trust* [2001] EWCA Civ 1703, [2002] 1 WLR 210.

[3] For a helpful analysis, see Dyson LJ, 'Expert Witnesses under the Civil Procedure Rules', Clinical Risk (2005); 11: 148–56.

[4] See *Midland Bank Trust Co Ltd v Helt, Stubbs & Kemp* [1979] Ch 384.

[5] Surveyors, accountants, and experts in foreign law may also give factual evidence.

other issues relating to a homicide. The boundary line between opinion and factual evidence may be indistinct in some aspects of contemporary litigation. Nevertheless, where possible, it is desirable for the expert to limit his evidence to the 'opinion issues' rather than the factual issues. It is open (and to be encouraged) to the expert, however, to provide opinion on different potential factual scenarios in anticipation of the judge's findings of fact.

In addition an expert is on occasion requested to conduct an inquiry on behalf of the court and then report back his conclusions to the court and to the parties.[6] **6.06**

Assessors (who are usually appointed for their particular expertise) sit with a judge to assist him to understand the complexities of technical evidence given in court. (See Chapter 8 below.) **6.07**

C. The Need to Restrict Expert Evidence

The seminal work in this area was carried out by Lord Woolf in his two reports entitled *Access to Justice*.[7] In para 2 of the Final Report, Lord Woolf criticized the development of 'A large litigation support industry, generating a multi-million pound fee income . . .', which meant that 'Many potential litigants do not even start litigation because of the advice they are given about costs', which he described as: **6.08**

> 'as great a social ill as the actual cost of pursuing litigation'.

His strong view was that the (over) use of experts had inexorably increased the complexity and delay of legal proceedings. As great a mischief was the disproportionality of costs to damages which in many cases was caused in part by the expense of experts. This had prevented 'access to justice' across the board. **6.09**

D. The Control of Expert Evidence

With a determination to effect change, Lord Woolf proposed that he would make recommendations to: **6.10**

- distinguish between the fact-finding and the opinion-giving roles of experts;
- increase the independence of experts and to reduce their partisan use by the parties;

---

[6] See *Tingle v Lannen*, 1992, unreported, where Ward J (as he then was) ordered a court inquiry as to whether the claimant was a patient within the Mental Health Act 1983. The experts for respective parties' experts had disagreed.

[7] See Interim Report (June 1995) <http://www.dca.gov.uk/civil/interim/woolf.htm> and Final Report (July 1996) <http://www.dca.gov.uk/civil/final/index.htm>.

- encourage the use of experts to narrow rather than multiply issues in dispute;
- reduce the delay and expense resulting from the use of experts; and
- ensure the parties and the court reduce to a minimum the inconvenience caused to experts in the conduct of their professional life by having to give evidence.[8]

6.11 His trenchant view was that it was necessary to implement wholesale reform of the court rules and procedures so better to define the inter-relationship between the court, the expert, and the parties, and to achieve the goals as set out above. All this was to be constructed within the constraints of the adversarial system as developed over the centuries by English common law.

6.12 The Civil Justice Council[9] was set up as an Advisory Public Body by the Civil Procedure Act 1997 (which was the statute containing the Woolf reforms) with responsibility for overseeing and coordinating the modernization of the civil justice system as laid out in Lord Woolf's reports, *Access to Justice*. The Council published a protocol in June 2005 offering guidance to experts.[10] Many organizations and bodies have been set up to develop good practice for the conduct of experts (and lawyers) in litigation.[11]

E. Independence of Experts

6.13 Up until the publication of the CPR, the duties and responsibilities of experts were uncodified and had developed at common law in a piecemeal way, no less since the introduction of the Civil Evidence Act 1972. Training in the writing of reports and the giving of evidence was virtually unknown in the United Kingdom prior to 1996. As a result, the duties and responsibilities of experts were disparate and in practice often ignored.

6.14 The decisions in the *The Ikarian Reefer*[12] and *Whitehouse v Jordan*[13] had *inter alia* set out some of the responsibilities of experts. Taken together they emphasized that expert evidence should be independent of the instructing parties and that an expert witness should state the facts and assumptions on which his report was based. (See Chapter 11 below.)

6.15 The CPR now codifies the extent of the expert's duties to the court once proceedings have begun. The CPR recognize, however, that there is an 'advisory role' for experts prior to the commencement of court actions.

---

[8] *Access to Justice*, Interim Report, ch 23, para 4.

[9] At <http://www.civiljusticecouncil.gov.uk>.

[10] See *Protocol for the Instruction of Experts to give evidence in civil claims* (June 2005) <http://www.civiljusticecouncil.gov.uk/914.htm>.

[11] For example, Clinical Disputes Forum in clinical negligence cases <http://www.clinical-disputes-forum.org.uk>.

[12] See (1993) 2 Lloyd's Rep 68.   [13] [1981] 1 WLR 246.

F. Special Protection to Experts:
Immunity from Suit in Negligence

For reasons of public policy the long-established common law rule was that **6.16** both advocates and experts were immune from suit in negligence or breach of contract, the latter probably as a witness in the proceedings. The rationale for such experts' immunity was so that experts were to speak freely at trial. The origins of the rule were traced to the judgment of Kelly CB in *Dawkins v Lord Rokeby*.[14]

The paramount issue for many litigants who have been seriously economically **6.17** damaged by allegedly poor expert advice and performance in court was whether such immunity from action continued in the modern world. A good example arose in the case of *Stanton v Callaghan*.[15] In this case the expert witness surveyor had been engaged by the claimant. He had indicated that the claimant's property required total underpinning, not the partial underpinning undertaken by the claimant's insurers. On the basis of this expert advice, the claimant issued proceedings against his insurer. Long after proceedings had been issued and substantial costs incurred, and after a meeting between the experts, the experts agreed that the 'gap solution' was the most effective (and by happenstance) the cheapest option. As a result the claimant was forced to settle the claim with his insurers on disadvantageous terms.[16] The claimant then sued his expert in contract and negligence.

When considering the question of the immunity of the expert and his report **6.18** from suit in negligence and/or breach of contract, Chadwick LJ, in the Court of Appeal, stated as follows:

> What, then, is the position in relation to expert reports? It seems to me that the following propositions are supported by authority binding in this Court: (i) an expert witness who gives evidence at trial is immune from suit in respect of anything which he says in Court, and that immunity will extend to the contents of the report which he adopts as, or incorporates in, his evidence; (ii) where an expert witness gives evidence at trial the immunity which he would enjoy in respect of

---

[14] (1873) LR 8 QB 255, 263–5. Kelly CB concluded that 'no action lies against a witness upon evidence given before any court or tribunal constituted according to law'.

[15] [2000] 1 QB 75.

[16] Proceedings were commenced in August 1986; the trial was fixed for 11 January 1990; the experts meeting took place on 14 December 1989: 'the Plaintiffs were faced with the choice of accepting his advice or instructing another expert' ([2000] 1 QB 75, 87, per Chadwick LJ).

that evidence is not to be circumvented by a suit based on the report itself; and (iii) the immunity does not extend to protect an expert who has been retained to advise as to the merits of a party's claim in litigation from a suit by the party by whom he has been retained in respect of that advice, notwithstanding that it was in contemplation at the time when the advice was given that the expert would be a witness at the trial if that litigation were to proceed.[17]

6.19 Thus the law was unambiguous in respect of evidence given at trial. Immunity from suit was absolute. The actual expert report was also immune from suit lest any disappointed litigant tried to circumvent the principal rule.

6.20 It was less straightforward in relation to the work where an expert acted 'to advise as to the merits of a party's claim'. Precisely what the court meant by this remains unclear.

6.21 The trend in recent years has been to establish culpability and to abolish immunity[18] and, until the decision of *Arthur JS Hall & Co v Simons*,[19] the clear authority was that 'provided the test of "principle and proximate connection" is satisfied, the pre-hearing work of an expert will come in the protective circle of the witness immunity principle'.[20]

6.22 However, in the case of *Hall*, the House of Lords considered the extent to which the allegedly negligent conduct of a lawyer in conducting his client's case in the litigation was immune from suit. The majority held that in the modern world none of the previously stated reasons for immunity subsisted (i.e. divided loyalty, the cab rank rule, the witness analogy, and the collateral challenge) and accordingly the administration of justice no longer required advocates to enjoy such immunity.

6.23 This was a big blow to the legal profession. In the course of the judgments, their Lordships also gave consideration to the immunity allowed to experts. This was in response to counsel acting for the legal profession who argued that a sturdy plank in the defence of the status quo was to align the immunity which experts enjoyed, by analogy to lawyers. It was argued that the lawyer and the expert were performing the same function in assisting the court. In considering this analogy, Lord Hoffmann said:

5. The witness analogy

No one can be sued in defamation for anything said in court. The Rule confers an absolute immunity which protects witnesses, lawyers and the judge. The

---

[17] [2000] 1 QB 75, 100.

[18] See *Kent v Griffiths and London Ambulance Service* [2001] QB 36 where emergency services were confirmed to be liable in negligence.

[19] [2002] 1 AC 615.

[20] *Raiss v Palmano* [2001] PNLR 21, per Eady J. Surprisingly the judge also thought that the dishonest representation of panel membership by the expert was also covered by the immunity—ibid para 9.

administration of justice requires that participants in court proceedings should be able to speak freely without being inhibited by fear of being sued, even unsuccessfully, for what they say. The immunity has also been extended to statements made out of court in the course of preparing evidence to be given in court.[21]

6.24 In refusing to allow continuance of this immunity to advocates, Lord Hoffmann confirmed (on a number of occasions in his judgment) that the immunity still applied to witnesses, including expert witnesses. His bold and unambiguous assertion was: 'A witness owes no duty of care to anyone in respect to the evidence he gives to the Court. His only duty is to tell the truth.'[22]

6.25 Nevertheless, it is undoubtedly true that the immunity for experts is not considered to be absolute and the principle of 'proximate connection' still applies.[23] In other words, not all work undertaken by experts during the litigation is protected. There is no legal certainty as to how far this immunity protects experts. Evidence at trial, attendance at experts' meetings, and preparation of reports have all been declared either immune from suit or protected by legal privilege.

6.26 It seems clear that advisory reports, i.e. opinions written before proceedings are commenced, do attract a potentially tortious relationship. What is more opaque is the protection afforded to those experts' reports prepared by 'shadow experts' (for example, those instructed to comment on disclosed or joint experts' reports) or those prepared after proceedings have commenced, but not utilized in the proceedings, or those experts who fail to follow precise instructions.[24] It cannot be long until the courts are asked to rule on the precise extent of the 'circle of immunity'. In *Meadow v General Medical Council*,[25] Collins J held that an expert witness is immune from disciplinary proceedings, as a corollary to the immunity from suit in negligence, save where the trial judge chooses to report the expert to the statutory regulator.

6.27 There is considerable difficulty in establishing with any rigour the exact extent of the immunity and this has led to significant debate. For example, there can be a substantial time lag between instruction of experts and trial. Indeed, Lord Hoffmann thought that the difficulty was so great that this was in the context of advocate's immunity, '. . . another reason why the [advocate's] immunity should

---

[21] [2002] 1 AC 615, 687.   [22] ibid 698.
[23] See also 'reports . . . prepared with a view to giving evidence': *Darker v Chief Constable of West Midlands Police Force* [2000] 1 AC 435, 447, per Hope LJ.
[24] See also the Protocol for the Instruction of Experts, para 5.1: 'Advice which the parties do not intend to adduce in litigation is likely to be confidential'.
[25] [2006] EWHC 146 (Admin). The General Medical Council has applied to the Court of Appeal for permission to appeal: see Chapter 9 below.

be altogether abolished'.[26] Similar views were held by Lord Hope of Craighead and Hutton LJ.

6.28 It is not inconceivable that in the future the courts will emphasize the analogy between the expert and the advocate and follow the example of Lord Hutton (in respect of advocates) in *Hall*:

> because of the difficulty of drawing a clear line to fix the boundaries of the immunity and because in civil proceedings the error which is alleged to constitute negligence, even though committed in court, will often be attributable to a decision taken . . . in the relevant tranquillity of barristers' chambers and not in the hurly burly of trial, I consider that, when this is linked to the public perception to which I have referred, the balance falls in favour of removing the immunity in civil matters.[27]

and therefore abolish the present immunity given to experts.

6.29 Can it be said that experts write their reports in tranquil offices outside 'the hurly burly of the trial' in practice? Indeed para 1.2 of the CPR Part 35 Practice Direction requires that: 'Expert evidence should be the independent product of the expert uninfluenced by the pressures of litigation'. This is an acknowledgement that best practice is to write reports distanced from clients' legal representations capable of influencing the scope and nature of experts' reports.

6.30 Is there a distinction between a report written by an accountant for the purposes of a court trial (many months or years before that trial) or, say, for a large financial institution or government department outside the litigation process, save that in the former case the law allows the accountant immunity from suit in negligence or breach of contract? Although expert immunity seems to be established by case law, the trend suggests otherwise. The courts may already have laid the groundwork for the demise of any immunity. At the very least we can expect a fairly strict definition of how wide the 'circle of immunity' is to extend.

G. No Immunity from Order against Expert Witness to Pay Litigant's Costs

6.31 Although an expert may be immune from a negligence claim when he gives evidence in court, it is not inconsistent with that principle for an expert to pay wasted costs if the expert is in flagrant disregard of duties owed to the court.[28] The incurring of substantial and unnecessary legal costs by an unsuccessful litigant, let down by a hopeless expert, is likely to be a significant part of the

---

[26] *Arthur JS Hall & Co v Simons* [2002] 1 AC 615, 707.   [27] ibid 729.
[28] See further Chapter 9 below.

economic harm suffered. In many cases, though not all, this will be the only loss suffered, since with credible expert advice, presumably litigation would not have been initiated in the first place. Costs can run into many thousands of pounds. Experts should be wary of supporting actions on flimsy grounds.

In *Phillips v Symes*,[29] a consultant psychiatrist had expressed the view that **6.32** Mr Symes had been incapable of managing his own affairs since 1980, which had in the judge's words resulted in 'serious consequences' to Mr Symes. The question which occupied the court was to what extent, if at all, Mr Symes had a right of redress if the expert was immune from suit in negligence and breach of contract. The logical next step was to consider where an order for costs against the expert was available, but there was precious little warning to experts that this was a potential risk. However, the Protocol for Instruction of Experts reproduced in the Part 35 Practice Direction indicates as follows:

> 4.7 Experts should be aware that any failure by them to comply with the Civil Procedure Rules or court orders or any excessive delay for which they are responsible may result in the parties who instructed them being penalised in costs and even, in extreme cases, being debarred from placing the experts' evidence before the court. In *Phillips v Symes* Peter Smith J held that the courts may also make orders for costs (under section 51 of the Supreme Court Act 1981) directly against expert witnesses who by their evidence cause significant expense to be incurred, and do so in flagrant disregard of their duties to the Court.

Moreover, para 2.4 of the Part 35 Practice Direction contains the mandatory requirement that each report be signed off by the expert with the statement that: 'the opinions I have expressed represent my true and complete professional opinion'.

In de-coupling expert immunity from a wasted costs application, Peter Smith J **6.33** said:

> It seems to me that in the administration of justice, especially, in spite of the clearly defined duties now enshrined in CPR 35 and PD 35, it would be quite wrong of the court to remove from itself the power to make a costs order in appropriate circumstances against an Expert who, by his evidence, causes significant expense to be incurred, and does so in flagrant reckless disregard of his duties to the Court.
> I do not regard the other available sanctions as being effective or anything other than blunt instruments.[30] The proper sanction is the ability to compensate a person who has suffered loss by reason of that evidence . . . I do not accept that Experts will, by reason of this potential exposure, be inhibited from the fulfilling their duties. That is a crie de cour [sic] often made by professionals, but I cannot believe that an expert would be deterred, because a costs order might be made against him in the event that his evidence is given recklessly, in flagrant disregard

---

[29] [2004] EWHC 2330, [2005] 1 WLR 2043.
[30] 'Committal, reporting to professional bodies and the like'.

for his duties. The high level of proof required to establish the breach cannot be ignored. The floodgates argument failed as regards lawyers and is often the last resort of court . . .

The idea that the witness should be immune from the most significant sanction that the court could apply for that witness breaching his duties owed to the court seems to me to be an affront to the sense of justice.[31]

6.34 Peter Smith J ordered that there be an inquiry into the expert's conduct in the case, in particular to establish whether or not the evidence he gave was in 'flagrant breach of his duties'. Experts did not need a specific warning as to the risks as to costs. The risk was self-evident from CPR r 32.14 which applies to all experts as well as lay witnesses and states:

Proceedings for contempt of court may be brought against a person if he makes, or causes to be made, a false statement in a document verified by a statement of truth without an honest belief in its truth.

So the expert's declaration which is a mandatory requirement indicates that the expert could be the subject to contempt proceedings and also for perjury.[32]

H. Privilege from Disclosure of Some Experts' Reports

6.35 The doctrine of legal professional privilege applies to communications between clients and their lawyers. It also encompasses the preparation of witness statements and expert reports, as long as they are made in the contemplation of litigation. Since the development of the CPR and in particular the 'cards-on-the-table approach', the question of privilege from disclosure of some expert reports has become an important issue as one party attempts to gain advantage over the other. Now that the principal duty of the expert is to the court (once proceedings have begun) some have argued that all expert reports are disclosable to the opponent, no matter when (in relation to the state of proceedings) such report had been commissioned or written.

6.36 This has always been an over-enthusiastic view, because from the inception of the CPR there was a recognition of the distinction of the expert who owed a duty to the court, and one who did not, namely 'A reference to an "expert" . . . is a reference to an expert who has been instructed to give or prepare evidence for the purpose of court proceedings' (CPR r 35.2). Self-evidently an expert could not owe a duty to the court if proceedings had not yet been issued. This

---

[31] [2004] EWHC 2330, paras 95–96, 98.
[32] The procedure by which allegations of interference with the course of justice are brought—see the Contempt of Court Act 1981. Perjury would lie only if the expert has given evidence as to factual matters. Perjury cannot lie for an expression of opinion, which is a matter of judgment. A dishonest opinion might contribute to perverting the course of justice.

'advisory' expert owes a primary duty to the client and, as we have seen, may not be immune from an action in negligence or breach of contract.

This position is in contrast to where experts are instructed to provide reports **6.37** when proceedings have commenced. These reports are addressed to the court signifying that the expert's duty is to the court rather than to his instructing party, with the consequent benefit of immunity from suit.

The timing of the commencement of the expert's duty to the court is, however, **6.38** not clear. Lawyers began to face potential problems with regard to which experts' reports were said to be disclosable. Was it, for example, all expert reports commissioned after proceedings had begun, or was it restricted to expert reports where (and when) the court gave permission[33] to a party to rely on an expert in a particular field? Some experts took the view that all reports were potentially disclosable to the court and were written accordingly.

The reality is that in virtually all litigation the case develops after the process **6.39** of discovery of documents and exchange of witness evidence which usually precedes exchange of expert evidence. It would be surprising if an expert's view did not develop in tandem with this. It would be even more surprising if the expert's initial (out-of-date) views were to be disclosable to the court and to the opponent.

The Court of Appeal in *Jackson v Marley Davenport Ltd*[34] considered whether **6.40** the claimants could withhold from disclosure an expert's preliminary report made in preparation of his final report and Longmore LJ stated:

> There can be no doubt that, if an expert makes a report for the purpose of a party's legal advisers being able to give legal advice to their client, or for discussion in a conference of a party's legal advisers, such a report is the subject matter of litigation privilege at the time it is made. It has come into existence for the purposes of litigation. It is common for drafts of expert reports to be circulated among a party's advisers before a final report is prepared for exchange with the other side. Such initial reports are privileged.
>
> I cannot believe that the Civil Procedure Rules were intended to override that privilege.[35]

The effect of this decision is to make de jure that which already had been de **6.41** facto.[36] Of course, experts and lawyers on each side had been collaborating in the light of further evidence garnered as the case progressed. Many had spent considerable time maintaining the fiction that only the disclosed report was in

---

[33] Usually at the case management conference some time after legal proceedings began.
[34] [2004] EWCA Civ 1225, [2005] PIQR P141.   [35] ibid paras 13 and 14.
[36] Longmore LJ specifically placed reliance on the Code of Guidance on Expert Evidence which made provision for amendments to be made to the report.

existence. The condoning of such practice by the Court of Appeal may in some minds detract from the stated intention of the reforms to make experts more independent and less partisan. Certainly, the case recognizes the necessary balance between the team approach vis-à-vis experts and lawyers as the litigation develops and the duty of the expert to the court to give evidence which is honest and impartial.

I. Evolution of Expert Evidence

6.42 For those outside the litigation process it is often difficult to understand how expert evidence develops over the life of the case, to its pinnacle of testimony at trial. Frequently, an expert's involvement in the process can begin with a telephone call and grow into the sapling of an initial report, drafted to advise the party even before proceedings are begun. This advisory evidence is crucial to the litigation process. Without it many cases would wither and die. For this reason such reports are owned by the instructed party and are protected from disclosure to the opponent and to the court by legal professional privilege.

6.43 It is self-evident that, notwithstanding the commencement of proceedings, the case will continue to develop and the expert will be showered with further evidence. Indeed usual case management requires that, before exchange of expert evidence, there be proper discovery of documents and materials and the exchange of witness statements. Prior and during this process the expert's report is still protected by legal professional privilege and is not disclosable to anyone other than the instructing parties. It is only when the evidence and investigation is complete that the report blossoms into a fully disclosable report in a final form.[37]

6.44 Nevertheless it is important to emphasize that instructing parties expect the same standards of independence, objectivity, and honesty no matter when the report is commissioned. The semantic difference of 'advisory' and 'court' reports is only relevant because in the former status lawyers expect the possibility of change, whereas in the latter status such change can only be rare and exceptional.

J. Instructions to Experts

6.45 An important weapon to strengthen the independence of the expert and to emphasize his duty to the court was to remove the right of the party to claim legal professional privilege over his instructions to the expert. An expert is now

---

[37] See *Jackson v Marley Davenport Ltd* [2004] EWCA Civ 225, [2005] PIQR P141.

required to set out in his report 'the substance of material, instructions whether written or oral' (see CPR r 35.10(3)).

6.46 This logical requirement, imposing an open understanding as to the purpose of expert instruction, was supplemented with a new requirement that such instructions were not to be privileged from the disclosure but that:

> (4) The instructions referred to in paragraph (3) shall not be privileged against disclosure but the court will not, in relation to those instructions—
> (a) order disclosure of any specific documents; or
> (b) permit any questioning in court, other than by the party who instructed the expert, unless it is satisfied that there are reasonable grounds to consider the statement of instructions given under paragraph (3) to be inaccurate or incomplete.[38]

6.47 In considering which instructions were available for disclosure and therefore not privileged Longmore LJ in *Jackson v Marley Davenport Ltd* stated that these were those that related 'to the expert's intended evidence, not to the earlier and privileged draft of what may or may not in due course become the expert's evidence'.[39]

6.48 This is a sensible and pragmatic approach by the Court of Appeal. It allows the instructions to the expert to develop naturally with the case. An issue, which might have seemed important to a party at the outset, may have receded, while another may have become redundant and yet another the crucial point in the case. It is unproductive and irrelevant to show this development either to the court or to the opponent. This is providing the expert complies with the duty as set out in the Protocol for the Instruction of Experts as follows:

> 15.2 Experts should not be asked to, and should not, amend, expand or alter any parts of reports in a manner which distorts their true opinion, but may be invited to amend or expand their reports to ensure accuracy, internal consistency, completeness and relevance to the issues and clarity. Although experts should generally follow recommendations of solicitors with regard to the form of reports, they should form their own independent views as to the opinions and contents expressed in their reports and exclude any suggestions which do not accord with their views.

6.49 Before disclosure of any report, the expert should be given the opportunity to review and, if necessary, update the contents of the report.

6.50 The requirement of openness of instruction, together with the removal of privilege where instructions appear 'inaccurate or incomplete', provides a strong deterrent for experts becoming too imbedded in the one-party team approach.

---

[38] CPR r 35.10(4).
[39] *Jackson v Marley Davenport Ltd* [2004] EWCA Civ 1225, [2005] PIQR P141, para 14.

K. Range of Opinion

6.51 In yet a further mechanism to overcome the 'hired gun' approach, para 2.2(6) of the Part 35 Practice Direction requires an expert to consider not just his own view, but:

> where there is a range of opinion on the matters dealt with in the report—
> (a) summarise the range of opinion, and
> (b) give reasons for his own opinion.

6.52 This is also supplemented by the requirement in para 1.4 of the Practice Direction that 'An expert should consider all the material facts, including those which might detract from his opinion'.

6.53 Strict adherence to the Practice Direction by the expert requires an analysis of not only how he came to his own opinion, but also what other experts are likely to think within the context of the case. In effect this 'justification analysis' provides a counter-check to the expert's own analysis and logically leads to the deliverance of a more independent opinion. This process is particularly important in professional negligence cases where there may be a range of practice which could be considered by the court to be acceptable.

L. Attendance at Court

6.54 An expert must understand that he may be required to attend trial. Usually a solicitor is able to give proper notice of this because the trial is fixed in advance. Sometimes the expert is unable to attend for good reason and the courts will try to ensure that the expert's diary is taken into account and that he can attend at a convenient time. Some experts require witness summonses to be served to secure attendance; others do not. Common courtesy requires the instructing solicitors to ascertain which their expert prefers. In *Brown v Bennett*,[40] an expert was successful in setting aside a witness summons where a party wished to call her as a expert but could no longer afford her fees.

6.55 The courts have also become much more flexible as to the method of delivering expert evidence at trial. The use of video link and telephone is now relatively commonplace.

---

[40] 2 November 2000, unreported.

M. Form and Content of Experts' Reports

General format

Guidance as to the general format of an expert's report (see also Chapter 3 **6.56** above) is contained in CPR r 35.10 and in further detail in para 2 of the Part 35 Practice Direction. The requirements can be summarized as follows:

(1) The report should be addressed to the court so as to emphasize the expert's duty in this regard.

(2) The report should provide details of the expert's academic and professional qualifications as well as his experience. The more esoteric the case, the more detail is required in this respect. See *Stevens v Gullis*.[41]

(3) The report should set out the source and details of the material instructions.

(4) The report should make clear the facts upon which the expert bases his opinion. Any assumptions made should be clearly set out.

(5) The report should set out the range of opinion and provide compelling reasons for the expert's own opinion. It is sensible to set out carefully how and on what basis the material, practice, or school of thought this range of opinion subsists.

(6) The report should summarize the expert's conclusions. This can be either at the beginning or the end of the report.

(7) The report should set out any qualifications to the opinion (i.e. the report is subject to findings or fact, the interpretation of results outside of the expert's field, the provision of additional material information, or expert advice (see CPR r 35.9)).

(8) If an expert interviews a witness for the purpose of his report, the note of the interview should be disclosed by annexing it to the report.[42]

(9) The report should identify and annex plans, photographs, models, etc referred to in the report.[43]

---

[41] [1999] EWCA Civ 1978: 'The requirements of the Practice Direction that an expert understands his responsibilities and is required to give details of his qualifications . . . are intended to focus the mind of the expert on his responsibilities in order that litigation may progress in accordance with the overriding principle', ibid 6, per Lord Woolf.

[42] See *Bank of Credit and Commerce International SA (In Liquidation) v Ali (No 3)* [1999] 4 All ER 83.

[43] See CPR r 33.6 which specifically requires special notice (21 days before the trial) to be given if reliance is to be placed on this material if it is 'not contained in an . . . expert's report'.

Liability reports

6.57 A good liability report should deliver the following:[44]

(1) An objective and forensic reconstruction of the events using the factual witness testimony, the documents, and other material which are available to the expert. It may be necessary for the expert to provide an opinion on alternative factual scenarios.

(2) The methodology utilized and in particular whether any tests were carried out and, if so, by whom and under whose instruction.

(3) An explanation of the technical, scientific, or medical terms used in the report.

(4) A conclusion based on the balance of probabilities that one factual scenario is to be preferred. This may arise where there is a factual dispute and the expert can reach this conclusion because of his particular speciality. For example, in a clinical negligence case, an expert may take the view that the symptoms of a medical condition are more likely to fit with, say, the claimant's account of events. This is controversial ground and needs to be well supported.

(5) In professional negligence cases, an opinion on whether or not the professional has acted or failed to act in accordance with the acceptable standards. Here the expert should consider each possible omission or commission and give reasons for his opinion.

(6) In the case of an expert opinion which seeks to criticize an omission, such as the failure to perform a particular task (prevalent in medical and professional negligence cases), the report must set out, on a hypothetical basis what would have happened, on the balance of probabilities, but for the omission.[45] This is a necessary speculation by the expert and the duty in this respect may be considered to be a blur between the role of the judge to make findings on fact and that of the expert who provides explanations with regard to probable 'hypothetical facts'. Needless to say this is a controversial area and the expert must take great care.

(7) Reference to the published (and if necessary unpublished) technical, scientific, and medical material in support of the expert's opinions with copies annexed to the report.

(8) A view as to whether in relation to the key issues, the result has been to cause or materially contribute to the alleged loss.

---

[44] Model forms of experts' reports are available from the Expert Witness Institute and the Academy of Experts. Most instructing solicitors are likely to be able to supply a model report for experts to consider.

[45] *Bolitho v City and Hackney Health Authority* [1998] AC 232.

(9) An admission of any issue in the case that falls outside the expert's expertise.

(10) A summary of any missing information or material that is important to the case.

Declaration of truth

It is mandatory for all reports to be signed and for the expert to make the following declaration of truth: **6.58**

> I confirm that insofar as the facts stated in my report are within my own knowledge I have made clear which they are and I believe them to be true, and that the opinions I have expressed represent my true and complete professional opinion.[46]

This declaration of truth is the basis of the expert opinion to the court, the one upon which ultimately the court can enact perjury or contempt proceedings. In the case of *Stevens v Gullis*[47] the court held that if an expert disregards his duty to the court his expert opinion may be excluded, resulting in the instructing party losing the case. **6.59**

N. Amendments to an Expert's Report

In the modern practice of litigation it is almost inconceivable that an expert's report will be suitable for disclosure after the first treatment. It is inevitable that whenever an expert is instructed and the report written, the lawyer will wish to seek a clarification. This may be prompted to avoid opposing counsel doing so pursuant to the provisions of CPR r 35.6 which allows written questions to be put to the expert for such purpose. Indeed the court by this very provision and by decisions stretching from *Whitehouse v Jordan*[48] to *Jackson v Marley Davenport Ltd*[49] have condoned the practice. Experts need not be embarrassed; it is a fact of litigation life. **6.60**

Nevertheless, the courts have also been at considerable pains to emphasize that over-ambitious lawyers should not be permitted to direct the expert away from his overriding duty to the court (objective and impartial) towards the much condemned status of the (partisan) 'hired gun'. Therefore, amendments are allowable, with strict guidance. **6.61**

---

[46] Part 35 Practice Direction, para 2.4.

[47] [1999] EWCA Civ 1978. The court was doubtful about the qualifications of an 'expert' to give evidence. In any event the expert had failed to comply with the directions of the court and the case was dismissed on this basis.

[48] [1981] 1 WLR 246.   [49] [2004] EWCA Civ 1225, [2005] PIQR P141.

6.62 The guidance given in para 15.2 of the Protocol for the Instruction of Experts has been set out at para 6.48 above, but is worth repeating in this context. It states:

> Experts should not be asked to, and should not, amend, expand or alter any parts of reports in a manner which distorts their true opinion, but may be invited to amend or expand reports to ensure accuracy, internal consistency, completeness and relevance to the issues and clarity. Although experts should generally follow the recommendation of solicitors with regard to the form of reports, they should form their own independent views as to the opinions and contents expressed in their reports and exclude any suggestions which do not accord with their views.

O. Duty of Instructing Lawyers and their Clients to Experts

6.63 The principal duty of instructing parties is the common courtesy to keep experts informed of the progress of the litigation. Particular matters that need to be addressed are:

(1) The service of statements of case, witness statements, documents, and other material.

(2) The exchange of experts' reports whether voluntarily or as a result of case management. Proper practice requires that the expert be given the opportunity to review his report prior to disclosure alongside the contemporaneous disclosed evidence (see above).

(3) Provision of information to the experts of the timetable set by the court which is usually in the format of an order for directions. Note that the court has the power to 'direct that a party be served with a copy of the directions' (see CPR r 35.14(3)). The word 'party' has been given a wide meaning to include experts.

(4) There is a responsibility to advise the expert of the name, address, and case number of the action in which the expert is advising. Moreover it is also sensible to give the expert the name of the Queen's Bench Master or district judge who has control of the action so that the expert can write direct to the court, if required, pursuant to CPR r 35.14.

(5) Instructing solicitors must fix the date for trial as conveniently as possible for the expert. They should obtain 'dates to avoid' and inform the expert of the date fixed for trial as early as possible.

(6) It is remarkable how often experts complain of a lack of knowledge that a case had settled and the trial date vacated. Again it is common courtesy to advise the expert of this. Indeed the team approach requires experts to be thanked and congratulated if they assist in a successful case.

(7) Lawyers must abide by the terms of their contract with experts and make reasonable efforts to fulfil them and to make payment of fees on time.

P. Change of Opinion

On grounds of public policy, experts have so far been given immunity from suit **6.64**
in negligence and/or breach of contract for evidence which they prepare, provided that it has a 'principle and proximate connection' with the evidence given
or to be given at trial. The philosophy behind the public policy was to ensure
that experts are able to speak freely in order to override the fear of suit arising
out of a change from a previously held position. No barriers must be erected by
the court or instructing lawyers or their clients to prevent an expert retracting
from an opinion with dignity and without damage to his bank balance.

The position was clearly set out by Chadwick LJ in *Stanton v Callaghan*:[50]   **6.65**

> It is of importance to the administration of justice, and to those members of the
> public who seek access to justice, that trials should take no longer than is necessary
> to do justice in the particular case, and that, to that end, time in Court should not
> be taken up with the consideration of matters which are not truly at issue. It is in
> that context that experts are encouraged to identify, in advance of the trial, those
> parts of evidence on which they are, and those on which they are not, in agree-
> ment. Provision for a joint statement, reflecting agreement after a meeting of
> experts has taken place, is made by Order 38 rule 38. [See now CPR r 35.12.] In
> my view, *the public interest in facilitating full and frank discussion between experts
> before trial does require that each should be free to make proper concessions without fear
> that any departure from advice previously given to the party who has retained him will
> be seen as evidence of negligence.* That, as it seems to me, is an area in which public
> policy justifies immunity. The immunity is needed in order to avoid the tension
> between a desire to assist the court and fear of the consequences of a departure
> from previous advice. (emphasis supplied)[51]

This passage was approved in *Arthur JS Hall & Co v Simons*.[52]

The principle is long established. The practice is now set out in para 15.4 of the **6.66**
the Protocol for the Instruction of Experts which states:

> Where experts significantly alter their opinion, as a result of new evidence
> or because evidence on which they relied has become unreliable, or for any
> other reason, they should amend their reports to reflect that fact. Amended
> reports should include reasons for amendments. In such circumstances those
> instructing experts should inform other parties as soon as possible of any change of
> opinion.

The clear message is for the expert to inform his instructing party as soon as **6.67**
possible. It is rarely necessary to amend the report, but it is always necessary for
the expert to set out in detail the precise reasons for the change of view.

---

50 [2001] QB 75.   51 ibid 101–102.
52 [2002] 1 AC 615, 698, per Lord Hoffmann.

Q. Expert's Withdrawal from the Case

6.68 It is not just a change of opinion which requires the expert to withdraw from a case. In that event, it is likely that the decision will be made (see *Stanton v Callaghan* above) by the instructing party rather than the expert. The principles of 'freedom of speech' coupled with the expert's duty to the court and to his professional body may, however, result in withdrawal from the case in other circumstances.

6.69 The position is summarized in para 10.1 of the Protocol for the Instruction of Experts:

> Where experts' instructions remain incompatible with their duties, whether through incompleteness, a conflict between their duty to the court and their instructions, or for any other substantial and significant reason, they may consider withdrawing from the case. However, experts should not withdraw without first discussing the position fully with those who instruct them and considering carefully whether it would be more appropriate to make a written request with directions from the court. If experts do withdraw, they must give formal written notice to those instructing them.

6.70 The advice is sound. Nevertheless, any instructing solicitor would advise experts against seeking unilateral directions from the court without the fullest discussion between the expert, the solicitor, and the client. In effect writing to the court for guidance will make public the reason for withdrawal and may have consequences for the case which the instructing parties may wish to avoid. Ultimately however the expert may feel it necessary to seek direction from the court to withdraw from the case against the wishes of the instructing parties.

R. Numbers and Disciplines of Experts

6.71 CPR r 35.1 states that 'Expert evidence shall be restricted to that which is reasonably required to resolve the proceedings'. The previous practice of using a 'hired gun' to bolster cases was fundamentally condemned by Lord Woolf. Active management of cases from an early stage has cut down the over-use of experts in litigation. Judges are now required to accept 'lesser' evidence to help establish a fact. For example, the value of property, motor vehicles, the cost of nursing care, and earnings have all been determined on readily available publications rather than expert evidence. The court has recently held that expert evidence was not needed from an accountant on the meaning and interpretation of standard accountancy documents.[53]

---

[53] *LHS Holdings v Laporte* [2001] EWCA Civ 278.

The CPR fail to define what expert evidence is 'reasonably required', perhaps, **6.72** because this is case and fact sensitive. An important power is provided by CPR r 35.4(4) which states that 'The court may limit the amount of the expert's fees and expenses that the party who wishes to rely on the expert may recover from the other party'.

In *ES v Chesterfield and North Derbyshire Royal Hospital NHS Trust*[54] the general **6.73** principle of CPR r 35.1 to limit expert evidence to that which is reasonably necessary to resolve the proceedings was acknowledged. The court suggested however that: 'It would be wrong to approach this question with the predetermined belief that to instruct more than one expert in the same discipline will always be excessive'.[55]

What is required is 'fact sensitive' to each case. In *ES*, an obstetric negligence **6.74** case, the defendants intended to call three treating consultant obstetricians as factual witnesses at the trial. The Court of Appeal emphasized the importance of:

(1) the parties being on an equal footing; and
(2) proportionality between the value of the claim, the complexity of the issues, and the financial position of each party.

In ordering that the claimant be allowed to adduce evidence from two expert **6.75** consultant obstetricians, Brooke LJ said:

> Anybody watching the trial would be bound to be impressed by the fact that there was only one consultant obstetrician giving evidence for the claimant, while there would be three giving evidence for the defendant hospital trust, and those three would cover a much wider spectrum of personal experience than the single expert permitted to the claimant.[56]

This case demonstrates the flexible approach adopted by the Court of Appeal **6.76** which also emphasized that its judgment was restricted to the facts of the case, stating that 'the general rule must be . . . that in the vast majority of cases there should be no more than one expert in any one speciality'.[57]

S. Case Managers and Rehabilitation Experts

In *Wright v Sullivan*[58] the Court of Appeal had to determine the role of a **6.77** claimant's clinical case manager in the context of contested personal injury litigation. The Rehabilitation Code,[59] which applies to personal injury claims,

---

[54] [2003] EWCA Civ 1284, [2004] CP Rep 9.   [55] ibid para 17, per Brooke LJ.
[56] ibid para 24.   [57] ibid para 43(1).
[58] [2005] EWCA Civ 656, [2006] 1 WLR 172.
[59] See Annex D to the Pre-action Protocol for Personal Injury Claims.

recommends the appointment of clinical case managers to coordinate the rehabilitation process and to consider the claimants' future needs over a spectrum of clinical services, from nursing care to the provision of accommodation. The court in *Wright v Sullivan* held that a case manager owed a duty to act in the best interests of the patient alone. The appointment should not be made by the parties jointly and if such an expert was required to give evidence at court, she was a witness of fact. As a consequence she could attend a conference with the claimant's legal team. Brooke LJ stated:

> . . . It seems to me inevitable that the clinical case manager should owe her duties to her patient alone. She must win the patient's trust and if possible her co-operation in what has been proposed, and while it will be in her patient's interest that she should receive a flow of suggestions from any other experts who have been instructed in the case, she must immediately make decisions in the best interests of the patient and not be beholdened to two different masters.

> Needless to say, any communications the clinical case manager may have with the claimant's expert witnesses whose dominant purpose is not one which attracts litigation privilege . . . will be disclosed as a matter of course. But if the clinical case manager considers that it is in her client's interest that she should attend a conference with legal advisers at which advice is being sought then the privilege is not hers to waive, and I do not consider that the court would have any power to direct such waiver.

> . . The role of a clinical case manager, if she is called to give evidence at the trial, will clearly be one of witness of fact . . . She will not be giving evidence of expert opinion and the regime of CPR Part 35 and its Practice Direction will not therefore relate to her evidence.[60]

6.78 Thus the anomalous position of the duty owed by a case manager, who is clearly an expert in her field, has been clarified. It is evident that this individual may be giving expert testimony as to opinion one day, and witness evidence as to fact another day.

T. Scientific, Medical, and Technical Literature

6.79 All expert reports should be supported by reference to scientific, medical, or technical literature published either at the date at which the relevant facts took place or at the time of the trial (depending on the issues to be considered by the court). The more supportive the published material, the more likely it is that the expert's view will be convincing to the court (and to the opposition). Prudent lawyers also ask their experts to provide a list of published material which does not support the case, in readiness for the opponent's assault.

---

[60] [2005] EWCA Civ 656, [2006] 1 WLR 172.

DN v London Borough of Greenwich[61] involved the appropriate education to be **6.80** given to a claimant who suffered from Asperger's Syndrome. The defendants relied on their employed educational psychologist and failed to call an expert educational psychologist. The judge at trial relied to a large extent on the evidence given by the claimant's expert educational psychologist. There were serious deficiencies in the preparation of the case for trial and it was held that one of the lessons to be learned was that where:

> an expert refers to research evidence in his report, he must identify it in the report, so that it will be available to be considered by the other side without delay, and not merely four days before the trial starts.[62]

In *Wardlaw v Farrar*[63] the court approved the following standard directions **6.81** which is used in clinical negligence cases for the disclosure of unpublished material:

> Any published or unpublished literature upon which any expert witness proposes to rely shall be served at the same time as service of his statement together with a list of published literature and copies of any unpublished material. Any supplementary literature upon which any expert witness proposes to rely shall be notified to the party at least one month before trial. No expert witness shall rely upon any publications that have not been disclosed in accordance with this direction without leave of the trial judge on such terms [as to costs] as he deems fit.[64]

U. Expert-Shopping

It will come as no surprise that the courts take a dim view of lawyers who **6.82** practise in 'expert-shopping', i.e. the process of finding an expert to support a case whatever the truth. This concept is abhorrent to the principles of objectivity, independence, and duty to the court upon which rests the bedrock of expert opinion within the court system. It is likewise unsurprising that the practice is flourishing even since the implementation of the CPR.

Before the proceedings begin, the parties may legitimately take the view that the **6.83** expert simply has 'got it wrong', based on an objective analysis of the report. Such reports are protected from disclosure by the doctrine of legal professional privilege and the wide acceptance by the courts that 'advisory reports' are not disclosable. In practice, the same principles apply until, either by agreement or court order, the parties are required to serve or exchange expert evidence in the form of a report. No properly advised litigant is likely to rely on evidence which does not support the case without accepting the consequences.

---

[61] [2004] EWCA Civ 1659, [2005] 1 FCR 112. [62] ibid para 92(c), per Brooke LJ.
[63] [2003] EWCA Civ 1719, [2003] 4 All ER 1358. [64] ibid para 23.

6.84 There is, however, a category of case in which the opponent is aware of the discipline and identity of the expert instructed by the other side as a result of some involvement prior to disclosure. For example, a medical expert may have been asked to examine the claimant, a surveyor asked to inspect premises, or an engineer to inspect a machine. The courts have been asked to rule on the principle and conditions (if any) in such circumstances where the party wishes to instruct a new expert. Needless to say, the reason for wishing to instruct a new expert results from a serious loss of confidence in the previous expert.

6.85 In *Beck v Ministry of Defence*[65] the Court of Appeal considered:

> Whether it can ever be appropriate to allow a party to substitute one expert for another, without at some stage at least, being required to disclose the first expert's report.[66]

6.86 The defendants had lost confidence in their psychiatric expert and asked the claimants to provide facilities for examination by another psychiatrist. Understandably, the request was refused, no doubt for reasons of personal intrusion and tactics. The court agreed that unconditional submission to a further examination was inappropriate, with Ward LJ summarizing the position as follows:

> Nevertheless, expert shopping is to be discouraged and a check against possible abuse is to require disclosure of the abandoned report as a condition to try again.[67]

6.87 The case exemplifies the balancing act to be performed between, on the one hand, the principles of justice allowing one party to conduct the case as wished, against, on the other hand, the desire to avoid 'expert-shopping' and the implications of perpetuating the 'hired gun' approach.

V. The Relationship between the Report and Oral Testimony

6.88 It has been seen that the evidence of the expert evolves during the life of the litigation so that by the time of the trial there is a tendency for the expert to be a member of the instructing party's team. At trial the expert's overriding commitment is to be impartial and objective at all costs—the duty to the court must now be maintained. Indeed it is these qualities of independence and objectivity, coupled with consistency and sound knowledge, that makes the opinion of the expert attractive to the judge.

6.89 It is likely that the judge will have considerable experience in conducting cases, but over a wide range of practice from criminal law to complex commercial

---

[65] [2003] EWCA Civ 1043, [2005] 1 WLR 2206. [66] ibid para 2, per Simon Brown LJ.
[67] ibid para 30.

matters. Even if the judge has experience in a particular area (say clinical negligence) he may not have previously encountered a dispute in the precise area of the instant case. Most judges are extremely conscientious and will 'read into a case' prior to the trial. The judge will want to understand the nexus of the dispute. 'Reading in' is almost certainly the best way for the judge to achieve this. It is crucial therefore that experts and those instructing them appreciate that experts' reports must be well presented, consistent, logical, and relevant. Judges, like anyone else, will be irritated if a report lacks any of these attributes.

Also by the time of trial, in most cases, the experts from either side will have **6.90** met. The judge will have available a copy of the document (including any agreed agenda) which will distil the remaining issues between the expert witnesses. Naturally, the judge will analyse the document recording the outcome of the experts' discussion carefully, particularly against the initial reports, so as to ascertain what concessions have been made by which experts. He will wish to satisfy himself that such concessions are logical, and derive from factors other than lack of knowledge, either in relation to the case or to the technical, scientific, or medical background (i.e. the expertise).

It must be clearly understood by all experts that the judge will have formed a **6.91** preliminary impression of their capabilities even before oral testimony begins. In that sense, the relationship between the expert's report and the oral evidence at trial is extremely close. Impressive reports lead to impressive testimony.

The modern trend is for the expert's report to be the essence of the expert's **6.92** evidence in chief. This assumption is codified by CPR r 32.5(2) which states that 'Where a witness is called to give oral evidence . . . his witness statement shall stand as his evidence in chief unless the court orders otherwise'. This applies as much to experts' reports as it does to other witnesses' evidence.

Present-day practice is for the judge to allow the expert to expand on the evidence **6.93** contained in his report in relation to the matters in dispute, but this is likely to be curtailed in an effort to speed up the course of the trial and to save costs. The judge will want the first expert who gives evidence to explain the scientific, technical, or medical jargon. It is, therefore, important that an appropriate glossary and explanation is given in the expert's report. It is obviously helpful if these technical issues are agreed between the experts prior to the trial.

An important marker for independence will be the section of the report which **6.94** deals with 'range of opinion'. If this is not fully explored, particularly where there is an alternative scenario which might lead to a different conclusion, then the judge who reads the report and subsequently hears the evidence will believe that the expert is following the 'party line' rather than his duty to assist the court.

6.95 The substantive challenge to the expert evidence is likely not to come from the judge but from the opposing lawyer. His enthusiasm for upstaging the expert is perhaps best illustrated by the statement from Judge David Bazelon, Chief Judge of the US Court of Appeals for the District of Columbia, in 1984:

> Challenging an expert and questioning his expertise is the life blood of our legal system—whether it is a psychiatrist discussing mental disturbances, a physicist testifying on the environmental impact of a nuclear power plant or a General Motor's Executive assisting on the impossibility of meeting Federal Anti-pollution Standards in 1975. It is the only way a judge or jury can decide who to trust.

6.96 'Who (or whom) to trust?' is an apposite phrase because, in the end, this is likely to be the deciding factor in the judge's mind. 'Trust' is not just based on performance in the witness box. It goes to the heart of the case and to the analysis of the expert evidence from the initial expert's report until the last word in cross-examination, including his professional credentials and reputation within his expertise. Very often the judge is faced with having to decide between two or more experts. Providing the judge applies the correct legal tests to the evidence, and is courteous to the experts, his findings are almost unimpeachable. As Lord Bridge said in *Wilsher v Essex Area Health Authority*:[68]

> Where expert witnesses are radically at issue about complex technical questions within their own field and they are examined and cross-examined at length about their conflicting theories, I believe that the judge's advantage in seeing them and hearing them is scarcely less important than for when he has to resolve some conflict of primary fact between lay witnesses in purely mundane matters.

6.97 The clear and resounding message made time and again is that the trial judge is overwhelmingly the determiner of these issues. He is looking for truth and trust. As far as experts are concerned, this process begins with the exchange of expert evidence in report form. The position cannot be more succinctly set out than in the oft-quoted (for which no apologies) passage from Lord Wilberforce in *Whitehouse v Jordan*[69] as follows:

> While some degree of consultation between experts and legal advisers is entirely proper, it is necessary that expert evidence presented to the court should be and should seem to be, the independent product of the expert . . . To the extent that it is not, the evidence is likely to be not only incorrect but self-defeating.

---

[68] [1987] QB 730, 1091.   [69] [1981] 1WLR 246, 257.

7

QUESTIONS AND DISCUSSIONS

> The testimony relating to this footing of the case has been profuse and illuminating. As so often happens, the experts disagree, leaving the problem, as Tennyson might say, dark with excessive brightness.
>
> *International Pulverizing Corp v Kidwell* 71A 2d 151, 156 (NJ 1950) per Jayne J

A. Written Questions to Experts

Following the exchange of experts' reports, r 35.6(1) of the Civil Procedure **7.01** Rules provides that:

> a party may put to—
> (a) an expert instructed by another party; or
> (b) a single joint expert appointed under rule 35.7,
> written questions about his report.

The questions may be put only once, and must be put within 28 days of service of the expert's report. Somewhat enigmatically, the CPR r 35.6(2)(c) further provides that the questions:

> must be for the purpose only of clarification of the report, unless in any case—
> (i) the court gives permission, or
> (ii) the other party agrees.

It is not always easy to draw a clear distinction between questions 'for the **7.02** purpose only of clarification of the report' and those put as a challenge to the expert's views. The Protocol for the Instruction of Experts, para 16.3, advises:

> Where experts believe that questions put are not properly directed to the clarification of the report, or are disproportionate, or have been asked out of time, they should discuss the questions with those instructing them and, if appropriate, those asking the questions. Attempts should be made to resolve such problems without the need for an application to the court for directions.

Timetable

7.03 While CPR r 35.6(2)(b) clearly states that the questions must be put 'within 28 days of service of the expert's report', neither Part 35, nor the Protocol suggests a timetable for replies. There seems to be a general assumption that a further 28 days is a reasonable time. But where there is no response, if the expert does not answer the questions, then:

> the court may make one or both of the following orders in relation to the party who instructed the expert—
> (i)   the party may not rely on the evidence of that expert; or
> (ii) that the party may not recover the fees and expenses of that expert from any other party.

See CPR r 35.6(4)(b). Payment for the work involved in answering questions is the responsibility of those originally instructing the expert. Once the questions have been answered, para 16.2 of the Protocol makes clear that:

> Experts' answers to questions automatically become part of their reports. They are covered by the statement of truth and form part of the expert evidence.

7.04 It is clearly essential that if questions are to be asked, and answered, this exercise should take place before any discussions between experts, for the experts' reports are not truly complete until the answers to the questions have been incorporated within them. In practice, procedural judges seldom leave time for questions to be both posed and answered between the date set for the exchange of expert evidence and that for the expert discussion. Perhaps for this reason questions, at least in the author's experience, are seldom asked. They do, however, present an excellent opportunity, in appropriate cases for the eradication of kite-flying.

B. Experts' Discussions

7.05 Discussions between opposing experts have, in some part of the civil jurisdiction, been a feature of civil litigation for many years, for instance in the construction industry and in family courts. In *Access to Justice*,[1] Lord Woolf sought to broaden the scope of such discussions:

> Among the criticisms I made in my interim report was that the present system does not encourage narrowing of issues between opposing experts, or the elimination of peripheral issues. There has been widespread support for my suggestion that experts' meetings were a useful approach to narrowing issues. In areas of litigation (such as the Official Referees' Business) where experts' meetings are already the

---

[1] Final Report (July 1996) ch 13, para 42 <http://www.dca.gov.uk/civil/final/index.htm>.

usual practice, there is general agreement that they are helpful. In areas where they are not at present widely used, including medical negligence, the majority of respondents accepted that they could be helpful.

The purpose

In 1998 the CPR gave the courts power (CPR r 35.12) not only to direct a **7.06** discussion between experts but also to specify the issues the experts were to discuss. The stated aim was to:

(a) identify and discuss the expert's issues in the proceedings; and
(b) where possible, reach an agreed opinion on those issues.

The Protocol for the Instruction of Experts (para 18.3) goes further in estab- **7.07** lishing the purpose of discussions between experts. It should be, wherever possible, to:

(a) identify and discuss the expert issues in the proceedings;
(b) reach agreed opinions on those issues, and, if that is not possible, to narrow the issues in the case;
(c) identify those issues on which they agree and disagree and summarise their reasons for disagreement on any issue; and
(d) identify what action, if any, may be taken to resolve any of the outstanding issues between the parties.

The aim therefore of these discussions is: **7.08**

(1) to narrow the issues between the experts;
(2) to save time at trial.

In fact, experience suggests that a successful discussion can often obviate a trial **7.09** altogether. At the end of a discussion between experts in which the issues are properly defined the parties are better able to assess the risks of litigation and so compromise the case.

When and where

In construction cases experts frequently meet on site at the very beginning of the **7.10** dispute and may continue to do so as the case unfolds. In the majority of civil actions, however, the experts will not be able to have a meaningful discussion until there has been an exchange of expert view. That usually means after expert reports have been disclosed.

CPR Part 35 does not stipulate how discussions are to be arranged. Lord Woolf **7.11** expressed the view that in order to save costs.[2] 'In the more straightforward

---

[2] ibid ch 13, para 47.

cases, it may be possible to hold a "meeting" by using telephone conferencing . . .'. Paragraph 18.4 of the Protocol stresses the need for proportionality. Certainly, in the simpler cases, a telephone discussion may be a reasonable way forward, but in the more high-value cases, particularly where there are complex documents that need to be seen by both at the same time, there is no escaping a face-to-face meeting. While undoubtedly increasing the cost, such meetings have distinct advantages.

Role of the lawyer

7.12 For the most part, experts, even in a face-to-face discussion, will meet alone. There is, however, pressure in some quarters for lawyers to be present. Lord Woolf flagged up this difficulty:[3]

> In areas of litigation where the use of experts' meetings is well established, it seems to be accepted that there is no difficulty in allowing them to be conducted in private, with no-one present apart from the experts themselves. In other areas, it has been suggested that experts' meetings should take place only in the presence of the parties' lawyers, or of a neutral third party such as an independent lawyer or the procedural judge. In medical negligence, for example, it is thought that such an arrangement would be needed to overcome the traditional attitude of suspicion between the parties. In particular, it is said that private meetings between experts would not be acceptable to patients, because of the common perception that doctors 'hang together'.

7.13 Indeed it is in the field of clinical negligence that the pressure is greatest for lawyers to attend. A number of reasons are put forward why in the special circumstances of a clinical negligence action the expense of lawyers' presence is justified. The first is that identified by Lord Woolf, that the claimant, already injured by a clinical accident, will feel excluded from the process and, should the meeting result in the case collapsing, will feel once again 'stitched up' by the doctors. A second reason, and a more practical one, is that the issues between the parties in such cases are often of a highly complicated technical nature. The lawyers, present to hear how the experts have reached their conclusion, are in a much better position to understand the strengths and weaknesses of their case and better able to arrive at a prudent settlement. It is much easier for lawyers to explain to their lay clients why the experts have come to the view they have (particularly if it is to their disadvantage) when they have been present at the discussion.

7.14 The arguments for and against were set out in a footnote by Adrian Whitfield QC to the Guidelines on Experts' Discussions in the Context of Clinical Disputes.[4]

---

[3] ibid ch 13, para 49.   [4] Clinical Risk 2000; 6: 149–52.

From the viewpoint of the expert there seems little disadvantage in having the lawyers present provided that they abide by the admonition in para 18.8 of the Protocol: 'If lawyers do attend they should not normally intervene except to answer questions put to them by the experts or to advise about the law'.

There may even occasionally be an advantage for the expert. There are some **7.15** medical experts whose performance at experts' discussions is so maverick and unpredictable as to disrupt the meeting. The presence of a lawyer or two may act as a corrective to such behaviour.

The Court of Appeal has, on one occasion, declined to order the attendance of **7.16** lawyers. *Hubbard v Lambeth Southwark & Lewisham Health Authority*[5] concerned four separate actions for the three Hubbard children, all of whom suffered from a congenital progressive movement disorder, dystonia. The Queen's Bench Master directed that the expert neurologists should meet, but the claimant objected on the grounds that the neurologists would be overawed by the reputation of the paediatric neurologist at the centre of the claim. The Court of Appeal upheld the master's order and then considered whether lawyers should attend the discussions, the master having decided against it. The Court of Appeal declined to vary the order, but Hale LJ suggested that the two sides might sensibly agree to have an 'independent neutral person' to chair the meeting, although there does not appear to have been any take-up of the suggestion. Pointing to the analogy of the guardian ad litem in family cases, Hale LJ (as she was then) suggested at para 29 that such a person 'would probably be legally qualified and have experience in the field of litigation involved'.

Some lawyers are ambivalent about experts' discussions, fearing that they may at **7.17** this time lose control of the case. The answer to this concern lies in the setting of a clear agenda. In my experience, the success or failure of the expert discussion is principally determined by the agenda.

Agenda for experts' meetings

The agenda is usually preceded by a preamble, the purpose of which is to set out **7.18** the law for the benefit of the experts. The quality of these preambles is variable. Since the principles are the same in all litigation, there seems no reason why there should not be a standard preamble if properly drafted so as at least to get the law right. There is of course no guarantee that, even with a preamble, the experts will apply the right test and in the case of *Temple v South Manchester Health Authority*[6] one of the experts was criticized both by the trial judge and by

---

[5] [2001] EWCA Civ 1455.   [6] [2002] EWCA Civ 1406.

the Court of Appeal because he applied the wrong test in answering questions about causation. The preamble stated, 'The experts are reminded that civil cases operate on balance of probabilities, that is more likely than not'. But the expert, when giving his answers, clearly applied a test more appropriate to aetiology, as understood by doctors, requiring a confidence level of 95 per cent. His answers, therefore, were misleading.

7.19 While expert advice will be required in setting the agenda, the responsibility for it must lie with the lawyers. Lord Woolf envisaged that: 'At least in the heaviest cases where expert issues are likely to be most complex, the agenda for the experts' meetings should be set by the court'; but in practice that rarely happens, for the court, in the person of the procedural judge, does not have a sufficient grasp of the detail to be able to identify the issues for discussion.

7.20 Paragraph 18.5 of the Protocol for the Instruction of Experts advises that 'The parties, their lawyers and experts should co-operate to produce the agenda for any discussion between experts, although primary responsibility for preparation of the agenda should normally lie with the parties' solicitors'. Paragraph 18.6 goes on to stipulate that 'The agenda should be circulated to experts and those instructing them to allow sufficient time for the experts to prepare for the discussion'.

7.21 In clinical negligence cases, this is the part of the process most likely to stall. There appear to be two principal problems. The first is that few lawyers seem to exhibit the skills required for drawing up an agenda. Requirements will vary according to the nature of the case, but at least in clinical negligence cases there are clear guidelines[7] setting out how it is to be done. The Guidelines suggest that the process should be initiated by the claimant's lawyers (with expert advice) who should send to the defendants a draft agenda some 28 days before the agreed date for the discussion. The defendant should then within 14 days agree the agenda or propose amendments. Seven days after that, the claimant's lawyers should agree the agenda. That then gives the expert seven days to prepare for the meeting. In practice, such a timetable is scarcely ever achieved, partly because the courts set impossible timetables and partly because agreement is not forthcoming. Each side raises objections to the other side's questions and it is not infrequent for the experts to be faced with two separate agendas, one from the claimant and one from the defendant, there being no common ground between the parties. At other times, the agreed agenda arrives so late that the experts have no time to prepare for the discussion.

---

[7] Guidelines on Experts' Discussions in the Context of Clinical Disputes. Clinical Risk 2000; 6: 149–52.

The way in which questions are framed will vary according to the discipline **7.22** involved. Again, in clinical negligence cases there is much to be said for closed questions and the Guidelines[8] are unequivocal:

> The agenda should consist as far as possible of closed questions; that is questions which can be answered with 'yes' or 'no'. The questions should be clearly stated and relate directly to the legal and factual issues in the case.

There are those who object to closed questions on the basis that medicine **7.23** cannot be reduced to a yes or no answer. That is to misunderstand wholly the legal process. In the end, the court will have to decide, on a probability basis, whether the critical answers are yes or no, and will have to eschew equivocation. If the matter is complex, a series of closed questions, rather than a single question, may be necessary in order to elucidate the answer. To ask open questions is to invite textbook chapters for answers; it breeds equivocation and avoidance. The place for long technical explanations is in the experts' reports; by the time of the meeting, the court needs unequivocal responses to relevant key questions.

Where facts are in dispute, it is essential that the questions are not framed **7.24** in such a way as to require the experts to determine the disputed facts. They must instead be asked for their opinion on both factual bases. It will be for the court to decide on the facts. The correct legal test must be applied and the experts should not be asked (and should certainly not answer) questions outside their field of expertise. Many agenda contain matters irrelevant to the action.

How—arrangements for the meeting

The logistics of the meeting, if it is to be face-to-face, also deserve some detailed **7.25** consideration. Lawyers often set out with the idea that the meeting should be on 'neutral ground', but experts are usually willing to meet in one or other expert's office. The latter arrangement has the inestimable advantage that it permits the preparation of the final report during the course of the meeting. With the aid of a laptop computer, or secretarial assistance, the answers to questions can be recorded as the meeting proceeds and at the end the signing off of the document is a matter of minutes. On neutral ground it is often not possible to achieve such a convenient arrangement.

The documents to be provided must be stipulated with the agenda and should **7.26** normally include the particulars of claim, the defence, all of the experts' reports, answers to any supplementary questions, and all of the literature upon which

---

[8] ibid.

the experts rely. The other documents will depend on the nature of the case. Again, in a clinical negligence case, it is essential that the original medical records should be available. Photocopies are all very well, but it is seldom possible to tell from a photocopy what has been missed on the back of a document, often of more importance than what is on the front! In particular, those documents that are hard to photocopy (such as cardiotocograph traces, often several metres long) are provided in the original.

The report

7.27 CPR r 35.12(3) permits the court to direct that 'following a discussion between the experts they must prepare a statement for the court . . .'. The Protocol goes further (para 18.10) and states that 'At the conclusion of any discussion between experts, a statement should be prepared . . .'. This may most readily be achieved when the experts meet face-to-face. As explained, the final report of the meeting is constructed as the meeting proceeds and is ready at the end to be printed off and signed. Provided the document can be agreed and signed before the experts leave the room, there is no opportunity for backtracking subsequently. Lord Woolf warned about undue control by the lawyers when experts were instructed either not to agree or to refer back any points of agreement for ratification:

> This subverts the judge's intention in directing the experts to meet, because the decision as to what to agree becomes a matter for the lawyers rather than the experts . . .[9]

Failure to agree a note at the end of the meeting can only lead to endless delays and frequent attempts at 'editing' what has been agreed.

7.28 In telephone discussions the production of the final document is more difficult, but the obstacles are not insuperable. One neat solution is for one (or both) experts to have a dictation machine into which they dictate both sides' answers in the hearing of the other expert. At the close of the meeting the dictated note, with both sides' comments on it, is immediately typed up and e-mailed so as to achieve a rapid agreement, preferably without the temptation to refer answers back to the instructing lawyers.

7.29 While the content of the discussion between the parties is privileged and shall not be referred to at the trial unless the parties agree,[10] the report becomes part of the experts' evidence at trial.

---

[9] *Access to Justice*, Final Report (July 1996) ch 13, para 43.   [10] CPR r 35.12(5).

Experts' discussions—do they work?

Anecdotal evidence would suggest that on many occasions cases are comprom-   **7.30**
ised at the end of an expert meeting, so as to avoid trial. Even in those cases
which go to trial, some of the issues, previously thought to be live from the
statements of case, need not trouble the court. In other cases, the discussion
leads to no development in the position of either expert, and simply adds to the
cost of the action. From reading the experts' reports, it is usually possible to
identify areas in which the experts could be expected to move together. Where
the experts are substantially in agreement, or at the other extreme where they are
clearly poles apart, it is doubtful whether much can be achieved by discussion.
At present, there seems to be a somewhat uncritical attitude by the procedural
judges and expert discussions are ordered without much consideration of their
likely success. While no longer a novelty, the procedural device of experts'
discussions is still a judicial toy; it needs to be further refined and developed in
civil litigation.

8

ASSESSORS

It might be beneficial, in strictly scientific cases, to appoint assessors to sit with the judge, but only so long as the final decision always remained with the judge.

Sir Page-Wood, Vice-Chancellor, when chairing the meeting of the Royal Society of Arts in 1860, reported in RA Smith, 'Science and our Courts of Law' (1860) 7 Journal of Society of Arts 135, 146

A. Introduction

Although the court may call an expert witness of its own motion (but probably **8.01** then only with the consent of the parties), it rarely does so; this is because the court adheres to the established practice of leaving the calling of expert witnesses to the parties in dispute. Nevertheless, the court has a complete discretion to appoint assessors to sit with it, in order to assist upon those aspects of the case which require specialist knowledge for their comprehension and adjudication, such specialist knowledge not being confined to specialist classes or professional disciplines.

The underlying necessity for expert evidence has never been better expressed **8.02** than by Chief Baron Pigot in the Irish case of *MacFadden v Murdock*,[1] where he emphasized that experience as well as qualification could constitute expertise, so that the subject to which this kind of evidence is applicable is not confined to classes and specified professions and points to the potential use of assessors. It is applicable wherever peculiar skill and judgment, applied to a particular subject, are required to explain results or trace them to their cause. Chief Baron Pigot went on to say:

> Such evidence ought, as all evidence of opinion ought, to be received and con-
> sidered with narrow scrutiny and with much caution. But, without such evidence,

---

[1] [1867] 1 Ir CLR 211.

a jury will in some cases find it difficult and in some cases almost, if not wholly, impossible to arrive at a just conclusion; because the subject matter may be, to a great extent, or altogether, without the range of their own observation and experience, and not belonging to ordinary occurrences or transactions among men.[2]

8.03 In addition to the general power, there are provisions of a similar kind within specific High Court jurisdictions, such as the Patents Court, the Admiralty Court, and the Lands Tribunal[3] and under other statutes on specialist topics. There is also a specific provision for the appointment of assessors (to include a taxing officer and a practising solicitor) in disputes as to the taxation of costs. There is additionally a provision for the appointment of a 'scientific adviser' to assist the judge as to technical matters, either by sitting with him at trial, or 'by inquiring and reporting on any question of fact or of opinion not involving a question of law or construction'. The use of a 'scientific adviser', rather than assessor, seems to be confined to patent cases.

B. General Power

8.04 The general power is contained in s 70(1) of the Supreme Court Act 1981. It provides:

> In any cause or matter before the High Court the court may, if it thinks it expedient to do so, call in aid of one or more assessors specially qualified, and hear and dispose of the cause or matter wholly or partially with their assistance.

8.05 Long before CPR r 35.15 brought in a replacement for the practice of approving assessors, it was manifest to anyone that the non-disclosure of the advice which assessors gave to the court breached Article 6 of the European Convention on Human Rights. Ever since the case of *Re Hannibal* in 1867[4] the die was cast, in terms of the fairness of the trial. At the conclusion of his judgment, Sir Robert Phillimore assumed that 'for the future in causes of collision and salvage, heard before the Trinity Masters, he [the judge] should not sum up the evidence, but that the court and the Trinity Masters would retire and, on their return, the judgment of the court would be given'. That practice which persisted for over 100 years could not survive the requirement of a fair trial, whether at common law or under the Convention. As the European Court of Human Rights put it

---

[2] ibid 218.

[3] See T Hodgkinson, *Expert Evidence: Law and Practice* (1995) 68. Assessors may be used in administrative tribunals, where the principles of fairness will apply: see Stanley Burnton J in *Watson v General Medical Council* The Times, 7 October 2005.

[4] (1867) LR 2 A&E 53, 66. The dicta of Sir Robert Phillimore in *Re Hannibal* was specifically disapproved 137 years later in *The Bow Spring* [2004] EWCA Civ 1007, [2005] 1 WLR 144, para 60.

in *Ky Ma v Czech Republic*.[5] 'the concept of a fair hearing . . . implies the right to adversarial proceedings according to which the parties must have the opportunity not only to make known any evidence needed for their claims to succeed, but also have knowledge of, and comment on all evidence adduced or observations filed with a view to influencing the court's decision'. This conclusion in common law jurisdictions was arrived at by the Supreme Court of Canada in *Porto Seguro Compantia de Seguros Gavis v Belcan SA*.[6] Mrs Justice McLachlin (now Chief Justice of Canada) giving the judgment of the Supreme Court of Canada held that the practice in the Admiralty jurisdiction of the English High Court (adopted in Canada) of assessors privately assisting the trial judge over expert evidence violated the principle of justice and fairness. Assessors should be free to assist judges in understanding technical evidence; they may go even further and advise the judge on matters of fact in dispute between the parties, but only on condition of disclosure of their advice and a right of response from the parties sufficient to comply with the requirements of a fair trial. In the Canadian case the trial judge had refused to permit expert evidence where assessors had been already appointed to assist the judge in maritime matters (that English rule was modified in the Civil Evidence Act 1972 making expert evidence admissible without otherwise altering the assessor system).

The Canadian Supreme Court concluded that the modern conception of how **8.06** assessors may assist a judge included a need to disclose the advice and provide an opportunity for comment by the parties. 'Allowing expert evidence and providing transparency in the interaction between judge and assessor', the court concluded, 'works to ensure that the judge does not abdicate his or her role in favour of the assessor'. While the Woolf reforms made no reference to the illuminating and helpful criticism of the assessor system by the Canadian higher judiciary, the system clearly could not survive procedural reform, further promoted by the direct application of Article 6 of the European Convention on Human Rights, scheduled to the Human Rights Act 1998. And so CPR r 35.15 seeks to modernize the assessor system. Does it succeed?

C. Assessors Post-Woolf

CPR r 35.15(4) now provides for the disclosure and use at trial of such experts' **8.07** reports which the court asks for. Paragraph 7.4 of the Part 35 Practice Direction indicates that each of the parties is to be sent copies of any report prepared by

---

[5] App No 35376/97, 3 March 2000, para 40.
[6] [1997] 3 SCR 1278. See also the Australian case, *Re JRL, ex p CJL* (1986) 161 CLR 342, 351, per Mason J, and *Generics Institute Inc v Kirin-Amgen Inc (No 2)* (1997) 149 ALR 247, [1998] FCA 740.

the assessor. But para 7.4 provides specifically that the assessor will not give oral evidence; neither will the assessor 'be open to cross-examination or questioning'.

8.08 In *The Bow Spring*,[7] the Court of Appeal held that fairness requires that the parties should be given the opportunity to contend that the judge should or should not follow the assessor's advice, and that the opportunity would be exercised by way of comment in the course of final speeches to the judge.

8.09 In *The Global Mariner*,[8] Gross J, noting the Court of Appeal's judgment in *The Bow Spring*, set out the procedure for future cases. First, the range of topics on which advice might be sought from assessors should be canvassed with counsel for the parties by, at the latest, the stage of final submissions. Secondly, the questions ultimately put by the judge, together with the answers given by the assessor, should be in writing, which will be considered by the judge before finalizing the judgment. Counsel would be given a full opportunity to make submissions to the judge, whether or not the advice should be followed. The submissions should ordinarily be made in writing, but exceptionally they might be delivered orally. Thirdly, it should be unnecessary for any further submissions, following the consideration of the written submissions by the judge and assessors. The judge will invariably state in the judgment whether or not the assessor's advice has been accepted, and the reasons for so doing.

8.10 There is no indication, post-April 1999, that the assessor system under its updated procedure, has been used other than in admiralty cases, and even then only sparingly. The decision in *The Bow Spring* would seem to endorse the view that the general power in s 70(1) of the Supreme Court Act 1981, as practised under CPR Part 35 provisions, is not other than Convention-compliant. Is the fact that the assessor cannot, unlike anybody else giving evidence, be questioned (even less cross-examined) acceptable? Does the requirement of parties having the opportunity to comment on the assessor's advice suffice to comply with Article 6? Comment on evidence often demands an explanation of the material susceptible to intelligible comment. The assessor's immunity from direct questioning may mean that misunderstanding of advice to the court will remain uncorrected.

D. General Application of the Assessor System

8.11 In his interim report on *Access to Justice*, Lord Woolf commented that 'in complex litigation, it could often be of considerable assistance to the judge if he was provided with an assessor', and Lord Woolf specifically noted that the Admiralty

---

[7] [2004] EWCA Civ 1007, [2004] 1 WLR 144.   [8] [2005] EWHC 380, Admiralty.

Court practice 'should be extended', presumably to other types of litigation involving scientific or technical issues. Following that recommendation, Lord Woolf in his final report nevertheless noted that there had been some resistance to the extended use of the assessor system 'on the grounds that an assessor would usurp the rule of the judge'. Lord Woolf thought that such a situation would at least not arise where there are 'complex technical issues' when the assessor's function would be to *educate* the judge, enhancing the ability to reach a 'properly informed decision'.[9] Lord Woolf noted, *en passant*, that the function might be performed by two assessors, one instructed by each party—hardly in line with Lord Woolf's desire to cut costs.

8.12 The use of assessors has so far not been employed under the general power. Hence, it must be assumed that in s 70(1) of the Supreme Court Act 1981, a dormant provision lies, and has, not yet, experienced enlivening under CPR r 35.15.

8.13 The only explanation for this state of affairs is that litigating parties, under the influence, if not direction of their legal representatives, will not yield to any practice over expert evidence which they cannot procedurally control. The innovation of court management has, so far, not encompassed an imposition of a court-directed assessor system. Has the time come for a review of the court's powers to impose an assessor in those few cases where the complexity and controversiality of scientific and technical issues demands some court surveillance over the parties' expert witnesses, at least to provide the means of interpreting scientific or technical issues?

---

[9] *Access to Justice*, Final Report (July 1996) ch 13, para 59.

9

REMEDIES AGAINST THE DEFAULTING EXPERT

> Neither party, witness, counsel, jury or judge can be put to answer, orally or criminally, for words spoken in office.
>
> Lord Mansfield in *R v Skinner* (1772) Lofft 54

A. Introduction

If an expert has been carefully selected and instructed (see Chapter 3 above) **9.01** serious performance problems should not arise. But if they do, the options are limited. The law has so far not provided any means of redress for a serious failure of an expert witness to perform his duties to the court and to the litigant-client in the exercise of his skill and knowledge. But there are signs that the courts are beginning, under the impetus of CPR Part 35, to flex their muscles in respect of seriously defaulting experts. Peter Smith J's decision in *Philips v Symes*[1] to the effect that, in principle, an order for wasted costs could be made against an expert who is in serious breach of his duties to the court by acting recklessly and irresponsibly, indicates that in extreme cases judges may be willing to provide some redress against wholly incompetent expert witnesses.

B. Market Remedies

The market for expert witnesses is very fragmented, and information about the **9.02** performances, good, bad, or indifferent, of expert witnesses does not necessarily travel far or fast. But the 'hired guns', who were not an uncommon feature of the pre-CPR era, seem to have receded in the last few years. Also a grapevine

---

[1] [2004] EWHC 2330, [2005] 1 WLR 2043, ChD.

operates among specialist solicitors and counsel, for example in professional negligence and commercial claims, particularly in relation to experts who perform well or badly giving oral evidence. The marketplace will quickly sideline the bad expert; his services to the administration of justice will be a thing of the past.

C. Non-Payment or Reduction of the Expert's Fee

9.03 If an expert witness fails to produce a report at all, or on time, when an important deadline was made clear (usually to comply with a court order for disclosure) or the expert fails to declare an interest until late in the day, the client may justifiably decline to pay the contracted fee. Litigants may on occasion suggest that the expert should not be paid when the advice or report is not favourable to the client's case. The solicitor must explain, however, that the expert's duty is to the court, and that withholding a fee in these circumstances would be a breach of contract. Paying a reduced fee may also be justified if the expert's advice or report is so poor or partisan that it shows that the expert was not honest about his expertise or completely misunderstood his duty to the court. Similarly, it may be reasonable not to pay additional fees if the expert fails to complete his assignment, by declining or delaying to answer questions on his report, or refusing to take part in the required discussion with the other party's expert, or is uncooperative about arranging to attend trial.

9.04 But litigants and their lawyers should check their contract with the expert carefully before refusing to pay or reducing the fee concerning, for example additional fees for additional work, disbursements incurred by the expert (unless no consent was obtained when the contract specified this), or for cancellation fees (see Chapter 3 above).

9.05 Often the simplest remedy against an expert who underperforms is to decline to re-instruct him. But should the expert be told why? Experts frequently complain that they receive no feedback at all on their reports, positive or negative. How can an expert improve if he is not told why his reports are unsatisfactory? Several expert witness databases or directories ask for solicitors' references. It is perfectly legitimate for a solicitor to refuse to provide a reference if the expert has performed poorly.

D. Criticism by the Judge

9.06 It is a trial judge's function to evaluate the expert evidence upon which the parties rely. If a judge prefers one party's expert evidence to another's, he should give reasons in his judgment. Occasionally, a judge will go further and comment adversely on a particular expert's report or performance at court. The following are some examples of judges criticizing experts:

(1) An expert with close connections with the client, proceeding without written instructions and with limited knowledge of CPR Part 35. In *SPE International v Professional Preparation Contractors (UK) Ltd*[2] the trial judge ruled as inadmissible a report from an 'expert' on the calculation of losses in a very technical dispute in the shot-blasting industry, which he had prepared without any written instructions, and which was outside his expertise, he was an ex-RAF officer, and a management consultant to the claimant. In fact his wife had carried out most of the work for the report.

(2) An expert acting as advocate in the client's cause. In *Cairnstores v Aktiebolaget Hassle*,[3] a patent case, the defendant's expert was criticized by the judge for acting when he put forward untenable theories, possibly because of 'over-exposure' to the defendant's case, having been instructed by that party in similar litigation in several other countries.

(3) An expert who failed to review the evidence properly. In *Phillips v Symes*[4] at a preliminary hearing to decide whether Mr Symes, a bankrupt, had the mental capacity to conduct the litigation, an expert witness, a consultant psychiatrist, concluded that the bankrupt had not had capacity to manage his affairs for the previous 20 years, following a stroke. The judge, Peter Smith J, seriously criticized the psychiatrist for not investigating the issue of capacity adequately (he saw Mr Symes for a total of one hour and only reviewed some of the other evidence), for persevering with his opinion for much too long in the face of the other evidence, and for 'assuming the role of advocate' for Mr Symes.

(4) In *Great Eastern Hotel Co Ltd v John Laing Construction plc*,[5] a case involving a long delay in the completion of a hotel refurbishment, the trial judge heavily criticized one of the defendant's experts, a programming manager, for asserting the defendant's competence in the management of the project when he had not investigated their terms of engagement, did not know exactly what they had done, and when he failed to take into account admissions of neglect by one of the defendant's witnesses of fact. His evidence was rejected as he 'had no concept of his duty to the court as an independent witness'.

A senior judge suggested in a public lecture (which the author attended) that **9.07** lawyers might be negligent if they did not check whether judges had commented adversely about an expert before they instructed him. This author

---

[2] [2002] EWHC 881.   [3] [2002] EWHC 309.
[4] [2004] EWHC 2330, [2005] 1 WLR 2043, ChD.   [5] [2005] EWHC 181, TCC.

begs to differ. It is possible to carry out searches of judgments in some internet databases, but this is time-consuming, and an expert is not necessarily completely unsatisfactory, simply because one judge has criticized his work in one case.

E. Complaining about the Expert

9.08 If the failings of an expert witness are sufficiently serious, such as accepting or continuing with instructions when there is a conflict of interest, or producing blatantly biased or very incompetent evidence (both of which could be a serious breach of the expert's duty to the court) the client, a lawyer involved in the case, or, on occasions, the judge might be justified in making a complaint to the expert's employer, professional body, or to the expert witness organization of which he is a member. Complaints to the individual organization which had recommended that expert, or to the publishers of the directory or database from which he was selected, might also be considered, for instance, if the expert's references are found to be false or unsubstantiated, or the description of, or his claims for, his expertise prove to be inaccurate. Any substantiated complaint might adversely affect the expert's future work as an expert witness but a complaint to his professional body could have even more serious implications for his entire professional career, and should not, therefore be undertaken lightly.

F. Reporting to the Professional Body

9.09 It is not possible to ascertain how many expert witnesses have been the subject of complaints to their professional bodies arising from their expert witness work. Most professional bodies now report the outcome of disciplinary hearings on their websites, but not of other complaints which are resolved at an early stage, or which are not considered sufficiently serious to progress to a formal hearing. In at least two reported civil cases since the implementation of the CPR, trial judges have referred complaints about an expert witness to the expert's professional body. In only one instance to date has the outcome been reported. That case concerned an architect, Michael Wilkey, who was instructed as an expert witness by the publicly funded architect claimant in *Pearce v Ove Arup Partnership Ltd*.[6] The claim was that a leading international architect, Rem Koolhaus, had copied Pearce's plans for a building. The claim failed and Jacob J (now Jacob LJ), in his judgment, was very critical of the claim as a whole, and of

---

[6] (2002) 25(2) IPD 25011.

Mr Wilkey's evidence in particular, which he described as biased and irrational. The Architects' Registration Board (the ARB) duly considered Jacob J's specific criticisms at a disciplinary hearing in February 2003, and made the following findings:

(1) Mr Wilkey did not visit the building in question before writing his report, nor make it clear that he had not done so—the ARB found that the Legal Services Commission had refused funding for a visit and that as the claim concerned copying plans, a visit was not essential;

(2) he had not read or understood an important document, the design brief for the building, which was attached to his report—the ARB found the judge was wrong, in that the brief was not annexed to the expert's report;

(3) he failed to inspect all the drawings for the building held at an architectural institute in the Netherlands—the ARB found that the expert had recommended such a visit to his client, but instructions were not given for him to go (possibly for lack of funding), and that the defendant's legal and expert team made copies of the drawings available in any event;

(4) the expert said Rem Koolhaus must be lying if he denied copying the plans—the ARB found that Mr Wilkey did not make such an accusation in his report, and only did so orally under the pressure of cross-examination by the defendant's counsel and questioning by the judge. The ARB did comment that Mr Wilkey was unwise to answer the question, and should have replied that whether Mr Koolhaus lied was a matter for the judge to decided not for an expert witness.

No finding of serious professional misconduct was made against Mr Wilkey.

9.10 It is perhaps surprising that the ARB did not apparently investigate, or at least comment upon in their findings, the more general and more serious allegation that Mr Wilkey displayed bias. But the case illustrates that complaints about expert witnesses to a professional body do need to be carefully and precisely formulated, and that perhaps judges are not always best placed to make such complaints, not least because they cannot participate in the detail of the disciplinary process.

9.11 The other case in which a judge raised a complaint about an expert witness was *Hussein v William Hill Group*.[7] This was a personal injury claim in which the claimant had greatly exaggerated his injuries and was awarded only £50. He relied upon two medical reports from doctors who were his personal friends, a GP and a consultant psychiatrist. The judge did not believe their evidence and particularly criticized the consultant psychiatrist for allowing himself to be

---

[7] [2004] EWHC 208, QB.

brought into the case at a late stage, simply to support it. The judge asked for the papers to be referred to the General Medical Council (GMC). At the time of writing (March 2006), there is no report on the GMC's website of any disciplinary hearing involving either doctor.

9.12 Complaints or cross-examination by lawyers can be effective in bringing to light an expert witness's deficiencies for action by relevant regulators. Barian Baluchi claimed to have a PhD and be a consultant psychiatrist. In fact in the 1990s he had bought his PhD in the United States and had obtained a false medical registration in the United Kingdom by assuming the identity of a former trainee doctor whose professional registration had lapsed. He frequently acted as an expert witness preparing medical reports in asylum cases. A lawyer became suspicious and involved the GMC. In September 2003 the GMC suspended the 'doctor' pending police investigations. In January 2005 Mr Baluchi admitted 30 charges, including obtaining a false medical registration, and perjury, and was imprisoned. In March 2005 the High Court extended his suspension from practice until March 2006, presumably to enable Mr Baluchi to seek advice before the GMC made a final decision about his registration.

G. Expert Witness Immunity[8]

9.13 Expert witnesses cannot be sued for what they say in court proceedings. The reasons that the courts have given for this privileged position for witnesses is that it is in the interests of justice that witnesses generally can express themselves freely without fear of repercussions, and to minimize the occasions when parties try to prolong litigation by attacking witnesses, rather than accept the outcome of a trial that was not in their favour. The leading recent case on experts' immunity is *Stanton v Callaghan*[9] which concerned the alleged negligence of a surveyor expert witness. The Court of Appeal concluded that the immunity extends to the expert's oral evidence at trial and to the contents of the report on which his oral evidence is based. However, the court held that the immunity does not extend to protect an expert who has been retained to advise as to the merits of a party's potential claim, even if proceedings are contemplated at the time the advice is sought.

---

[8] See Chapter 6 above for a longer discussion on immunity in relation to reports and oral evidence.

[9] [2000] 1 QB 75.

H. Immunity in Relation to Professional Disciplinary Proceedings—the *Meadow* Case

The extent of the disciplinary powers of regulatory bodies to entertain complaints against expert witnesses from third parties (other than from the court in which the complaint arose) has for the first time been canvassed in the courts, before Collins J in the Administrative Court on appeal from a ruling of the General Medical Council's Fitness to Practice Panel (FPP) on 15 July 2005.[10] **9.14**

Professor Emeritus, Sir Roy Meadow, a consultant paediatrician and former President of the Royal College of Paediatrics and Child Health, had for many years been forensically engaged in the country's child protection system and was notably the author of a controversial theory about child abuse, called Munchausen's Syndrome by Proxy, which has frequently figured in evidence by Sir Roy Meadow in both criminal courts and in family court proceedings. Specifically, he had given evidence for the Crown in the prosecution of Mrs Sally Clark in a trial for the murder of two of her three infant children at Chester Crown Court in October 1999.[11] **9.15**

The essence of the complaint to the GMC was that Sir Roy Meadow had repeatedly stated that the risk of two infants dying of SIDS (Sudden Infant Death Syndrome) in a household such as Mrs Clark's was '1 in 73 million', whereas the incidence of two SIDS deaths in a single family was far greater than Sir Roy had stated. Sally Clark's appeal was successful, but not on the ground that Professor Meadow's '1 in 73 million' statistic had influenced the jury. The GMC's Fitness to Practice Panel concluded that he had gone outside his field of expertise (paediatrics) and that he had given misleading and erroneous statistical evidence, he not being a statistician. The FPP specifically found that in giving that evidence he had acted throughout in good faith. **9.16**

In concluding that Sir Roy Meadow's misleading evidence to the criminal court amounted to 'serious professional misconduct' (leading to his erasure from the medical register) the FPP alluded, in passing, to the context of the 'misconduct'. It stated: **9.17**

> The Panel has noted with care the argument put forward on your behalf that others within the court system did not question your erroneous application of statistics in

---

[10] The hearing of the appeal took place on 23–25 and 27 January 2006, when judgment was reserved until 17 February 2006. In his judgment, Collins J allowed the appeal (*Meadow v General Medical Council* [2006] EWHC 146). The GMC has subsequently indicated that it will seek permission to appeal to the Court of Appeal.

[11] Mrs Clark's conviction was ultimately quashed by the Court of Appeal (Criminal Division) on 29 January 2003 (on a second appeal, she having failed on an earlier appeal see: *R v Clark (Sally)* [2003] EWCA Crim 1020, [2003] 2 FCR 447).

the police statement, Magistrates' and Crown Courts. You, however, were the expert witness, you provided the statistics, spoke to them with authority and it was your expert evidence which was relied upon by the other parties to the court proceedings.

Expert witnesses are a crucial part of the judicial process and their evidence is relied upon by others who do not possess that expertise. The Panel cannot know to what extent your evidence influenced the jury in the Sally Clark case and that has never been an issue in this case.

The FPP did not examine Sir Roy's statistical evidence in the context of the criminal proceedings before and during the trial.

I. Implications of the Judgment in *Meadow v General Medical Council*

9.18 The Meadow case raised directly the question whether a witness's immunity from suit should be extended to provide an expert witness's immunity from disciplinary proceedings before his or her professional body; and, if so, whether there are any qualifications which are appropriate if that extension is in principle justified. On the particular facts of the case, the judge in *Meadow v General Medical Council*[12] held that the lapses in Sir Roy Meadow's evidence did not justify the finding of 'serious professional misconduct'. The judge held that the FPP decision bordered on the irrational. The FPP said that Sir Roy's conduct was fundamentally incompatible with what is expected by the public from a registered medical practitioner.[13] That was an alternative (and successful) ground of appeal to the question of the GMC's jurisdiction to entertain the complaint.

9.19 Collins J concluded that, given the law's concern to protect the administration of justice, likewise disciplinary proceedings should be precluded. Collins J did not allude to the fact that one of Lord Mansfield's five actors in the court proceedings—namely, counsel as the advocate in court—had lost its traditional immunity. (It appears from the judgment[14] that the question of the jurisdiction of the GMC's FPP, on the ground of witness' immunity, had not been raised either before the FPP or in the grounds of appeal. It was a point the judge raised at the outset of the oral hearing.)

9.20 The question instantly occurs as to whether the advocate's loss of the immunity meant that other actors in the courtroom were in jeopardy of losing their protection. More specifically, where does the expert witness stand in this regard? The question is touched on at para 6.24 above, where it is noted that there is a

---

[12] [2006] EWHC 146, Collins J.   [13] ibid para 57.   [14] ibid para 8.

powerful argument to the effect that the expert witness is more akin to that of the advocate than is the ordinary witness giving evidence exclusively as to factual matters.

The potential distinction between the ordinary witness and the expert witness **9.21** has been judicially noted. It formed part of the reasoning of Lord Hoffmann and Lord Hutton in *Arthur JS Hall & Co v Simons*[15] in considering the function of public policy and determining any immunity (see Chapter 6 above). But before the advocate lost the immunity, the distinction had been alluded to. Nourse LJ in *Stanton v Callaghan*,[16] after noting that the extent of an expert witness's immunity from suit was still in course of development—and would or should be developed on a case-by-case basis—said:

> I see no justification for distinguishing between an expert and a lay witness either on the ground that the expert is usually remunerated for his services or on the ground that he might be less likely than a lay witness to be deterred from giving evidence. . . . An immunity founded on a requirement of public policy that witnesses should not be inhibited from giving frank and fearless evidence cannot afford to make distinctions such as these.

Post-*Hall v Simons*, there is a distinction, not mentioned by Nourse LJ, that **9.22** might lead the courts, in future, to align the position of the expert witness to that of the advocate rather than to the ordinary witness. The distinction depends on the particular evidential status of the expert witness. No witness may give opinion on the factual matters which he relates, although in practice he is likely to draw inferences from the factual material. Opinion evidence ordinarily is inadmissible; that is why the judges had to create an exclusionary rule of evidence so as to admit evidence on scientific and technological issues beyond the knowledge of the court.

The expert witness who is called by one or other of the parties to litigation—the **9.23** same is broadly true of the single joint expert and the expert in criminal proceedings—is propounding an opinion that will tend to coincide, at least by the time the case comes to trial, with the client's case being advanced by the advocate. The expert derives the factual material, upon which his scientific or technological opinion is sought, from all the material supplied to him by the instructing party or assembled by the expert from investigations. The expert neither agrees nor disagrees with the facts. The expert's function is not to evaluate or assess the accuracy of the statements of the witnesses. The ordinary witness is susceptible to a charge of perjury; there is judicial authority for the proposition that an expert cannot commit perjury because he is giving only an honest and frank opinion. Only facts are either true or false.

---

[15] [2002] 1 AC 615, [2000] 3 WLR 543.   [16] [2000] 1 QB 75, 109.

9.24 Lord Wilberforce said in *Roy v Prior*[17] that 'immunities conferred by the law in respect of legal proceedings'—*a fortiori*, in disciplinary proceedings because the function there is to control professional conduct and not to compensate a complainant—'needs always to be checked against a broad view of the public interest'. Collins J's acknowledgement that the judiciary may prompt disciplinary proceedings imports a qualification on the immunity that produces an anomaly. If the regulator—the GMC, a statutory body—has no jurisdiction to entertain a complaint, it cannot have jurisdiction conferred on it other than by statute. Was Collins J, by implication, construing s 40 of the Medical Act 1983 so as to confer the power of reference to the GMC by the judiciary in the case of expert witnesses? Neither the Medical Act 1983, nor other legislation setting up disciplinary proceedings for other professional bodies, specifically excludes from or includes within its jurisdiction the disciplining of its members in their capacity of expert witness.

9.25 Contrary to the judgment in *Meadow v General Medical Council*, if the courts were to decide that an expert witness no longer has the benefit of the immunity, the context of the legal process, in the course of which the expert's impugned conduct is being judged by the disciplinary tribunal, would be the prime consideration for that tribunal. This might entail the receipt of a report from the court where the complaint arose. There is the further consideration that the European Court of Human Rights is not inclined to support immunities. But experts have a right to freedom of expression under Article 10 of the Convention: this would tend to support an immunity. Likewise freedom of expression would operate to restrain the exercise of any disciplinary function.

J. Would Accreditation of Expert Witnesses Assist?

9.26 Some professional bodies have specific codes of conduct for their members who act as expert witnesses (for example the RICS, with the GMC developing one also), and as a result of an initiative by the Civil Justice Council, the EWI, the Academy of Experts, and the Council for the Regulation of Forensic Practitioners are considering the preparation of principles to guide professional bodies in accrediting their expert witness members (see Chapter 2 above). Some commentators have suggested that the problems discussed above might have been avoided if there was an official system for accrediting expert witnesses. The author disagrees, because in relation to Barian Baluchi (para 9.12 above), once a professional person has obtained registration with his professional body any accreditation scheme is unlikely to pick up a false registration. Also

---

[17] [1971] AC 470, 481.

professionals with years of experience, especially once they have achieved some success in their field, are hardly likely to be refused accreditation.

K. Scrutiny of Expert Evidence before Trial

The CPR require experts to attach to their reports all research or literature on **9.27** which they rely, and to hold experts' discussions (with the preparation by the experts at or after the discussion of a note of areas of agreement or disagreement). This should alert the parties and the trial judge in civil cases to the more obvious 'kite-flying', at least when evidence is being given by more than one expert from a discipline. But there are still risks when one expert is pre-eminent in his field and the other less so, or where the crucial evidence is given by a single joint expert who may not even be cross-examined.

One solution might be for the courts to subject expert evidence in difficult or **9.28** sensitive cases to more rigorous examination before it is presented at trial. In the United States some courts will only allow in 'scientific' evidence that appears to be subjective if it is supported by appropriate validation, such as peer review, and or has gained widespread acceptance in the scientific community. The evidence is 'tested' at pre-trial deposition hearings. This would add to the costs in the short term but there could be costs savings if the trial was shortened as a result.

L. Actions for Contempt or Perjury

In theory, proceedings for contempt of court can be brought against an expert **9.29** witness for making a false statement in a report dishonestly. This could be about his qualifications or experience, or about the findings of his investigations in the case (but not his opinion). Sanctions for contempt include fines and imprisonment of up to two years. But there are no reported cases when experts have been sanctioned, probably because opinion evidence can never amount to perjury. A false statement on oath in oral evidence could amount to perjury, a criminal offence, but the prosecution would have to prove beyond reasonable doubt that the expert witness knew the statement was false, and made the statement deliberately. Again there are no reported cases, although it seems that Barian Baluchi (see para 9.12 above) admitted several counts of perjury, presumably because he had said that he was qualified as a psychiatrist, when he was not.

M. Experts and Wasted Costs Orders

9.30 Section 51 of the Supreme Court Act 1981 gives the court the power to make a costs order against a person who is not a party to the proceedings. CPR r 48.2 sets out the procedure for making such an application. The Court of Appeal has said that such orders should be exceptional (see *Symphony Group plc v Hodgson*)[18] and should be made only when the non-party is guilty of wholly unjustifiable conduct, or there was a cause of action against him. A second important criterion is the extent to which the conduct of the non-party caused loss to the applicant, in the sense of occasioning or increasing costs. Orders tend only to be made when the non-parties have been 'maintaining' (i.e. financially supporting) an action that failed, or played a substantial part in running or guiding such an action for their own interests.

9.31 The courts also have the power, under CPR r 48.7, to make 'wasted costs' orders against solicitors and advocates whose improper, unreasonable or negligent act or omission caused the applicant to incur unnecessary costs. The procedure for a non-party costs order under CPR r 48.2 is to apply to the court for permission to add the person as party to the proceedings for the purposes of costs only, and for the person to be given a reasonable opportunity to attend the hearing when the court considers the matter further. Similarly, an application for a wasted costs order is heard after the conclusion of the proceedings, and the court must give the respondent a reasonable opportunity to attend a hearing to give reasons why it should not make an order (CPR r 48.7(2)).

9.32 There are no reported examples of costs orders being made against expert witnesses, and only one against a witness of fact.[19] But in *Phillips v Symes*[20] the court permitted an expert witness to be joined as a party to the proceedings for the purposes of costs. The aspect of the case in which the expert witness was involved concerned whether Mr Symes, a bankrupt, had the mental capacity to conduct the litigation. A consultant psychiatrist concluded that he had not had capacity to manage his affairs for the previous 20 years, following a stroke. Peter Smith J seriously criticized the psychiatrist for not investigating the issue of capacity adequately.

9.33 The claimants applied for an order that the psychiatrist could be joined to the action as a respondent for costs purposes, because Mr Symes, as a bankrupt, would not be able to pay any of the costs. The expert defended the application

---

[18] [1994] QB 179.

[19] *Locabail (UK) Ltd v Bayfield Properties Ltd (No 3)* [2000] 2 Costs LR 169, The Times, 29 February 2000.

[20] [2005] EWHC 2330, [2005] 1 WLR 2043, see also para 9.06 above.

on the grounds of expert witness immunity. Peter Smith J decided that a claim for costs could be pursued against the expert and that witness immunity did not extend to an application for costs. He concluded that, given the expert's duties to the court under CPR r 35.3, a costs order would not operate generally as a deterrent to experts giving evidence. He also said that the other available sanctions against incompetent expert witnesses, for example reference to the expert's professional body, were nothing more than '*blunt instruments*'. But Peter Smith J made it clear that a high level of proof would be required to establish a 'gross dereliction of duty or recklessness' by an expert to found a costs order. He said that the claimants would have to prove that the psychiatrist was:

> in serious breach of his duties to the court by acting recklessly, irresponsibly and wholly outside the bounds of how any reasonable psychiatrist preparing an opinion for the court would properly have acted.[21]

(See Chapter 6 above).

N. Conclusion

The decision in *Phillips v Symes*, although it is only at first instance, seems to provide a tangible means of redress against wholly irresponsible and incompetent expert witnesses. But the test proposed is a higher one than to establish mere negligence, and it is not clear from the judgment whether any eventual order might be that the expert witness must pay the costs of the losing party (as in a non-party order) or must pay the costs specifically incurred and wasted by his actions (as in a wasted costs order). At the time of writing (March 2006), the court decision has not been taken to the next stage, probably because the main litigation against Mr Symes is still continuing. **9.34**

---

[21] ibid para 18.

10

ALTERNATIVE DISPUTE RESOLUTION

> The ability to reach an early resolution of disputes—without the need to invoke the procedures which the state provides through its courts—is of importance and value to citizens in a civilized society.
>
> Chadwick LJ in *Expert Witness Institute v Commissioners of Customs and Excise* [2001] EWCA Civ 1882, [2002] STC 1, para 30

A. Introduction

A visitor to the Royal Courts of Justice in the Strand would, several years ago, **10.01** have encountered at the entrance to the Law Courts a sandwich-man carrying a board with the sign 'Arbitrate, don't litigate'. This was an early instance, long before the era of Woolf reforms, of advocacy for an alternative method of resolving disputes between parties. Arbitration probably pre-dated any established legal system. The role and function of the expert witness in arbitration proceedings, however, does not essentially differ from that in the civil jurisdiction of the courts, in the sense that any expert participates in a confrontational, litigious process between rival disputants.

Today, the plea from inside the Law Courts is 'mediate, mediate, mediate', a **10.02** distinct variant of the traditional alternative to litigation. Mediation has become the flavour of the judicial approach to litigation, prompted by CPR r 1.4(2)(e) which, post-April 1999, states that the court, in pursuance of its engagement in active case management, should encourage the parties to use an alternative dispute resolution (ADR) procedure 'if the court considers that appropriate', and to facilitate the use of such procedure. The Court of Appeal has evinced the view that the parties themselves have a duty to consider seriously the possibility of ADR procedures being utilized for the purpose of resolving their claim, as particular issues within it, when encouraged by the court to do so. Citing such an approach in the remarks of Brooke LJ in *Dunnett v Rail Track* *plc*,[1] the Court of Appeal in the twin cases of *Halsey v Milton Keynes NHS Trust* and *Steel v Joy and Halliday*[2] said that it had the power to deprive a successful litigant of costs, if the winning party had unreasonably declined to adopt a recommendation from the court that the parties should mediate. The Court of Appeal further indicated how it would approach the question of penalizing a winning party by not awarding costs. While it was fully recognized that the courts cannot positively order mediation against the wishes of an intransigent litigant, the threat of finding themselves unable to recover costs will be ever-present if a party declines to heed the voice of judicial recommendation to go to ADR.

B. Arbitration

10.03 Arbitration, the provenance of which can be traced back to the marketplace of medieval England, is an alternative, adjudicatory process which determines the rights and wrongs of claim and counterclaim, unencumbered by the rules of court, and with its own methods of adducing evidence towards the producing of an award by the arbitrator(s). This process is distinguishable from the court procedure only in that it is conducted behind closed doors, is much less formal in its hearings and potentially acts expeditiously, at supposedly less cost to the parties. An award effectively finalizes the dispute. Any challenge in the courts is strictly limited under the Arbitration Act 1996 to appeals on a point of law.

10.04 There are many types of arbitration from the 'look–sniff' arbitration in the commodities market at one end of the scale, to a full-blown oral hearing at the other. The expert may be appointed to act as arbitrator—in which case he or she brings to the reference a technical knowledge and expertise that would otherwise be lacking, or the expert may be instructed by either party to appear as an expert witness giving independent evidence of opinion to the arbitrator sitting as a tribunal. The oral hearing has all the marks of a trial in court, but there are several, important differences.

10.05 In England and Wales a single arbitrator is usually appointed under the Arbitration Act 1996. The purpose of this Act is expressed very clearly in s 1 which states the following principles:

    (a) the object of arbitration is to obtain the fair resolution of disputes by an impartial tribunal without unnecessary delay or expense;

---

[1] [2002] EWCA Civ 303 (costs judgment), para 12, per Brooke LJ, citing the note in the Autumn 2001 edition of the *White Book Service 2001*, p 18, added 'Skilled mediators are now able to achieve results satisfactory to both parties in many cases which are quite beyond the power of lawyers and courts to achieve' (para 14).

[2] [2004] EWCA Civ 576.

(b) the parties should be free to agree how their disputes are resolved, subject to such safeguards as are necessary in the public interest;

(c) in matters governed by this Part [Part I, Arbitration pursuant to an Arbitration Agreement], the court should not intervene except as provided in this Part.

The expert may act as a non-legally qualified 'lay' or technical arbitrator and once appointed can conduct the dispute in such a manner as accords with the duties of the arbitrator, as set out in s 33 of the 1996 Act: **10.06**

(1) The tribunal shall:
   (a) act fairly and impartially as between the parties, giving each party a reasonable opportunity of putting his case and dealing with that of his opponent, and;
   (b) adopt procedures suitable to the circumstances of the particular case, avoiding unnecessary delay or expense, so as to provide a fair means for the resolution of the matters falling to be determined.
(2) The tribunal shall comply with the general duty in conducting the arbitral proceedings, in its decisions on matters of procedures and evidence and in the exercise of all other powers conferred on it.

The parties are consulted by the arbitrator at the start of the arbitration reference after the arbitrator has satisfied himself that the appointment has been properly made, the arbitration agreement is in writing, and what specific rules or conditions have been adopted by the parties. A flexible procedure and timetable will be set by the arbitrator to resolve the dispute in a way that is tailored so as to narrow differences and distil the issues in dispute through the most appropriate, cost-effective and timely methods available. **10.07**

The arbitrator sits in a quasi-judicial role and actively manages the reference to make sure that the claimant has a fair opportunity to present his case and that the respondent has the same opportunity to defend the claim and present any counterclaim. This is the mirror version of a 'fair trial before an independent and impartial tribunal'—the familiar phrase of Article 6 of the European Convention on Human Rights. **10.08**

Processes used in arbitration vary from issue to issue, and might involve site inspections, look-sniff, flip-flop (where the arbitrator must decide the case by either granting the requested award or dismissing the claim), documents only, or a full oral hearing on specific issues. At the end of submissions, there can be a period of limited disclosure, exchange of lists and inspections before the preparation for an oral hearing, witness statements of fact, expert witness reports, meetings of experts, and a pre-hearing review. Interlocutory meetings are held to deal with issues that arise during the course of the reference. The strict legal rules of evidence do not apply in arbitration, but specific rules of conduct will be imposed by the arbitrator. The arbitrator's award is final on each issue, and there is no appeal against his findings and his determination of facts, **10.09** except on limited grounds on a point of law. The award is treated for all purposes as a court judgment and is directly enforceable through the courts.

10.10 Since there is no evidential rule that restricts the expert's evidence to an opinion, based on factual material supplied to the expert, the expert's expertise may be opinion-giving interspersed with an analysis of factual material (frequently a feature of evidence, impermissibly given by forensic accountants in fraud trials in the criminal courts). Since arbitration is not hidebound by rules of evidence constructed by the law in court proceedings, experts can expect to have great latitude in the manner in which they communicate their expertise.

10.11 The dilemma which the expert faces in civil litigation, where a dual—ex facie conflicting—duty is owed to the court (which is said to be overriding) and to the party which calls them, is happily absent from the arbitral process. The expert's duty will be to exercise skill and judgment on behalf of the client hiring the expert to give evidence to the arbitrator. Any duty to the arbitrators will exactly replicate the duty to the client—no more and no less.

C. Arbitral Variables

10.12 There is a process known as 'Med-Arb', where a reference by two parties to an independent neutral person as mediator, if not successfully resolved by mediation, immediately becomes a failed meditation and switches to a formal arbitration. The same independent neutral person allegedly swaps hats in mid-stream and becomes an arbitrator, thus saving on the costs of new submissions by both parties. It is frequently the case, however, that a mediator will know much more than he or she should about a particular party's position and vulnerability, in consequence; and there is a difficulty whether this extraneous knowledge (too much information) can be put out of mind when weighing the evidence actually presented by the parties as part of the arbitral reference. There are those that argue that the mediator is inevitably biased and that 'Med-Arb' is fatally flawed as a technique. But in certain circumstances it can be very effective. If a different person were subsequently appointed as arbitrator, after a failed mediation, any apparent lack of independence is overcome, although the advantage of the knowledge of the actual issues in dispute is lost.

D. The Expert in Arbitration

10.13 The arbitrator in his quasi-judicial capacity decides on the number of expert witnesses and the appropriate qualifications of the expert whose evidence he will admit in the reference, which will be agreed in advance after consultation with both parties. In the situation that a technical (lay or non-legally qualified) arbitrator requires additional expert advice on a technical point, or a legally qualified (non-technical) arbitrator needs expert advice, then both have the power under s 37 of the Arbitration Act 1996 to appoint their own expert. Section 37 states:

(1) Unless otherwise agreed by the parties—
   (a) the tribunal may—
      (i) appoint experts or legal advisers to report to it and the parties or,
      (ii) appoint assessors to assist it on technical matters; and may allow any such expert legal adviser or assessor to attend the proceedings; and
   (b) the parties shall be given a reasonable opportunity to comment on any information, opinion or advice offered by any such person.
(2) The fees and expenses of an expert, legal adviser or assessor appointed by the tribunal for which arbitrators are liable are expenses of the arbitrators for the purposes of this Part.

10.14 The expert appointed in the capacity of a 'tribunal expert' has the ideal opportunity of demonstrating independence from either party to the arbitrator. There is a danger, however, that the material issue or issues before the arbitrator (as a tribunal) might be seen to be determined by the expert. Every expert must strongly resist any temptation to tell the arbitrator, judge, or tribunal what the expert considers is the correct answer; the sole function of a tribunal-appointed expert is to advise and guide the tribunal on technical issues, and not to turn himself into a decision-maker.

10.15 All experts accepting an appointment as expert have a duty to ensure that they possess the relevant technical knowledge or expertise, are up to date with technical or scientific developments in their own profession or area of expertise, and are fully conversant with what is required of them as an expert witness. Self-appraisal (with its inherent defects) is something every expert should regularly undertake before accepting specific assignments, as well as ensuring that it is possible to meet the tribunal-imposed timetable and that report/witness statement deadlines can be met and to make themselves available for any joint meetings of experts, or to attend oral hearings. Expert witnesses should also invite feedback from their instructing parties at the completion of each assignment to focus immediately on any weaknesses in presentation skills or knowledge base.

E. Other Tribunals

10.16 Experts may be appointed to assist parties in specific disciplinary cases, such as proceedings before a court-martial. They may also assist in hearings before immigration tribunals, employment tribunals, professional conduct tribunals.

VAT and Duties Tribunals, the Lands Tribunal, or the General and Special Tax Commissioners. This list is not exhaustive, but it illustrates the diversity of tribunals that might call for the assistance of an acknowledged expert to understand fully a complex technical issue outwith general public knowledge. The rules of each tribunal or panel will be different, and it is the duty of all experts to familiarize themselves with these rules before commencing work on any assignment.

F. Mediation

10.17 The concept of introducing a third person to intercede in legal proceedings between rival disputants is not new. Throughout the ages, cultural and ethnic groups have sought the device of an intercedent to assist or conciliate in situations of social conflict. What is new is the declared statement of the contemporary legal system that the resolution of disputes can more readily and cheaply be achieved by diversion from the ever-growing cost of legal services and often the delay in bringing disputes to adjudicatory process and a final conclusion. Mediation seeks, moreover, to deflect the exacerbating qualities of the adversarial system that promotes confrontation and accentuates litigation neuroses.

10.18 The essential characteristic of mediation has been best described by Leonard Riskin:[3]

> The central quality of mediation lies in its capacity to reorientate the parties towards each other, not by imposing rules on them, but by helping them to achieve a new and shared perception of their relationship, a perception that will redirect their attitudes to one another.

And, one might add, lead them to compose their differences and end their dispute according to their views and interests, regardless of any rights and wrongs.

10.19 On the face of it, there is no role or function for the expert as a provider of an opinion supporting one party or the other. Nor indeed is there any adjudicator to whom an expert's opinion would be subjected to questioning and determination. But there is nevertheless a role to be played by someone who possesses an expertise in the subject-matter of the dispute referred by parties to mediation.

---

[3] 'Toward Newer Standards for the Neutral Mediator' 26 Arizona Law Review 329–62 (1994), cited in F Strasser and P Randolph, *Mediation: A Psychological Insight into Conflict Behaviour* (2005) 62.

G. Expert Mediator/Mediator Expert

There is intrinsic merit in a mediation if the parties share a feeling that their **10.20** mediator is a specialist in the substantive issue in the dispute. This feeling highlights the current debate in mediation circles whether it is better that the mediator should be skilled in the art of mediation or whether the expertise on the subject-matter should take preference. The answer will depend primarily on whether the purpose of the mediation is purely facilitative or evaluative. If the latter, the expert will supply a dimension to the process of mediation that the non-expert will lack. If the purpose is facilitative, the skills that pertain to a renowned mediator will be the more valuable. The answer is probably, 'horses for courses'. Experts can expect to be called on to mediate whenever the parties will feel most comfortable with a mediator who has particular understanding of the topic that lies at the root of their dispute. The confidence in the process of mediation is enhanced if the mediator has this knowledge and not solely the qualities of a skilled mediation.

In mediation the parties are in absolute control of the process. It often leads to **10.21** a compromise resolution which may then be reduced to a formal binding legal agreement, to be signed by both parties or their authorized representatives. Apart from acting as a mediator, the expert has an important part to play in pre-mediation meeting work helping to prepare opinions on settlement proposals, advising on technical matters, or answering specific questions referred by the mediator or the parties. The expert, although engaged and paid by one party, is still under his duty to remain impartial and comment to assist the tribunal, in the same way as if the dispute was going to trial under the CPR or to arbitration. The expert should consider the party's claim or defence and scrutinize the case of the other party and test it against accepted technical and scientific data and standards.

A mediation usually begins with an initial joint meeting chaired by the **10.22** mediator, where the position of each party's case is stated in turn. Once progress falters, the mediator will break the meeting into caucus sessions which he will hold with each party and their teams of advisers in their own break-out or retiring rooms. The mediator may organize separate meetings for different parts of opposing teams during the course of the mediation, including separate meetings of experts to agree technical points, narrow issues, or agree facts.

Meetings between the experts during the course of mediation frequently enable **10.23** the parties to arrive at a greater understanding of their respective views and interests. This can be achieved after a without-prejudice, open discussion, often without the presence of lawyers. Experts' meetings, and indeed the whole mediation process, is conducted on a without-prejudice basis, for negotiation of a settlement that can be effectively suggested by and be acceptable to the parties. If a settlement, however, is not achieved, it is difficult for either party not to be aware of the true nature of the other party's case, and arguments will emerge that would not normally be fully disclosed in litigation, at least not until substantial other legal costs will have been incurred. The outcome of a mediation often includes elements that would not be part of a court judgment or arbitration award, such as the inclusion of an apology where appropriate, as in libel disputes, or the restatement of contracts and the commitment to undertake further trade for a specified period. Mediation is quite creative and involves less lawyerly tactics. The parties are in contact throughout the mediation and each expert acts at all times directly on the instructions of his party. At the end of the day or at a convenient point, the mediator may summon another plenary session and see if a negotiated settlement will emerge. If it does, the lawyers on the parties' teams will work together on a legal settlement contract for all parties to sign.

H. Other Forms of Alternative Dispute Resolution

Conciliation

10.24   Conciliation is an evaluation of a dispute by a neutral person who proposes a solution to the parties. It is non-binding and differs from mediation which is a facilitation by a neutral person, an independent third party, who helps each party to explore their own position and reach their own agreement to settle their dispute. Conciliation is a rather 'take it or leave it' form of ADR, and there is no role for an expert, except to act as conciliator.

Executive tribunal

10.25   Another voluntary non-binding procedure is that of the use of an 'Executive Tribunal' or a 'mini trial', where a panel is made up of the senior members of an organization chaired by a neutral facilitator. The panel has decision-making power to negotiate between the parties in dispute and, if necessary, impose a settlement on them. This method is often used where trade secrets or commercially sensitive 'know-how' is involved. Privacy and confidentiality that are essential to the organization are preserved in a closed environment. There is a role here for an expert, if instructed by any party to assist in understanding and explaining complex technical or scientific issues to the panel/tribunal/facilitator and to enable the instructing party to understand the issues.

Neutral evaluator

In certain circumstances a 'neutral evaluator' may be appointed, prior to the **10.26** trial of issues in litigation, to give a private, non-binding opinion. Such experts are often legally qualified, and take the role of an independent intervener, paid equally by both parties. Names of suitable experts to act as Dispute Resolution Advisers or to form a Dispute Review Board or Panel are usually obtained by the parties or their solicitors from the appropriate professional body.

Housing adjudicator

The final non-binding ADR technique considered here is specific to the con- **10.27** struction industry; it was introduced in the Housing Grants, Construction and Regeneration Act 1996 (HGCRA 1996) and gave 'immunity' to the adjudicator after 1 May 1998. An adjudication decision is binding on the parties until any further dispute resolution procedure is involved, rather like sticking a plaster on the wound of the dispute. The key points, set out in s 108 of the HGCRA 1996, are as follows:

(1) *Notice.* Any party to a construction contract must have the right to give notice at any time of their intention to refer a particular issue or issues to an adjudicator.

(2) *Appointment.* The method for securing an adjudicator's appointment and briefing within seven days of the referral to adjudication must be provided in the adjudication agreement (mandatory).

(3) *Timescales.* The adjudicator's decision must be issued within 28 days unless the referring party consents to a maximum 14-day extension or all parties agree a longer extension of the timetable.

(4) *Impartiality.* The adjudicator is impartial as regards either party to, or any issue in, the dispute and may not accept an appointment if he is conflicted (mandatory).

(5) *Inquisitional.* The adjudicator, however he sees fit, must do everything that is necessary to ascertain facts and law and investigate the issue or issues.

(6) *Binding.* The adjudicator's decision is binding and final until other legal proceedings, arbitration, or agreement are commenced.

(7) *Immunity.* The adjudicator has immunity from any claim against him unless he has acted in bad faith.

The expert might become involved if he is qualified to act as the adjudicator or **10.28** if he is asked to be involved in the adjudication process as a party expert to give oral or written evidence. However, the main point of adjudication is its very strict and short timetable so there is only a limited role for expert evidence, unless the quantum in dispute is substantial or the expert is already engaged before the dispute arises and can assist in ascertaining facts and law in the form of evidence to put to the adjudicator.

Expert determination

10.29 Expert determination is another form of ADR, where an expert is agreed by both parties and jointly instructed by both parties to determine a dispute. In the event of a failure to agree on the expert, a third party nominated by the parties, such as the President of the Law Society, has the power to appoint the expert for them. The agreed expert is selected, using criteria specified by the parties concerning their geographic area of practice, technical expertise, and other specified qualification or expertise.

10.30 The expert is approached and, once he has confirmed that he has no conflict in accepting the appointment, agrees the terms of his engagement and the scope of his instructions with both parties. At the same time, the expert will write to the parties and asks them to provide him with an outline of the dispute and the key issues. The expert will then decide what further investigations, inspections, and tests need to be undertaken. The expert has a duty to do everything that is necessary to enable him to reach his own independent opinion on the issues in dispute between the parties. He is not obliged to involve the parties in his inquiries or discuss his findings with them—his sole obligation is diligently and scientifically to make his inquiries and issue his determination written in terms that are clear to the parties. The parties have no control and may not have any involvement in the determination procedure, apart from their agreement to the expert's appointment and to be bound by the expert's determination. The parties do, however, have an opportunity to go to court to have the determination reviewed or set aside as non-binding, but that is a matter of finality and enforceability for the courts. Expert determination is typically used for share valuation; liability certificates for performance bonds; actuarial issues relating to pension schemes; and the valuation of goods, stock, or businesses.

10.31 The problem with all these ADR techniques, apart from arbitration, is that they are not binding without the specific consent of the parties. If the inclination is to adopt a form of ADR only after litigation has begun, the parties are unlikely to agree on anything, even the time of day. ADR is at its optimum if it is brought into play as an *early* diversion from litigation and the expert has a major role to play in clarifying technical issues. Cajoling by the court is almost always too late.

11

DUTY TO THE COURT

The bare ipse dixit of a scientist, however eminent, upon the issue in controversy, will normally carry little weight, for it cannot be tested by cross-examination nor independently appraised, and the parties have invoked the decision of a judicial tribunal and not an oracular pronouncement by an expert.

The Lord President, Lord Cooper of Culross in *Davie v Magistrates of Edinburgh* 1953 SC 34, 40

A. Introduction

When the common law judges adopted the exclusionary rule of evidence, **11.01** whereby expert opinion on scientific and technological issues might be admitted in order to assist the court on such matters outside its knowledge and experience, the expert witness became not only under a duty of care to the party calling him, to exercise his skill and judgment, but also a like duty to the court. That was so in pre-Woolf days[1] and CPR r 35.3(1) now so states, uncontroversially. Everyone in the legal proceedings may justifiably look to the expert for assistance on matters beyond the court's knowledge and experience.

CPR r 35.3(2) provides, however, somewhat enigmatically, that the duty to **11.02** the court 'overrides' any obligation the expert owes to those instructing him or by whom he is paid. The enigma seems to be resolved in judicial minds by the notion that expert evidence to the court should be, and be seen to be, 'the independent product of the expert, uninfluenced as to form or content by the

---

[1] *The Ikarian Reefer* [1993] 2 Lloyd's Rep 68, 81, and 82, per Creswell J; *Cala Homes (South) v Alfred McAlpine Homes East Ltd* [1995] FSR 818, per Laddie J; *Cantor Fitzgerald v Tradition UK* [2000] RPC 95, per Pumfrey J. The Scottish courts have adopted, with approval, the formula set out in *The Ikarian Reefer*: see *Elf Caledonian Ltd v London Bridge Engineering Ltd*, 2 September 1997, unreported, per Lord Caplan and *McTear v Imperial Tobacco Ltd* [2005] CSOH 69, per Lord Nimmo Smith.

exigencies of the litigation'. That formula was first expressed by Lord Wilberforce in 1981 in *Whitehouse v Jordan*,[2] and reinforced post-April 1999, by emphasis on the impartiality and independence of the expert in providing unbiased opinion in relation to matters within his expertise.[3] In that case, both the Court of Appeal and the House of Lords were critical of the manner in which some of the expert evidence was prepared, appearing to have been 'settled' by counsel; this may explain the exaggerated language used by Lord Wilberforce. The reality is that experts' reports would not, nor could not, exist other than for the requirements of litigation.

11.03 Tristram Hodgkinson[4] states that 'the conventional view of expert witnesses is that, although they are called by a party *they do not share that party's interest* [italics supplied], and therefore give independent and fair evidence to the court'. The duty and dilemma facing the expert witness have not been better described judicially than in the judgment of Thorpe LJ in *Vernon v Bosley (No 1)*,[5] if only because the Lord Justice drew extensively on his experience in the family court jurisdiction under the Children Act 1989 where the proceedings are not purely adversarial. In this case, one in which the trial judge had found that the medical experts had 'lost objectivity and became *parti pris*', Thorpe LJ stated:

> The area of expertise in any case may be likened to a broad street with the plaintiff walking on one pavement and the defendant walking on the opposite one. Somehow the expert must be ever mindful of the need to walk straight down the middle of the road and to resist the temptation to join the party from whom his instructions come, on the pavement. It seems to me that the expert's difficulty in resisting the temptation and the blandishments is much increased if he attends the trial for days on end as a member of the litigation team. Some sort of seduction into shared attitudes, assumptions and goals seems to me almost inevitable.[6]

The Queen's highway may not provide the happiest of metaphors, because jaywalking is not perceived to be a safe or sound practice for pedestrians, and in any event a point equidistant between the position of two litigating parties will not necessarily produce the correct answer; so long as the careless pedestrian stays off either pavement he will remain unidentified with either side. (Perhaps the expert, as a special witness, should be travelling vehicularly.) But the metaphor does indicate what the judiciary perceives as the necessary independence and impartiality in the development of the expert witness's expertise, although Thorpe LJ is suitably mindful of the dilemma facing the expert wary of not appearing to maintain his objectivity. Thorpe LJ's passing shot—paradoxically,

---

[2] [1981] 1 WLR 246.
[3] *Anglo Group plc v Winther Brown* (2000) 72 Con IR 118, para 109, per Judge Toulmin QC.
[4] *Expert Evidence: Law and Practice* (1990) 111.   [5] [1997] 1 All ER 577, 612.
[6] ibid 612.

since forensic experience might instil the requisite impartiality—reveals a judicial predilection for the part-time expert with less experience of the courtroom ethos. He said:

> I would more tentatively hazard that it is likely to be easier for the expert holding a current NHS consultancy or a chair in medicine to maintain detachment than one whose principal responsibility is to undertake medico-legal work. The responsibilities and anxieties of the clinician presumably help to maintain a balanced perspective of the court room contribution.[7]

B. Scope of the Duty

The duty under CPR Part 35 arises only as and when the expert has been **11.04** instructed to give or prepare a report for the purpose of court proceedings. In many cases, the expert witness will have been approached by a prospective claimant before the expert is brought within the terms of Part 35, where his opinion will have been sought as to the strength or weakness of any case which might be fought in legal proceedings. If the pre-Part 35 opinion from the expert is favourable to the client, the expert is likely then to prepare a report with a view to litigation. Independence and impartiality which the law imposes on the expert witness who has not given prior advice to a client may not be so readily attributed to the expert witness who has committed himself to the client's cause. The seduction, to which Thorpe LJ alludes, will have occurred long before the expert's appearance as a witness in court. A litigant, who is told that the expert witness whom his legal representatives have chosen to call as a witness in support of his case, might justifiably exhibit astonishment, however, when told that the expert did not necessarily serve the client's interest in pursuing the claim to a successful conclusion.

A distinguished Sheriff and academic lawyer in Scotland, Sir Gerald Gordon **11.05** QC, once wrote:[8]

> To say that the [the expert witness] must give his evidence impartially, that he appears as an independent witness and not as an advocate for the party who calls him, is true but rather insulting, since it applies to all witnesses. The difference is that an expert who is giving opinion evidence cannot literally fulfil his oath to tell the truth etc, since only facts are true or false. He fulfils his oath by giving his opinion frankly and honestly, without minimising any difficulties it may cause or suppressing any doubts which he has.

The court is entitled to expect an expert witness to apply his expertise frankly, honestly and objectively to the facts of the case, whether these are facts that he is

---

[7] ibid.   [8] In S Mclean (ed), *Legal Issues in Medicine* (1981) 214.

in a position to verify, or facts that he has been given in the course of his instructions from legal representations. The expert must not, of course, express an opinion that he does not genuinely hold; nor should he allow his opinion to be coloured by considerations of what could be advantageous to the party instructing him. The problem arises not from an expert who consciously and dishonestly misleads a court by expressing an opinion contrary to the opinion which he truly holds. It is the unconscious shading of view, to accord with the client's interests or wishes, that is the insidious danger to the unbiased opinion 'uninfluenced as to the form or content by the exigencies of the litigation'.

11.06 Apart from the expert witness who has not had any connection with the case before becoming bound by CPR Part 35, the reality of the expert who has advised a party prior to involvement in producing a report for the court will have been asked to formulate an opinion on the facts put to him. Discussion between the expert and the party's legal representatives will almost invariably have taken place. There will be conferences with counsel, at which the client will be present and will doubtless communicate his strong desire to succeed in his claim. The expert may or may not display enthusiastic support for his opinion and for the client's case. However the expert conducts himself in his report and in his dealings with the client and legal representatives, both pre-trial and during the vicissitudes of oral proceedings in the courtroom, the expert is, or is seen to be, a part of the claimant's team. Even if the expert is not ostensibly an advocate for the client, he must inevitably be engaged in persuading the court of the correctness of his opinion favourable to the client. And his persuasiveness may be affected by the expert's commitment to some social policy, for example abortion, mental disorders, or smoking.[9]

11.07 Frankness and honesty, as well as an adherence to the etiquette of his own professional rules, demand that the expert should vigorously guard against allowing his opinion to be influenced by what he knows will assist the client to win his case. He needs to maintain a balanced attitude to any challenge of his opinion during the questioning in the courtroom and not adopt the pose of an advocate. But all of this is encompassed by the duty of care which the expert owes to his client.

---

[9] See *McTear v Imperial Tobacco Ltd* [2005] CSOH 69, para 5.18, per Lord Nimmo Smith where experts who were members of the pressure group ASH were considered by the judge not to be instinctively regarded as impartial men giving evidence on behalf of a claimant who had suffered from lung cancer resulting from heavy smoking.

C. The 'Overriding Duty'

Given the background to the expert's involvement in adversarial legal proceed- **11.08**
ings, what then constitutes his 'overriding' duty to the court? What, in fact, does
it override? The answer in CPR r 35.3(2) to the question is, 'any obligation' to
the client. The Protocol for the Instruction of Experts explained: 'experts must
not serve the exclusive interest of those who retain them', which seems to say
nothing more than that the expert has a duty to assist the court in addition to
assisting his client. Can the obligation to assist the court involve, however, a
duty that is not owed similarly to the client? The expert has no obligation to his
client to do otherwise than apply his expertise objectively to the facts as they are
put to him (the facts may, of course, alter in the course of the litigation, in which
case the expert may adjust his opinion, but in doing so he will be performing his
duty to the client to exercise his skill and judgment, frankly and honestly).

The client, just as much as the court, is entitled to expect advice which is **11.09**
objective, which expresses the opinion truly held by the expert, and which, in
arriving at that opinion, the expert has been careful not to allow himself to be
influenced by the client's aims in the litigation. If the expert does otherwise, he
is likely to lead his client to expensive disaster, and in that event the client would
be entitled to be aggrieved, and to consider that the expert had failed him. In
that event, there is nothing to 'override'.

D. Duty to the Client

Looking at the matter another way, there are duties which an expert owes to his **11.10**
client and which he continues to owe, notwithstanding any duty to the court.
An expert owes his client a duty to present his evidence as clearly and per-
suasively as possible; he has a duty to identify clearly the facts on which his
opinion depends, to consider, and be in a position to explain in evidence, how
his opinion would be affected if the facts were found to be different from those
for which his client contends, and to explain clearly the process of reasoning by
which he supports his opinion. In stating his opinion, the expert is required by
para 2.2(6) of the Part 35 Practice Direction 'where there is a range of opinion'
to '(a) summarise the range of opinion, and (b) give reasons for his own opinion'. At first sight, the requirement that an expert should indicate any opinions
contrary to his own would appear not to be in the interests of his client. But the
expert who fails to address honestly any view contrary to his own, will readily
lose the favour of the trial judge, and thus do a disservice to his client. It is not
unacceptable to recognize that the expert has a persuasive, rather than a merely
informative role to play. In doing these things, the expert can be said to owe

obligations to his client which go beyond the duty to help the court, and are not overridden by such duty. In an adversarial process, the overriding duty might be said positively to reside in the duty to the client.

11.11   The 'overriding duty' owed to the court under CPR r 35.3(2) is, almost certainly, of no legal effect. It is also in conflict with the nature of civil litigation which remains adversarial, despite the introduction of court management. It is the failure of the Woolf reforms to address the inherent contradiction between litigation that is left in the hands of disputant parties and legal proceedings which seek to provide the court with the equipment to adjudicate fairly on scientific and technological matters outside the experience of the judiciary. Engrafting inquisitorial concepts onto an adversarial process produces an awkward compromise.

11.12   If, however, the 'overriding' obligation is no more than exhortative, there can be little objection to its use.[10] But, if more is sought for the obligation, it should be abandoned, both for its inutility and ambiguity. The obligation of the expert in CPR r 35.3(1) 'to assist the court' should suffice.

---

[10] Anecdotally it is said, both by litigators and judges, that it does do good—there are less over-partisan experts. But this may also be the result of the expert's declaration.

12

TRAINING

[I regard] with a degree of indifference verging on contempt the criticism of judges that demands for them a type of training which would render them more like assessors or expert witnesses than judges of fact and law.

> Lord Hailsham of St Marylebone (when Lord Chancellor) in his Hamlyn lecture, 'Hamlyn Revisited: The British Legal System Today' (1983) 50; cited by Pannick, *Judges* (1987) 69

A. A Responsibility to Be Trained

Anyone holding themselves out to be a professional, has, by definition, a duty to ensure that he or she remains up to date. This is so, whether or not the relevant professional body requires its members to undergo continuing professional development training. For expert witnesses, this duty goes further. As well as keeping up to date in their field of expertise, they must also ensure that they are likewise aware of the duties and responsibilities of an expert witness in relation to court practices and procedures. **12.01**

Expert witnesses who are not sufficiently aware of their duties as an expert witness are taking big professional and financial risks. In the case of *Phillips v Symes*[1] Peter Smith J ruled that 'in appropriate circumstances a third party costs order can be brought against somebody who was a witness and as a result of the manner in which he gave evidence'. (In this particular instance, the witness was an expert in psychiatry.) Counsel in that case both agreed that 'when an expert is cross-examined as to his credit as an expert, that can involve necessarily an examination of his duties, his understanding of his duties, and putting to him whether or not he has discharged those duties'. **12.02**

---

[1] [2004] EWHC 2330, [2005] 1 WLR 2043, ChD. See also Chapter 9 above.

12.03 At present the law does not require expert witnesses to receive training in what it is to be an expert witness. However, following the well-publicized appeals in the so-called 'cot death cases', involving flawed evidence from medical experts,[2] Baroness Kennedy QC recommended in 'the SUDI Report'[3] that trial judges should operate a checklist and question:

- What is the expert's area of practice?
- Is the expert still in practice?
- What is the expert's area of expertise?
- To what extent is he or she an expert on the subject?
- To what extent is the expert's view widely held?
- When did the expert see a case of this particular kind in clinical practice?
- Is the expert in good standing with their medical Royal College?
- Is the expert up to date with continuing professional development?
- Has the expert received training in the role of the expert witness in the last five years?

12.04 The SUDI Report acknowledges that the ultimate responsibility to determine the competence of an expert lies with the judge. Nevertheless, the Report recommends that 'the Royal Colleges or specialty associations should accredit experts'.[4] Accreditation (see Chapter 2 above) is closely linked with the issue of training, but so far no Royal College has mandated its members to be accredited, or trained to practice as an expert witness.

12.05 Where the expert witness is giving exclusively opinion evidence (and is reliant upon factual material supplied by the instructing solicitor) the question of the truth of his evidence does not arise. In preparing written reports and giving oral evidence in support of disclosed reports, such expert witness 'should maintain professional objectivity and impartiality at all times'.[5] In so far as such expert witnesses appear in court to be questioned on their reports, training needs to be directed to an understanding of the forensic process and the concomitant duty to assist the court in resolving the scientific or technological matters in issue.

12.06 In many instances, however, expert witnesses may be asked to give evidence which combines both factual and opinion matter. For example, a forensic psychologist, in describing a person's mental health, will almost certainly have

---

[2] *R v Clark (Sally)* [2003] EWCA Crim 1020, [2003] 2 FCR 447 and *R v Cannings* [2004] EWCA Crim 01, [2004] 1 WLR 2607.

[3] Report of a working group convened by the Royal College of Pathologists and the Royal College of Paediatrics and Child Health, *Sudden Unexpected Death in Infancy* (September 2004) <http://www.rcpath.org/index.asp?PageID=455>.

[4] ibid 6.

[5] Protocol for the Instruction of Experts, para 13.2.

examined the patient in addition to relying on medical reports supplied by the instructing solicitor. Likewise, an accountant in a commercial litigation will often be preparing analyses of financial documents, as well as expressing an opinion on accountancy practices. In so far as more hybrid evidence is given by the expert witness, he or she is treated like any other witness of fact.

B. Training to Be a Witness

Some expert witness organizations, membership of which is entirely voluntary, **12.07** such as the Expert Witness Institute,[6] do require their members to be trained in the duties and responsibilities of an expert witness. Other organizations, which register expert witnesses as members and operate on a different basis, do not require them to be trained. Some do not vet members at all and pride themselves on their inclusivity.

In summary, there is no general professional requirement that expert witnesses **12.08** are trained in what it is to be an expert witness. Before giving evidence experts may, if they so wish, give evidence in court without ever having received any training as to their duties as an expert witness. However, the large number of commercial training providers offering suitable courses suggests that many experts increasingly take it upon themselves to undergo training. There are some professionals who will come to court infrequently, usually when the issue is particularly recondite and calls for a highly specialized expert. Training is more relevant for the medico-legal expert and other forensic specialties.

Suitable courses for experts cover matters such as the Civil Procedure Rules, **12.09** report writing, and giving oral evidence. The latter is now commonly known as 'witness familiarization' training; its purpose is to inform witnesses about the process of giving evidence; and to help witnesses to give evidence free from debilitating nerves. On this type of course, expert witnesses will be trained on practical matters such as how to prepare for giving evidence and what to expect in questions by counsel and judge. For example, the trainer might point out that cross-examining barristers will use leading questions and thereby suggest answers, which the expert witness witnesses are not obliged to accept. Experts will almost certainly also be advised that they must stay within their area of expertise and that if they do not know the answer, they should say

---

[6] The Expert Witness Institute was launched in 1996. It aims to support experts. EWI requires three satisfactory references from barristers or solicitors who have used the applicant as an expert witness. For full membership experts must also undertake training. Some of EWI's members choose to obtain ISO 9000 registration as a further means of demonstrating their quality. The website for EWI can be found at <http://www.ewi.org.uk>.

so. Witness familiarization training for experts usually includes some mock cross-examination.

C. Witness Familiarization

The view of the courts

12.10 Until recently, whatever witness-familiarization training there was had not attracted the attention of the judiciary. This changed in June 2004 with the ruling on the issue of witness familiarization by Pitchford J during the trial of a defendant on counts of attempted murder.[7] The judge's ruling has been developed by two Court of Appeal decisions[8] and a civil case of first instance.[9] In all three cases, the training involved witnesses of fact who were not experts. All witnesses (including expert witnesses on factual matters) have to stay on the right side of the distinction between witness familiarization, which is permissible, and witness coaching, which is not. The prudent expert witness will take careful note of these cases and ensure that he or she complied with the case law on witness-familiarization training. The consequences for an expert who underwent an improper training course could result in professional misconduct, costs orders, and proceedings for contempt of court.

12.11 The trial in *Salisbury* was heard at Chester Crown Court and concerned the allegation that a nursing sister at Leighton Hospital, Crewe, had attempted to kill patients in order to free up hospital beds. At the end of the first day of the trial, the defence learned for the first time that a number of Crown witnesses had undergone a witness-familiarization course which included mock cross-examination training. The defence applied to the judge to rule the evidence of all witnesses who attended inadmissible under s 78 of the Police and Criminal Evidence Act 1984, alternatively, for the proceedings to be stayed on the grounds of abuse of process. Pitchford J suspended the trial so that he could listen to evidence about the course provided by the training company InPractice. The trainer (a barrister) gave evidence of what happened. In deciding not to exclude the evidence of the witnesses, Pitchford J said:

> There is, in my view, a difference of substance between the process of familiarisation with the task of giving evidence coherently and the orchestration of evidence to be given. The second is objectionable and the first is not. . . . The course was

---

[7] *R v Salisbury*, 18 June 2004, unreported; ruling available at <http://www.inpracticetraining.com>.

[8] *R v Momodou and Limani* [2005] EWCA Crim 177, [2005] 2 All ER 571; *R v Salisbury* [2005] EWCA Crim 3107 (on appeal from Pitchford J).

[9] *Ultraframe (UK) Ltd v Fielding* [2005] EWHC 1638, ChD.

delivered by a member of the Bar I judge to have been well aware of the implications. She took pains to ensure that any witnesses who attended her courses knew of the possible consequences of collusion, and she forbade it. No attempt was made to indulge in application of the facts of this case, or anything remotely resembling them. True it is, that witnesses would have undergone a process of familiarisation with the pitfalls of giving evidence and were instructed how best to prepare for the ordeal. This, it seems to me, was an exercise any witness would be entitled to enjoy were it available. What was taking place was no more than preparation for the exercise of giving evidence.[10]

(Mrs Salisbury was convicted on two counts of attempted murder.)

Before her appeal was heard, the Court of Appeal dealt with the subject of witness-familiarization training in *R v Momodou and Limani*.[11] The background facts of that case were that there was a disturbance at Yarl's Wood Immigration Detention Centre which was run mainly by Group 4 staff. An initially minor incident escalated into major disorder; the cost of damage ran into millions of pounds. Mr Momodou and Mr Limani were put on trial at Harrow Crown Court, alongside other defendants. It emerged at trial that witness training had been arranged for some Group 4 witnesses who were to give evidence for the prosecution. When informed of it, counsel for the Crown, Mr Nigel Rumfitt QC, advised that it was wrong, and that the programme, which he thought might constitute contempt of court by Group 4 and the training providers, Bond Solon, must be stopped immediately. **12.12**

The trial proceeded on the basis that the case study written for a mock cross-examination exercise, the details of which appear in the judgment, was used by the training provider. The judgment found that it had such obvious similarities to the actual incident that it was an 'entirely inappropriate basis' for witness training. Group 4 denied that witnesses had been 'coached'—in other words advised what to say in their evidence or had their evidence inappropriately influenced by the training course and said that they had given instructions not to use the case study. It was agreed at trial by both defence and prosecution that the training offered was 'wholly inappropriate and improper'. The judge withdrew the case against another defendant because most of the witnesses who gave evidence against him had been trained. Mr Momodou and Mr Limani were convicted of violent disorder. They appealed their convictions. **12.13**

One of the main grounds of the appeal was that Group 4 witnesses who gave evidence against the appellants had been trained or coached while attending a witness-familiarization course. Though the appeal ultimately failed, the Court of Appeal set out detailed guidance on witness familiarization for criminal **12.14**

---

[10] Quoted in *R v Salisbury* [2005] EWCA Crim 3107, para 60.
[11] [2005] EWCA Crim 177, [2005] 2 All ER 571.

cases and in the absence of any case giving specific guidance for civil cases, 'it would be prudent to proceed on the basis that the general principles set out in *Momodou* also apply to civil proceedings'.[12]

12.15 The Court of Appeal in *Momodou* was not opposed to sensible witness familiarization. Judge LJ said that:

> Witnesses should not be disadvantaged by ignorance of the process, nor when they come to give evidence, taken by surprise at the way it works. None of this however involves discussions about proposed or intended evidence. Sensible preparation for the experience of giving evidence, which assists the witness to give of his or her best at the forthcoming trial is permissible. Such experience can also be provided by out of court familiarisation techniques. The process may improve the manner in which the witness gives evidence by, for example, reducing the nervous tension arising from inexperience of the process. Nevertheless, the evidence remains the witness's own uncontaminated evidence. Equally, the principle does not prohibit the training of expert and similar witnesses in, for example, the technique of giving comprehensive evidence of a specialist kind to a jury, both during evidence-in-chief and in cross-examination and, for example, developing the ability to resist the inevitable pressure of going further in evidence than matters covered by the witnesses' specific expertise. The critical feature of training of this kind is that it should not be arranged in the context of, nor related to any forthcoming trial, and it can therefore have no impact whatever on it.[13]

General principles

12.16 The general principles that emerge from the *Momodou* judgment about witness-familiarization training courses can be summarized as follows:

(1) Witness preparation training should normally be conducted or supervised by a solicitor or barrister, or someone who is responsible to a solicitor or barrister with experience of the relevant justice system, be it civil or criminal.

(2) The training provider should not have personal knowledge of the matters in issue at the forthcoming trial, and any attempt to discuss the forthcoming proceedings should be stopped immediately; advice given as to why it is impermissible should be noted in the form of a warning.

(3) Records should be maintained (who attended, the course materials, who delivered the course, who organized it).

(4) The training material should bear no similarity whatever to the issues in the forthcoming trial, and nothing should 'play on or trigger the witness's recollection of events'.

---

[12] Bar Council, *Guidance on Witness Preparation*, October 2005, available at <http://www.barcouncil.org.uk>.

[13] *R v Momodou and Limani* [2005] EWCA Crim 177, [2005] 2 All ER 571, para 62.

Bar Council guidance

In light of *Momodou*, the Bar Council issued guidance to practitioners.[14] The **12.17** guidance supplements para 705 of the Bar Code of Conduct: 'A barrister must not rehearse, practise or coach a witness in relation to his/her evidence'. This guidance deals with the 'line to be drawn between (a) the legitimate preparation of a witness and his/her evidence for a current or forthcoming trial or hearing and (b) impermissible rehearsing or coaching of a witness', and refers to *Momodou* in detail.

Regarding experts, the Bar Council's guidance says: **12.18**

> A barrister may, however, familiarise experts with the process of giving oral evidence, including:
> (1) explaining the layout of the Court and the procedure of the trial, and
> (2) providing guidance on giving comprehensive and comprehensible specialist evidence to the Court, and resisting the pressure to go further in evidence than matters covered by his or her specific expertise.
>
> . . . However, great care must be taken not to do or say anything which could be interpreted as manufacturing, or in any way influencing the content of the evidence that the expert is to give in the witness box.[15]

Mock cross-examination

In July 2005 in the case of *Ultraframe (UK) Ltd v Fielding*[16] Lewison J, sitting in **12.19** the Chancery Division of the High Court, delivered a lengthy judgment, a small part of which relates to a witness-familiarization course for witnesses of fact. The judge said that the mock cross-examination based on case studies provided by the course participants 'should not have happened'. He said: 'Given that the trainers do not themselves know the subject matter or scope of the forthcoming trial, it seems to me to be highly undesirable for the potential witnesses to compile their own case study, or choose their own topics for cross-examination'.[17] The judge highlighted the fact that if the mock cross-examination material is chosen by the witness, and it resembles the facts of the case, there is a danger of coaching.

It has been the practice of some expert witness training providers to ask expert **12.20** witnesses to bring 'old reports' from 'closed cases' for use in mock cross-examination. In light of *Ultraframe*, this must now be regarded as bad practice. Witnesses should not choose their own material for cross-examination. The trainer should use fictional case studies for mock cross-examination, so as to

---

[14] Bar Council (n 12 above). [15] Bar Council (n 12 above) para 16.
[16] [2005] EWHC 1638, ChD. [17] ibid para 29.

be sure that there can be no mistake and so that no dress-rehearsal for a real cross-examination can occur.

Postscript

12.21 In November 2005 the Court of Appeal considered *R v Salisbury* on appeal. Mrs Salisbury's defence team sought to rely on the fact of the prosecution witness-training course as one of their grounds of appeal. The appeal failed. The Lord Chief Justice, Lord Phillips of Worth Matravers, commented on the trial judge's witness-familiarization ruling:

> The judge gave a lengthy and fully reasoned ruling, entirely in accordance with the principles subsequently confirmed by the Court of Appeal in *R v Momodou and Limani* [2005] 2 Cr.App.R. 6 and in the unreported case of *Ultraframe v Fielding* (2003) EWCA Crim 3755 . . .
>
> It became clear during the limited cross-examination of witnesses who had attended the course that nothing untoward had taken place and that a warning in the most forceful and appropriate terms was sounded about the impropriety of discussing evidence. There was no question of any witness having a copy of his or her witness statement to study or pass around before the trial.[18]

The case adds little, to the existing judicial guidance, but it confirms once again that the Court of Appeal is not against sensible witness-familiarization training.

D. What Should Expert Witness Training Consist of?

12.22 Expert witness courses should cover the expert's duties to the court and give advice on how to comply with them. They should cover:

- Experts' duties under CPR Part 35.
- Key case law for expert witnesses.
- The Protocol for the Instruction of Experts.
- Report writing—structure, format, and formalities.
- The practices and procedures in the courtroom.
- The process of giving evidence.
- What to expect in cross-examination, for example that counsel will use leading questions to try to undermine the witness.
- Mock cross-examination.

The one topic that is potentially contentious is mock cross-examination, but only if it involves coaching. Sensible expert witness-familiarization training is

---

[18] *R v Salisbury* [2005] EWCA Crim 3107, paras 58 and 59.

expressly endorsed by the courts. Experts will find a number of reliable training providers who offer it.

The professional and financial stakes are high for an expert who enters the **12.23** witness box. It is the expert's responsibility, therefore, to undertake training on the role of the expert and how to perform properly. The courts do not require it, but in the interests of raising standards and of reducing the risk of failed justice, expert witnesses will be advised to engage in training and education about the expert witness system.

13

ONE EXPERT'S EXPERIENCE[1]

A court of justice was not a fit place for the exercise of inductive logic [of science], life was too short and it was impossible to give endless time to the examination of scientific theory for the benefit of one set of litigants.

Bowen LJ in *Fleet v Metropolitan Asylum Board*
(the Darenth Smallpox Case) (1886) 2 TLR 361, 363

A. Introduction

Epidemiology is a branch of medical science that seeks to distinguish between a mere association between exposure and disease and a relationship that is most likely to be causal. An epidemiologist's work is to conduct and interpret studies that throw light on the possibility of causative associations between exposure to potentially harmful (or beneficial) substances and disease. The study of various hormones—especially the pill or oral contraceptives—and the understanding of the effect they may have on subsequent disease has been the focus of my professional career. Hence my involvement as an expert witness in the proceedings brought by a number of women claimants who alleged that they had suffered illness as a result of taking the newly developed 3rd generation contraceptive pill.

13.01

One of the besetting problems of epidemiology is to detect the studies where there is inadvertent deception caused by confounding or other artefact. How to circumvent this in reliable studies is a core epidemiological activity. Confounding occurs when an association is established between a putative hazard and a

13.02

---

[1] Based on the appearance of Professor Klim McPherson, Visiting Professor of Public Health Epidemiology, Oxford University, as one of a number of expert epidemiologists in the matter of Oral Contraceptive Group Litigation, tried by Mackay J in the Queen's Bench Division of the High Court, between March and July 2002 (*XYZ and Others v Schering Health Care and Others* [2002] EWHC 1420, [2003] 70 BMLR 88).

disease that is not causal. The association arises because people exposed to the hazard are at greater risk of possessing characteristics that do cause the disease but are only coincidentally related to the hazard. For example, prescribing a certain kind of contraceptive pill differently to women who are at a high risk of a disease may give the impression of higher risk for that pill in epidemiological studies.

13.03 Since the 1960s (when the hormone dosages were much higher, with more side effects) new pill formulations had been developed and marketed to reduce the risks for women on hormonal contraception. Each required a new licence, and safety was assessed both in the laboratory and epidemiologically. In the case of 3rd generation pills and venous thromboembolism (blood clots in the leg or lung) I was of the view that the epidemiology was sound and there was indeed an increased risk. The case against the manufacturers of the new formulations, introduced in the 1980s, was to be tried in 2002. These new low dose pills which contained new progestogens had been heavily marketed for their putative cardiovascular safety relative to previous pills—known as 2nd generation.

13.04 From my membership of the Committee of Safety of Medicines (CSM) for several years I knew full well that differences of interpretation routinely occurred between the manufacturers of pharmaceutical products and the decisions of regulators on their safety or efficacy. But these conflicts were decided upon the opinion of dispassionate epidemiological expert opinion, balancing the possibilities of confounding with interpretations of causation for both risks and benefits of their products. This process was set in the context, which is different from the civil court, in which the regulators had but one responsibility—to protect the health of the public on a balance of risks and benefits. This context had explicitly to ignore the financial interests of the companies, and the ultimate costs to the NHS, in favour of a dispassionate, objective assessment of actual risks and benefits to patients. Liability per se is of no concern, except in an implicit transfer for the given indication to the regulator. Thus an obligation exists to warn of unsuspected side effects.

B. Scientific Background

13.05 For many years there had been surprising indications of an increased risk with the new 3rd generation pills of venous thrombosis. Venous thromboembolisms (VTEs) are quite rare as complications go: around 5 among 100,000 (normal fit non-contraceptive using) women per year. All oral contraceptive users have a higher risk. Accordingly, several studies had been tasked in the early 1990s with investigating the possibility of such an effect. The outcome was important, because the new 3rd generation pills had been developed and marketed in order to have a better cardiovascular safety profile when compared to their predecessors (2nd generation pills). The new progestogens (Desogestrel and Gestodene) had, it was believed on theoretical grounds, since they exhibited a greater beneficial effect on lipids, a better cardiovascular risk profile than the common progestogen used in 2nd generation pills, Levonorgestrel. All of these preparations by then contained low dosages of oestrogen. Hence the expectation was that they would be associated with lower cardiovascular risk.[2] By 1995 3rd generation pills, still in patent, had captured 50 per cent of the oral contraceptive market.

These epidemiological studies were published during late 1995 and early 1996. **13.06** There were then four of them—all showing a significant elevation of the risk of thrombosis among 3rd generation users compared with 2nd. Broadly, the relative risks—when adjusted for measured confounding—were around twofold. (That is the risk of thrombosis among 3rd generation users was around twice the risk among 2nd generation users. In absolute terms around 30/100,000 women per year compared to 15/100,000.) But in one study, conducted by the World Health Organization (WHO) the risks were nearly threefold. Based on pre-publication information supplied to the CSM, a 'Dear Doctor' letter was sent to all UK doctors in October 1995. This warned of the likely extra risk of thrombosis (appropriately emphasizing the low absolute risk among fit, non-pregnant, women) and advised women of higher intrinsic thrombosis risk to consider changing back to 2nd generation pills. As it happens, for reasons that remain obscure but are familiar, the 'Dear Doctor' letter caused a panic among women and their general practitioners (described as another 'pill scare'), who variously changed pills, or stopped altogether—resulting apparently in 30,000 unwanted pregnancies.[3] This CSM action, thought by many to have been precipitous, clearly annoyed the drug manufacturers and, possibly, the public. The manufacturers, and some prescibers, publicly held firmly to their claim that the increase was illusory, and that there was no increased risk of thrombosis caused by the new progestogens.

The context was thus fully set for a class action from women claimants against **13.07** three manufacturers (Schering, Wyeth, and Organon) of 3rd generation pills for damages for their venous thrombosis. A highly successful class of product, still in patent, had been criticized by the CSM. To remain a successful product, the current epidemiological interpretation obviously had to be resisted at all costs.

---

[2] Meade TW, Greenberg G, Thompson SG, 'Progestogens and cardiovascular reactions associated with oral contraceptives and a comparison of the safety of 50 and 30 mg preparations' BMJ 1980; 2: 1157–61.

[3] Wood R, Botting B, Dunnell K, 'Trends in conceptions before and after the 1995 pill scare' Popul Trends 1997; 89: 5–12.

The manufacturers needed to refute the decisions of regulators around the world, as well as a near unanimity of expert independent scientific opinion.[4] Few experts had serious doubts about an elevated risk in these products. But how elevated?

13.08 For completeness, it must be added that in 1997 (a mere two years after the original 'pill scare', based on the epidemiological findings) independent laboratory investigations of serum among around 175 women of an activated protein C sensitivity ratio (which is known to predispose to thrombosis) was compared among non-pill users, 2nd and 3rd generation users, and women with Factor V Leiden mutation, an especially vulnerable group at high risk of thrombosis. The results were startling. The gradient in response from non-users through to intrinsically high-risk women was linear and highly significant, with 3rd generation users exhibiting almost the same response as Factor V Leiden women and very significantly higher than 2nd generation users. These in turn were significantly higher than non-users, but only half the elevation found for 3rd generation users.[5] It is very rare for a 'surprising' epidemiological finding to receive such support, from an entirely non-epidemiological source, so quickly and so convincingly.

13.09 My involvement had begun in 2001. As it happens, this was three months after I had taken a new senior post with the Medical Research Council (MRC) in Bristol, having moved from a Chair at the London School of Hygiene. I underestimated the conflict that would result. To be on top of the proceedings would involve many hours in attendance at the Royal Courts of Justice, even when not appearing as a witness. My first meetings with counsel began in January 2002. The proceedings began on 4 March. My schedule for witness interrogation was to start on 26 April, but by that time other witnesses would have discussed many of the epidemiological issues. It was incumbent on me, therefore, to attend many of these hearings before giving oral evidence in court.

13.10 When I first attended the court towards the very beginning, when epidemiological principles and individual studies were discussed, several core features struck me. First, the number of lawyers and experts on each side was unbalanced. On the claimants' side were normally two barristers and two solicitors, and possibly two experts at any one time. On the side of the defendants, the situation was wholly different (and quite confusing). There were often six (and more) barristers, four solicitors, and eight experts and a number of other professionals serving their case. Their side of the courtroom was always crowded, the claim-

---

[4] World Health Organization, *Cardiovascular disease and steroid hormone contraception*, Report of WHO scientific group, WHO technical reports series 877 (1998).
[5] Rosing J, Tans G, Nicolae GAF et al, 'OC and venous thrombosis: differing sensitivities to activated protein C in women using a second and third generation oral contraceptives' Br J Haem 1997; 97: 233–8.

ants' side almost always empty. The courtroom was also replete with cabinets some six feet high, filled with documents of evidence. Hence, one had to seat oneself strategically in order to see the lawyers, the judge, and the witness— being able to see all three simultaneously was almost always impossible. The formality of the court was, to an outsider, surprising.

The epidemiological issues appeared relatively simple, but for the above reasons **13.11** the account below perforce must be complex. This, I think, is an underestimated consequence of transferring from one mode of assessment to another, when each has little in common. So often a description has to go back to its roots, when accepted by one mode, it appears opaque, even counter-intuitive, to another. Such a transfer promised to be exacting, but would be totally unproductive if the verdicts of each ended up having little in common, with no further insights into methodology. Indeed were this to happen, then definitive resolution is indicated. Society simply cannot have several responsible (and respected) assessment paradigms that yield opposed implications. In fact, history shows that if such circumstances do exist, then responsible social cohesion will be threatened. Either 3rd generation pills are more likely than not, in aggregate (when compared with 2nd generation pills) to cause individual thromboses, or they are not. It cannot be both. Nor can resolution ever be a matter largely of faith.

In the following text, I hope to illuminate the process as seen from the point of **13.12** view of a naïve expert witness in the hope of making such disparities less likely. I welcome coherent choices of the method of assessment with which I am most familiar. An expert witness can always be wrong. In the end, civilized society relies on the legal process ultimately to adjudicate. But in this instance, in my opinion, it failed. In part, that was my fault, and post hoc remedies as regards my conduct will be suggested below, together with some for the conduct of expert witnesses generally in civil litigation. It may be presumptuous to suggest remedies in court proceedings in cases of this sort, but nonetheless I will allude to some.

C. The Trial [6]

The judge had agreed with the parties' lawyers, in pre-trial hearings before my **13.13** involvement as an expert witness, the several demonstrations of fact that would be required for the claimants' case to succeed. These were, in turn, that:

---

[6] The claim was a class action, a type of legal challenge, that was not available in English legal history until the late 1980s: see *Davies v Eli Lilly* [1987] 1 WLR 1136, 1138, a unique action brought by, 1,500 plaintiffs against the manufacturers of Opren, a drug prescribed for arthritic patients.

(1) the risk of thrombosis is increased with 3rd generation pills compared with 2nd;

(2) the estimated Relative Risks (RRs) were not due to confounding;

(3) RR is greater than twofold, i.e. RR (thrombosis): 3rd/2nd >2;

(4) a biologically plausible mechanism exists;

(5) this defect could have been discovered in late 1989;

(6) there is no proven benefit of 3rd versus 2nd; and

(7) had the defendants complied, the claimants would not have been pre-scribed 3rd generation pills, or would have chosen an alternative form of contraception.

13.14 It is convenient to limit the following discussions exclusively to items (2) and (3) above, which were my, and other epidemiological experts', main concern. The first is necessary, but not sufficient—since it has to be demonstrated that on the balance of probability a thrombosis was caused by taking 3rd generation pills in preference to 2nd. This has a particular numerical implication, which it turns out is not all well captured by the third requirement, which is just wrong. The second requirement is crucial to the case and gave rise to the greatest opportun-ity for obfuscation from the defence. The biological explanation ((4) above) presented in 1997 remained unrefuted,[7] indeed had been confirmed experi-mentally.[8] Since the case failed at the two hurdles ((2) and (3) above) the others were not considered in court.

D. Balance of Probabilities

13.15 As soon as I was engaged, I suggested that the threshold relative risk of a thrombosis, when comparing 3rd generation with 2nd for assigning causation for an individual case, should not be twofold, i.e. on the balance of probability. In the generality of such cases of liability, claimants are exposed to some hazard. Then the epidemiology has to demonstrate that it is more likely than not that the event in question happened as a consequence of that choice of exposure. In probabilistic terms this means the extra absolute risk among those exposed is more than those unexposed. That is, in this case, more than twice as high (a relative risk) as those unexposed. Only then is it more likely than not that the event was a consequence of that exposure. This is because the extra absolute risk attributable to exposure is then greater than the baseline risk.

---

[7] Vandenbroucke JP, Rosing J, Bloemenkamp KWM et al, 'Oral contraceptives and the risk of venous thrombosis' NEJM 2001; 344, 20: 1527–35.

[8] Rosing J, Middeldorp S, Curvers J et al, 'Low-dose oral contraceptives and acquired resistance to activated protein C: a randomised cross-over study' Lancet 1999; 354: 2036–40.

Thus twofold relative risks have apparently become the legal yardstick for demonstrating causation (and thus ultimately liability). But, first, relative risks are the wrong metric. Secondly, this case is different, since exposure to 2nd generation oral contraceptives (OCs) is widely known and understood to cause a threefold excess risk of thrombosis compared with non-pill users anyway. This is, in part, why 3rd generation pills were developed—to mitigate this and other risks. The choice faced by a woman is not between exposure or not (where a twofold RR would be appropriate), but between exposure to a known hazard (2nd) and an unknown one (3rd)—in each case for the purposes of reliable contraception. The unknown hazard was thought to be less risky than the known one. The case rested (in part) on whether or not it was, and in part on whether or not any extra risk could have been known. It seemed obvious to me, therefore, that a logical extension of the principle of demonstrating causation in the balance of probability criterion was, in this case, to demonstrate that the attributable risk of 3rd generation pills of a thrombosis, above the risk of 2nd generation, should be at least as great as the attributable risk of 2nd generation pills above baseline. This is exactly the argument for a single putative risk over baseline, and is wholly consistent with the logic of the situation. Since women already underwent a well-known extra risk of a thrombosis with conventional pills, the issue of liability must hinge on the amount of absolute risk increase. Relative risks or risk ratios are no more than a shorthand alternative method of comparing risks, which happen readily to demonstrate the strength of any association. They say absolutely nothing of themselves about the balance of probabilities. The problem was that a relative risk of twofold had become established as the criterion in the most common of liability cases. In this case, for a woman choosing between the two hormonal products, the balance of probability would be satisfied when the relative risk was greater than 1.67 (actually 1.66 recurring). The reason is that the risk then added to the risk of a thrombosis by 3rd generation pills would be more than the added risk for 2nd generation pills above the baseline risk (since the RR = 3). The absolute risk would need to add at least as much again (twice the baseline risk). The situation is illustrated below.

The figure below shows absolute risks of a thrombosis on the left among all women not on hormonal contraception and then consecutively on 2nd generation pills (P2) and then hypothetically on 3rd generation pills (P3), with sufficient extra risk for an argument of causation on the balance of probabilities. This assumes, as one must in the absence of alternative explanations based on data, an additive model for these risks. The argument is, therefore, that the last of these is sufficient, and that hinges on an understanding of components of attributable absolute risk, and consideration of actual choices for women. It is vital to note that the baseline risk applies to all women all the

13.16

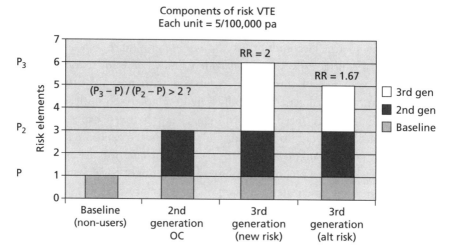

Attributable risks

time, while the court's criterion ((3) above) assigns this risk only to women on the 2nd generation preparations. Clearly, there has to be an important initial risk (which is causative in a legal sense) for this argument to cope with *reductio ad absurdum* criticisms. An extra attributable risk, which is small relative to the baseline, can easily be twice as large as the extra risk already existing and be of little consequence, since it would be swamped by the intrinsic baseline risk.

13.17 Very early on I discussed this interpretation with the legal team for the claimants. As described above, for the purposes of demonstrating causation, it was, in my view, necessary to establish a relative risk of 1.67. The team seemed happy, if a little sceptical, about the argument I put, which was supported by the other epidemiologist present. I understand it was considered by the legal team with other experts with a view to consider whether to put the argument, but my view was not accepted by other experts and was not regarded as addressing the correct legal question. On expert advice it had already been agreed that a relative risk of greater than 2 had to be established. My view was that this concession had probably been agreed in error by non-experts—but it remained unclear to me in law where that left the above-mentioned epidemiological argument. I had expected that any legal criteria would follow the giving of the expert evidence, and not pre-empt it. Reliance for the question had clearly to be on the legal representatives conducting the case. I learned only some time later that another expert had contradicted my advice when put to him by the claimants' legal team. But apparently, the question for the court had been, 'If the claimant had been taking the 2nd generation pill rather than the 3rd, is it more likely than not that the claimant would not have suffered the DVT?' In my view, the more pertinent question was, 'If a claimant on 3rd generation pills, having chosen between 2nd and 3rd generation, suffers a DVT, is it more likely than not that the DVT is a consequence of that choice?' The former unfairly loads the baseline risk only onto 2nd generation pills. But since, for both preparations, the baseline risk is identical, it cannot affect the choice. According to the first formulation above, it clearly must, which, in my view, is because the question is ill-directed. However, the latter formulation was not the question which was tried.

My draft expert report on the epidemiology nonetheless invoked the above **13.18** argument, judging the epidemiology on the basis of a relative risk of 1.67. It was made clear to me that this argument was not going to be advanced for the reasons already set out. I agreed to accept the legally imposed relative risk of 2, agreed previously. I did feel then that the case for the claimants might even be winnable on that criterion and the evidence. This, in my view, was in large measure why the case was lost—as we shall see. Certainly, with hindsight, I was not as forceful as I should have been in putting the epidemiological case. If I had been involved at the outset of the litigation, I would have been in a stronger position. I took, at the time, what seemed wiser counsel in circumstances that I then only poorly understood. Basically, the case was complex enough and I did not want to compromise the rest of the evidence by introducing what probably would be seen as something of a red herring, or possibly even special pleading. Clearly, establishing an RR of 1.67 is not as difficult as achieving an RR of 2— particularly given the epidemiological evidence, but that consideration played no part in the argument, which was based on relevant probability considerations entirely.

E. Confounding or Bias

The next complex set of epidemiological arguments in the court was also crucial **13.19** to the outcome. Again it was resolved unsatisfactorily. There is always a whole spectrum of possible biases that might explain an association between a possible hazard and a disease. The defendants had a limitless choice, and they pursued each with pronounced vigour. But the test must always involve, first, some explanation for an artefact; secondly, data demonstrating its plausibility; and thirdly, proper adjustment removing convincingly the measure of association (here the relative risk of 3rd versus 2nd for VTE). Clearly, invoking plausible explanations alone is not enough.

The defendants, for example, had claimed that the reason for the apparent **13.20** increased risk with 3rd generation products was a consequence of prescriber preferences for women at increased risk—since the product was thought to be safer (*prescription bias*). The defendants also contended, paradoxically, that there might be a diagnostic bias, in which doctors suspected the possible relationship between 3rd generation pills and thrombosis, and might be more inclined to diagnose a venous thrombosis among users than among women using the older pills. It was also thought possible that women dissatisfied with 2nd generation pills, because of unwanted side effects, would be at higher risk and more likely to switch (*selection bias*). Finally, any ill-effect may be more likely to manifest early in the use of any product and 2nd generation users would be survivors of this early effect compared to new 3rd generation users (*healthy user effect*). These arguments are all intrinsically plausible—but all have to be demonstrated by proper epidemiological analyses, which are generally quite difficult.

13.21 It is also worth saying that arguments such as these have dominated the question of the link between cigarette smoking and lung cancer, as well as hormone replacement therapy (HRT) and breast cancer, for far too long. In the latter case a large randomized trial has demonstrated a doubling of risk with long-term HRT use—and yet it is still denied by some with vested interests in the product. It is to be expected that manufacturers of a product will defend its safety, sometimes in the face of overwhelming evidence. Examples are legion. Indeed it is normal for confounding to be cited as the reason for any association that is unwanted as a causative one. When seriously unwanted, the arguments have to become seriously intense, unless of course the evidence for confounding is clear. This association was certainly seriously unwanted.

13.22 To reiterate, for any of these possible biases to be demonstrated, first, an important difference between users has to be shown with respect to the potential confounders. Then a difference in risk between persons subject to different levels of the confounding variable has to be shown. Once that is done, adjustment for this confounding has to demonstrate no residual risk associated with the exposure in question. For, while real confounding might well be present, that does not of itself necessarily exclude an important residual causative pharmacological effect. Clearly, there will often be difficulties in measuring some of these potential confounders, in which case ancillary evidence may be relevant.

F. Prescription Bias

13.23 Taking prescription bias first, the evidence was compelling that prescribing of the putatively safer pill to higher-risk women was likely, since surveys among doctors suggested that they would practise in that way. When their actual practice was examined, however, it went slightly in the opposite direction, or demonstrated no such prescribing bias. In other words, while doctors said they would differentially prescribe 3rd generation pills to higher-risk women, in fact they did not.[9]

The most crucial evidence against this explanation was provided by Professor **13.24** Alex Walker from Harvard University, who was another expert witness. His analysis[10] demonstrated beyond doubt that, to begin an account for a doubling of risk the potency of any prescribing bias, both with respect to the amount of actual discrimination and the different risks suffered by the two groups, were implausible, given the evidence. Groups of women, who did have highly elevated risk (for example, older women), were accommodated in the design of the studies by age-matching, or age was adjusted for in the analyses. Likewise, women with a history of a previous thrombosis or with Factor V Leiden mutation were excluded in all studies. There needed to be another potent (and recognizable) risk factor that gave rise reliably to the more likely prescription of 3rd generation pills. Walker's calculation demonstrated that since no sufficient increased risk could be demonstrated for any risk factor, and no such residual high-risk group could remotely be identified, this explanation was entirely fanciful, if initially plausible.

G. Diagnostic Bias

When studied, no evidence for such a bias could be discerned. Surveys of **13.25** doctors demonstrated no propensity to favour thrombosis as a possible explanation for symptoms among 3rd generation users.[11] Moreover, in a study that tried to culminate this bias, by matching cases and controls on the diagnosing physicians' tentative diagnosis, the relative risk estimate for thrombosis remained high and significant.[12] This evidence clearly does not satisfy the third criterion required to demonstrate a non-causal explanation. Indeed, not one of the criteria was satisfied.

---

[9] Dunn N, White I, Freemantle S et al, 'The role of prescribing and referrals bias in studies of the association between third generation oral contraceptives and an increased risk of thromboembolism' Pharmacoepidemiol Drug Safety 1998; 7: 13–14.

[10] Walker A, 'Gestodene, Desogestrel, and venous thromboembolism: a little risk after a long look. The safety of third generation oral contraceptives' J Clin Endocrinol Metab 1999; 84, 6: 1825–38.

[11] Heinemann LAJ, Lewis MA et al, 'Could preferential prescribing and referral behaviour of physicians explain the elevated thrombosis risk found to be associated with oral contraceptives?' Pharmacoepidemiol Drug Safety 1996; 5: 285–94.

[12] Bloemenkamp K, Rosendaal F, Buller H et al, 'Risk of venous thrombosis with the use of current low-dose oral contraceptives is not explained by diagnostic suspicion and referral bias' Arch Intern Med 1999; 159: 65–70.

H. Selection of Bias or Healthy User Effect

13.26 The general argument invoked was that there are complex selection processes, depending on past pill use, which gives rise to women at higher risk being more likely to prefer the new 3rd generation pills. Thus, the relative risk of around twofold can be explained, it was argued, by this selection, and not by the pharmacology of the newer pills. It would be tedious to go through the detail of all the arguments that were made to justify this belief. But the justifications are interesting and central to this case. What follows is tortuous, and perforce complex, but to do the argument complete justice would require much detail. Some detail, however, cannot be avoided. This part of the case caused some confusion both among the legal teams and the judge. I am not surprised that the court came to the wrong conclusion. The process involved complex statistical theory, highly complex epidemiological knowledge and experience and, in my view, provided scope for legal obfuscation. This aspect of the case painfully illustrates the point that abstract statistical scientific issues can sensibly be adjudicated upon in the courtroom, only by scientists. Otherwise, courts appear not to be well suited to the process of adjudicating on scientific theories for the benefit of individual litigants.

13.27 Expert witnesses answer questions put to them by counsel. If it is the case that the latter's comprehension is limited by their knowledge or experience, the issues will not be properly expounded in court. The arguments here are both complex and technical. Indeed professional—probably medical—colleagues in my experience, only rarely properly understand them after detailed explanation. It is wholly unreasonable to expect most lawyers, even if they are scientifically minded, to reach a level of comprehension that would enable proper cross-examination, without at least a great deal of tutoring. This, I think, is importantly unrecognized. It is too easily assumed that all, or at least sufficient technical knowledge can be readily absorbed. To admit to any deficit of understanding is unprofessional, if not undignified. Effective cross-examination requires a total understanding of highly technical material, which I believe in this sort of case, is only exceptionally achievable. Without it, obfuscation by expert witnesses can frequently serve an ulterior motive or purpose. In this case it did.

13.28 What was at stake was the strong belief by the defendants' team that the results of the large study (the Transnational Study) sponsored by the manufacturers, and published in the BMJ in 1996,[13] were an artefact of confounding. The

---

[13] Spitzer WO et al (Transnational Study), '3rd generation oral contraceptives and risk of venous thromboembolic disorders: an international case-control study' BMJ 1996; 312: 83–7.

adjusted, estimate relative risk published was 1.5, which every effort of adjustment in the analyses had failed to reduce further. The concluding remarks in the BMJ report were that, notwithstanding its own finding (described as a 'slight' increase), the results were most likely to be attributable to the various possible biases discussed extensively therein. Interestingly, no reference was made to the evidence accumulated from other studies, particularly those from independent sources suggesting a strong effect. After this publication, successive sponsored presentations to scientific meetings and the CSM continued to argue an ever-more complex and intricate case for an explanation of the higher risk of thrombosis being artefactual, and hence not causal. As I have argued, this is to be expected, but, if pertinent, must be properly justified.

13.29 From the above, it will be clear that extensive attempts to justify many of the possible biases failed. Such attempts continued after the 1995/6 publications. Studies, for example, restricted only to new pill users, thus eliminating the possibilities of healthy user effect or higher initial risk, demonstrated an increased risk for 3rd generation pills.[14] Indeed, the estimated relative risk was higher than threefold. A plausible case for important bias was never sustained by the kind of evidence required, in spite of a phenomenal effort from many independent and industry-sponsored quarters. Given this enormous effort, and the obvious need for such an explanation, it seemed clear that if such explanations existed they could have been found—supported with adequate evidence. They were not.

13.30 The sponsors of the Transnational Study continued to reanalyse their data, and to publish these analyses with a view to persuading the scientific community that their own results were biased and hence misleading. This simply ignored the accumulating evidence from, for example, the contemporary WHO Study,[15] which was likewise assiduously investigating artefactual explanations for their estimate of a relative risk approaching threefold. What is known to all epidemiologists is that a strong desire to eliminate an unwanted risk estimate by repeated reanalysis will often eventually succeed. This happens by evading or ignoring evidence that does not reduce the estimated risk, and by pursuing evidence from analyses that do. Such processes may also have to invoke unusual methodology. This process is known as data dredging. It has been common in medicine in the past and epidemiological methods have evolved largely to mitigate its effect. On the whole such dredging 'successes' should be ignored.[16]

---

[14] Herings R et al, 'Venous thromboembolism among new users of different oral contraceptives' Lancet 1999; 354: 127.

[15] Meirik O et al (WHO Study), 'Different progestogens on the risk of venous thromboembolism' Lancet 1995; 346: 1582–88.

[16] Vandenbroucke JP, Helmerhorst FM, Rosendaal FR, 'Competing interests and controversy about third generation oral contraceptives' BMJ 2000; 320: 381.

13.31 Thus the Transnational Study successively reported decreasing estimates of relative risks, whereas the WHO Study failed to do so. As we shall see the analyses conducted by the WHO Study were known to be wholly appropriate and legitimate. Those methods deployed by the Transnational Study became increasingly obscure and radical. Making these sorts of judgments, however, on methodological quality is complex, and of course can be controversial. But lawyers should not be the people to do that—it has to be performed by epidemiologists. In the court, experts on these methodologies, interrogated by lawyers, put the two sides.

13.32 There were two such publications central to this case. I will discuss one. This coup de grâce was a new analysis of the Transnational Study published in *Human Reproduction* in 1999.[17] This reanalysis succeeded apparently in reducing the estimated relative risk from 1.5 to 0.8, i.e. no increased risk of 3rd generation pills. In order to do justice to methods used for doing this, I have to describe some basic epidemiological principles.

13.33 First, the Transnational Study was a case-control study in which the past pill use of cases of VTE are compared with the pill histories of similar women without VTE. Cases (of women with VTE) and at least three controls, individually matched for age, hospital, and community, had been recruited and interviewed in 10 centres between 1993 and 1995. This is common method for investigating the aetiology of rare diseases. The alternative is a cohort study in which women using different pills are followed for enough years to have a reliable estimate of the relative risks. Case-control studies are retrospective, while cohort studies are prospective. The latter are thought to be generally more reliable, while the former are much more efficient.

13.34 The designs of these two types of study are different, as are the appropriate analyses, since the sampling methods are so different. One study selectively samples ill people, while the other samples particular types of pill users. This has profound implications on the study design to avoid bias and on the methods of analysis, which are consequently very different. These have evolved over the last 40 years as the theoretical characteristics of the sampling methods have been better understood and the appropriate methods of analyses developed.

13.35 The methodology utilized to reanalyse the Transnational (case-control) Study was highly novel, because it used the complex methodology developed for the analysis of cohort studies. Thus, the historical records derived retrospectively

---

17 Lewis MA, MacRae KD et al, 'The differential risk of oral contraceptives: the impact of full exposure history' Human Reproduction 1999; 14: 1493–99.

from the cases and controls were taken to be the prospective records of a cohort. The method assesses the spontaneous risk ratios from these records by analysing so-called 'risk sets' of contemporary participants (cases and controls in this case) at each diagnosis of VTE (in this case the recruitment of a case). In these analyses, adjustment can be made for possible confounding variables available in these records. It was these analyses that provided an estimate of relative risk less than unity.

The justification for this analysis was that complicated effects of past pill use, and of switching pills, could be adjusted out of the comparison and what would be left would be merely a biological effect. It was not clear which particular aspects would be removed, but what was clear was that switching from 3rd to 2nd generation pills, or vice versa, was part of the adjustment. But the problem here is that variables that describe this switching are logically, not coincidentally, related to the exposure variable. Hence adjustment would be bound to attenuate the measured effect—if there was one. But there was also a laborious argument involving the possibility of time dependency in the causal relationships, which might cover a multitude of effects—when the only one of interest might be a differential effect of duration of use, possibly conditional on past usage. **13.36**

In the court the deliberations of these analyses were confined by the judge to one part of the proceedings, with one expert on each side to examine the analyses. Before that had been decided, the claimants' solicitor asked me to write a report about the methodology used. Indeed, before the case began the judge had insisted that the data and the records used in these analyses be provided to the claimants' lawyers. They were indeed eventually provided, but were not allowed out of the offices of the solicitor, for reasons of confidentiality. I found this puzzling, since confidentiality is routinely guaranteed in epidemiological offices where analyses take place. Doing such analyses in someone else's office is often very problematic. Major problems were quickly identified, on detailed investigation of the computer files supplied, with the analyses performed and the results published, which were obscured by the scientific accounts in the publication. **13.37**

My report highlighted several core problems in the analyses, which would have rendered the publication unpublishable, had it been properly refereed. These had to do with breaking of the original matching, the unusually high incidence of disease (roughly 25 per cent, because thrombosis patients were selected as cases), and the adjustment for variables which themselves necessarily related strongly to exposure. Importantly, conventional case-control analyses could have accomplished all the putative benefits of these analyses, addressing exactly the same possibilities of confounding without any of these analytical problems. Hence, this new methodology was unjustified and confusing. Indeed, the **13.38**

WHO had undertaken the appropriate analyses, which had had no effect on estimates of risk.[18] Crucially, it was revealed that the defendants' definition of a risk set was incorrect, so much so that adjustment within each risk set involved utilizing data that were obtained after the time of the index event. Of course, this is only possible with data collected retrospectively and used as if prospectively collected. But, crucially, it involves adjustment for data derived from the future for each risk set, which is palpably absurd.

13.39 The dialogue in court was fascinating and tragic. I knew the defendants' expert extremely well (and had for many years). He was known as a competent expert witness whom I had come across quite often in my regulatory role on the CSM. He had worked for the tobacco companies, among many others.[19] When asked to describe his definition of a risk set, I thought it was obvious that he knew he was talking nonsense, even if it was engaging nonsense. The judge was elegantly bewildered. If there had been an assessor sitting alongside the judge, the epidemiological 'nonsense' would have been uncovered for what it was—nonsense.

13.40 As the description progressed, he was asked repeatedly by lawyers advised by Alex Walker—the claimants' expert on this issue—to redo the analyses, taking out, for example, the most blatant acts of epidemiological clairvoyance. He would reappear the next day having devised another solution. Tragically, he was one day found dead in front of his computer, having suffered a major heart attack. After that happened, further discussion on the topic was limited. It had been decided anyway beforehand that my report was outside the rules of engagement in civil proceedings. Thus a crucial question—the resolution of which was unambiguous—was left for the judge to decide upon. He, to his credit, contemplated taking impartial expert advice, but in the end forwent the opportunity. The claimants' legal team decided not to pursue the point on which an assessor might be asked to assist, having given the matter careful consideration and taken further independent statistical advice in the course of the trial. An assessor (or even a scientific adviser) on the Bench throughout the trial would have been invaluable, and in my view on this issue it was essential.

13.41 But from this moment the results of this faulty analysis were left hanging in the air. Apparently, I could not refer to them in subsequent deposition. Nor was I asked about them in the witness box, because the judge had ruled that I could not give evidence about it. (Whether this was after he had read my report on this matter, if he did, I have no way of knowing.)

---

[18] Poulter NR, Farley TMM, Chang CL et al, 'Safety of combined oral contraceptive pills' Lancet 1996; 346: 547.

[19] Obituaries: Kenneth David MacRae. BMJ 2002; 324: 1041.

I. Pooling all the Evidence

In court, many detailed discussions led to a consensus about the validity of the **13.42** various epidemiological studies and the most acceptable estimate of relative risk of thrombosis between 3rd and 2nd generation pills. These results are portrayed in the table below. The studies published in 1995/6 have been discussed above—in particular the WHO Study[20] and the Transnational Study.[21] The fourth study in 1995[22] was a study undertaken by Hershal Jick (another expert for the claimants), who updated his analyses in 2000[23] with more data and greater attention to the possibility of artefactual explanation. The remainder were published after the initial hiatus.

The technology of pooling studies is well established and essentially combines **13.43** the results together algebraically with appropriate weighting for their relative

All (accepted) studies, results agreed by the court

Study	Year	Adjusted RR (3rd/2nd)	95% confidence interval	Relative precision
Bloemenkamp[24]	1995	2.20	0.90–5.40	4
WHO	1995	2.70	1.60–4.60	11
Transnational	1996	1.73	1.07–2.79	13
Farmer (Mediplus)[25]	1999	1.35	0.74–2.39	8
Herings, all users	1999	2.30	1.50–3.70	16
Parkin[26]	2000	2.92	0.78–12.0	2
Jick (updated)	2000	2.20	1.50–3.30	20
Lidegaard	2002	1.40	1.00–1.90	26
Pooled estimate =		**1.89**	**1.59–2.25**	**100**

[20] Poulter N et al (WHO Study), 'Venous thromboembolic disease and combined oral contraceptives: results of an international multicentre case-control study' Lancet 1995; 346: 1575–82; Meirik O et al (WHO Study), 'Different progestogens on the risk of venous thromboembolism' Lancet 1995; 346: 1582–88.

[21] Spitzer W et al (Transnational Study), '3rd generation oral contraceptives and risk of venous thromboembolic disorders: an international case-control study' BMJ 1996; 312: 83–7.

[22] Jick et al, 'Risk of idiopathic cardiovascular death and nonfatal venous thromboembolism in women using oral contraceptives with differing progestogens components' Lancet 1995; 346: 1589–93.

[23] Jick et al, 'Risk of venous thromboembolism before and after 1995: cohort and case-control study' BMJ 2000; 321: 1190–95.

[24] Bloemenkamp K et al, 'Enhancement by Factor V Leiden mutation of risk of deep vein thrombosis associated with oral contraceptives containing a third generation progesteron' Lancet 1995; 346: 1593–96.

[25] Todd J, Lawrenson R, Farmer R, Williams T, and Leydon G, 'Venous thromboembolic disease and combined oral contraceptives: a re-analysis of the Mediplus database' Human Reproduction 1999; 14: 1500–5.

[26] Parkin L, Skegg D, Wilson M, Herbison G, and Paul C, 'Oral contraceptives and fatal pulmonary embolism' Lancet 2000; 355: 2133.

precision. There are two important features of this table. One is that the most reliable estimate of aggregate results of epidemiological studies is around 1.89— more than 1.67, but less than 2.00. The second, and possibly more important, is that the three studies funded by industry here yield low estimates of the relative risk. These are the Transnational Study, Farmer et al,[27] and Lidegaard et al,[28] the final results of which were published during the hearing.

13.44 These results were lower, and hence less alarming than the results from independent studies. The pooled estimates from industry, when compared with the pooled estimates from independent sources, were significantly different: 1.35 (95 per cent confidence limits 1.12–1.63) compared with 2.27 (1.72–3.00). Such a difference, without judging which are correct, is very likely to be an artefact of study design or analysis, and is most unlikely to be a chance occurrence.

13.45 There was no firm explanation for this, but it is a relatively common finding in the assessment of drug safety. Worse still, two of the studies had used the same data set—called the General Practice Research Database (GPRD). This is a record of a collection of all prescription drugs supplied to patients in a large number of general practices in the United Kingdom. It is used to identify cases and controls, and compare drug histories to elucidate possible side effects of drugs. Jick's analyses had used the GPRD, as had another expert, Richard Farmer, who had used the database for the same purpose. Farmer was an expert for the defendants, and obtained much of his research funding from the industry. His analyses of the same data provided estimates of relative risk far lower, 1.20 (0.90–1.70), than those of Jick, 2.20 (1.50–3.30). Since the former 'duplicates' the latter I have omitted it in the table at para 13.42 above in favour of the independent assessment. Whereas, in court, it was possible to investigate possible reasons for this discrepancy at a superficial level, the explanation was inconclusive. This is not surprising, since it would have involved a detailed investigation of every step in the collection and analysis of each study, much of which would probably not have been available for scrutiny. The argument hinged largely on the number of controls used in each analysis—and was essentially sterile.

13.46 There is strong prior evidence for this kind of bias, and strong evidence was provided to the court that vested interests can obtain results for important epidemiological associations tending to favour their belief. This was never properly and fully discussed in the court and seemed to me to be disparaged.

---

[27] Farmer et al, 'Population-based study of risk of VTE associated with various oral contraceptives' (Mediplus) Lancet 1997; 349: 83–8.

[28] Lidegaard et al, 'Oral contraceptives and venous thromboembolism: a five-year national case-control study' Contraception 2002; 65: 131–4.

Whenever I referred to it, the implications, which I felt to be important, were often dismissed by the judge.

The judgment was that the reanalysis of the Transnational Study may have been **13.47** valid. Indeed, the judge expressed great appreciation of the performance of the witness for the defendants on this question. If it was valid in his view, then indeed there was no extra risk. However, since this was the only study that was properly and fully discussed in the court, the fall-back position was that the relative risk was about 1.7 (higher, incidentally, than 1.67).

J. Conclusions

As an expert instructed by the losing claimants to assist the court, I clearly **13.48** have an interest in this account. I have argued elsewhere[29] that the case was inadequately tried, and that the judgment was wrong. It is, without doubt, held by the majority of the scientific community concerned with drug safety that this is indeed the case: many go further and have concluded that the legal system is deficient in this respect[30]—not a healthy state of affairs. In so far as this will ultimately turn out to be the perceived wisdom, it is worth examining why and how it happened. This case, and its judgment, and the bulk of those knowledge-able about contraceptive safety have apparently differing views about the effect of 3rd generation pills and thrombosis. In the minds of regulators and experts, widespread use of 3rd generation pills will cause more VTE. In the minds of the manufacturers there is no extra risk—amply supported by this judgment.

The judgment was that the reanalysis of the Transnational Study may have been **13.49** valid, and if so there was indeed no extra risk, and the manufacturers were entitled to succeed in their defence. This was the only justification based, as it was in my view, on faulty reanalysis. However, the judge adopted a fall-back position, that the relative risk was around 1.7. In the light of the agreed criteria for a successful claim of twofold, such an extra risk was insufficient to justify any claim against the manufacturers for an individual thrombosis. In my view, and that of many others, the Transnational Study reanalysis was epidemiological nonsense, a relative risk of 1.67 was sufficient, and anyway the real risk was probably of the order of 1.9, or greater, and causal.

---

[29] McPherson K, 'Epidemiology on trial—confessions of an expert witness' Lancet 2002; 360: 889–90.
[30] Skegg DCG, 'Oral contraceptives, venous thromboembolism, and the courts' BMJ 2002; 325: 504–5.

13.50 There has to be a high degree of collaboration between experts and lawyers, but its limits should be clearly defined. The issues of difference between members of the claimants' expert team should have been discussed well in advance. (There could have been no such reconciliation between the experts on the two sides.) It became apparent that my role as an expert witness was to consist solely of my evidence to the court—and that indeed was what happened. However, the option of pursuing evidence without collaboration, consultation, and agreement within the team, as I perceived it, seemed foolhardy. The balance of control does not favour the scientific expert.

13.51 My expert view did not prevail, for the reasons I have explained. First, I was too easily influenced by the vagaries of litigation and, secondly, I was not allowed by the judge to give evidence on one of the core issues, the reanalysis of the Transnational Study. The well-documented bias, in some instances essentially proven in court, of studies funded by industry was also inadequately dealt with. To do better, I would have required more experience in the proceedings of the court. If naïve expert witnesses are to serve a useful purpose, it is incumbent on the court to accommodate their naïvety fully, which requires nothing more than a better understanding of their deficiencies of experience. My first appearance was a learning experience for me, and next time I would do better. However, it is worth noting that, while giving my evidence, I could not require counsel for the claimants to interrogate me adequately, partly because, of course, all communication with them was forbidden at that time. Nor was I informed that some of my advice to them was given lower weight, presumably for valid legal reasons. It is therefore vital to ensure that experts are fully informed of, and well versed in, the idiosyncrasies of the adversarial system of civil litigation and that their expertise is well utilized by the court.

13.52 Even the most assiduous and able lawyer will lack the experience of professional epidemiologists. It might have been helpful in this case if the legal team had been afforded the continuous advice of an expert about how to proceed with all the witnesses who knew the subject well. Instead, it had the (possibly contradictory) advice of changing experts (there were, for example, five epidemiological experts for the claimants) who came and went (to and from the United States, for example) as the trial progressed. Contradictions between experts can be expected, but are often merely a consequence of simple misunderstandings and lack of early meetings to iron out the areas of disagreement and establish areas of agreement. Non-experts may not see that so clearly. But the progression of the case appeared anyway to develop in a piecemeal and incoherent way. It did not accommodate some vital discussion, for reasons of process, not logic. Clearly, the death of one expert for the defendants had a particular effect, which is unlikely to be repeated.

It was by no means apparent to the observer that the judge fully understood the **13.53** subtleties of the scientific case. Indeed, he candidly admitted as much. Nor for that matter were the subtleties well put in the court, partly because the proceedings were disjointed and partly because the claimants' lawyers were pursuing a legal hurdle, which was misplaced (in my view, because the RR>2 was very possibly too high) and forensically probably unattainable as the evidence progressed. A relative risk greater than 2 was never unambiguously supported by the data; to have been justified, one would have to understand completely the actual bias in industry (and other) funded studies, which is sadly beyond the most assiduous analyses. But it was not required on the evidence available. The whole proceedings seemed to me to be partly responsible for the disjointed nature of the case, since each part of the argument could be addressed once only, and the order and the significance of each part was determined by the court, in my view incoherently. Experts should have been involved in all parts of the case from beginning to end, with a clear definition of their role. They should have played their part in determining the forensic criteria and in the conduct of the trial. Some of the crucial issues—such as the role of industry in determining the risk of their products—seemed to be banned from full discussion. It was very relevant and remained poorly understood.

The judge could have taken expert advice on many of the difficult technicalities. **13.54** Indeed he confessed to a lack of mathematical sophistication on scientific issues. In my view, it was a mistake not to do so, for clearly he could not understand the detail of many of the arguments. For the reanalyses of the Transnational Study, the expert most cited by the defendants' witness was the eminent statistician who had developed the methodology used, Sir David Cox. He would have been perfectly acceptable to the claimants' team as the best impartial expert opinion by far on the suitability of these analyses. Could not the court, on its own motion, have appointed him as assessor?

The commercial world has different standards of assessment and evaluation of **13.55** long-term safety of their products than does the scientific world. This is why regulatory agencies exist. It is inappropriate if legal assessment inadvertently (or otherwise) adopts commercial standards when public health is the issue, at least without understanding the implications. This case was a lost opportunity for responsible pharmacovigilance—since it has affected marketing, sales, and use rates. That, in giving judgment, the judge commented adversely on all the expert witnesses for the claimants' side is one pertinent reflection, among others, of lack of professional empathy towards expert witnesses generally in the proceedings. This was misplaced, since it failed to address the scientific issues and relied upon judicial decision-making by way of preference of one expert rather than another, because he or she had the more impressive apparent credentials or performance. Lawyers and scientists may not share the same thought processes and may communicate in language that is not readily transmitted. Judges in the adversarial system of civil litigation may not be faulted for preferring one or other of the experts' evidence (or rejecting them all) if they find the scientific evidence difficult to comprehend. But to engage in the subjective and inexpert exercise of assessing credentials and the credibility of witnesses is highly unsatisfactory to the scientist, since it detracts from proper pronouncement on scientific issues.

13.56 Given the evidence and the criteria, both of which were inadequate, the judge really had little choice. To find in favour of the claimants would have taken an extra few weeks (for there were several criteria yet to try). Had the criteria been properly set, and the evidence properly interrogated, matters might well have been different. Nevertheless, the fault probably lies in a defective system of adjudication. Had the issue of the 3rd generation contraceptive pill been the subject of a public inquiry, the rules would have been different, less restrictive evidentially and procedurally. Since it resulted in litigation, blame needed to be apportioned, and the judgment was disproportionately influenced. This judgment was nonetheless wrong, even on its own criteria—the risk was indeed indicative of a causative effect on conservative assumptions.

14

CONCLUSIONS

In matters of science, the reasoning of men of science can only be answered
by men of science.

The claim by the Commission of Wells Harbour, Norfolk
in *Folkes v Chadd* (1782) 3 Doug 157

The Woolf reforms, embodied in Part 35 of the Civil Procedure Rules 1998, **14.01**
brought about no fundamental change in the expert witness system—if indeed
it is right to label the common law rule about opinion evidence, a string of
procedural rules and court practices, a system. Part 35, the Practice Direction,
and, belatedly in June 2005, the *Protocol for the Instruction of Experts to give
evidence in civil claims* have simply been bolted on to the basic rule of evidence,
created and sustained by the common law judges. That rule is that opinion
testimony of 'scientific men upon proven facts may be given by men of science,
within their own science',[1] although it is not necessary for the field of expertise
to be either subject to strictly scientific method or an organized branch of
knowledge.[2] The implementation of the CPR in 1999 sought to tackle the
further problems of costs and delay in civil litigation. So far as expert evidence is
concerned, something in that respect has been achieved. There is the notable
innovation of the single joint expert: this often reduces costs where the expert
evidence is uncontroversial but requires exposition for the court to understand.
And it has reduced costs in small[3] cases where the single joint expert is in effect
constituted the judge. The 1999 reforms appear to have achieved two other

---

[1] *United States Shipping Board v Ship St Albans* [1931] AC 632.

[2] *MacFadden v Murdoch* [1867] IR 211, per Chief Baron Pigot, and *Clark v Ryan* (1960) 103
CLR 486, per Dixon CJ and Menzies J at 501.

[3] The so-called fast track. The Civil Justice Council Annual Report 2004 noted at p 15 that
'Notwithstanding the success of the use of the single joint expert in the Fast Track the committee
has failed to detect any great enthusiasm for extending the practice up through the Multi-Track'
(see <http://www.civiljusticecouncil.gov.uk/164.htm>).

things in relation to expert witnesses: the greater use of meetings of experts to iron out matters not really in dispute, and a general raising of standards of expert evidence achieved through the expert's declaration and explicit statement that an expert's 'overriding' duty is to the court. Although this probably has no legal effect, there is a strong impression among the judiciary that the sobriquet of the 'hired gun' is less apposite than hitherto. If the use of the word 'overriding' is merely exhortatory, all well and good in order to encourage high standards of objectivity. If it is intended to mean more, it should be dropped from Part 35. The expert's duty to assist the court—CPR r 35.3(1)—should suffice.

A. The Exclusionary Role

14.02 Nobody concerned with the recent reforms, however, addressed the question of the exclusionary rule that introduced expert evidence in defiance of the rule against hearsay. More crucially, there has been no challenge to the central problem that the court is quintessentially a lay, i.e. non-scientific, body determining cases on detailed matters of expertise. In short, the challenge, handed down by Judge Learned Hand a century ago, lay unaddressed, particularly in those complicated cases which manifestly are beyond the understanding or appreciation of a lay tribunal, however resolutely committed to a fair determination of scientific evidence. The codes of procedural rules and case law neither provide a coherent system, nor encompass the jurisprudential concepts and functions in accommodating issues beyond the comprehension of courts without expert testimony.

B. An Australian Survey

14.03 It is an extraordinary fact that no one has been bothered to find out how well courts have assimilated scientific evidence, particularly where the experts have expressed conflicting views. At least the Australians have recently embarked upon a survey of how expert evidence plays a significant role in a wide variety of courts and tribunals. The survey in the late 1990s,[4] conducted under the auspices of the Australian Institute of Justice Administration, sought to gather information on judicial beliefs or approaches to the use of expert evidence. The survey's report disclosed three key outcomes: (a) the value of clarity in exposition of the expert evidence; (b) a quest for reliability in expert opinions; and (c) a desire that the courtroom be a truly accountable forum. Interestingly,

---

[4] I Freckleton, P Reddy, and H Selby, *Australian Journal Perspectives on Expert Evidence: An Empirical Study* (Australian Institute of Judicial Administration, 1999).

the recommendations for procedural reform were primarily designed to assist decision-makers to understand better and to evaluate expert evidence. The report concluded:

> The answers by judges to the survey instrument and their many comments and suggestions articulate a preparedness on the part of a substantial part of Australia's judiciary to confront in a flexible way the difficulties of complex and conflicting evidence of experts.[5]

14.04 A similar survey of the English judiciary would not go amiss. Such a survey needs, however, to be marked by a similar exercise among leading experts (the experience of Professor McPherson must be treated as a worrying feature of the contemporary scene). How best can expert evidence be adduced and, crucially, how can it be ensured that it is optimally understood?

C. Law and Science

14.05 Law and science are distinctive disciplines that meet one another in everyday life, not infrequently in the courtroom. Law is prescriptive. Science, on the other hand, aims to describe, interpret, and even predict the social and natural world. In decision-making, science is intrinsically probabilistic, non-hierarchical, and numerate. Courts of law seek an answer, if not certainty; they rely on precedent and are verbal in their processing of material. Scientists, always aware of the limited state of knowledge at any one time, are fearful of giving definitive answers to the law's quest for definite answers. Much scientific evidence comes nowadays from members of the medical profession. Science and medicine, are themselves uneasy bedfellows, never mind their relationship to the law. While science is seen as very much based on data collection and analysis, it is remarkable that only in the past few years have we talked about 'evidence-based medicine'. What was it before? Walter Gratzer[6] has written: 'Modern medicine has all the trappings of a science, and it undoubtedly makes use of discoveries in the biological sciences, but it remains perilously placed between science and "healing arts", based as much on superstition as logic'. By contrast, Carl Sagan stated that 'science is much more than a body of knowledge: it is a way of thinking'.[7]

14.06 Whatever discipline the expert professes, the problem remains of the communication of non-lawyer to lawyer. However competent and reliable the expert is, both as a scientist and accomplished witness, it is the understanding of the lawyer that is essential. Does the advocate appreciate the scientific issues

---

[5] ibid.
[6] W Gratzer, *The Undergrowth of Science: Delusion, Self-deception and Human Frailty* (2000).
[7] C Sagan, *The Demon-Haunted World: Science as a Candle in the Dark* (1997).

sufficiently? But above all, does the judge (or jury in a criminal trial) understand it? Legal institutions do not always adequately differentiate between reliable and unreliable expert evidence. Too often, it is asserted, courts are making decisions based upon unreliable techniques and ill-formed expert opinion. Faigman[8] has commented pithily that 'most lawyers have little or no appreciation for the scientific method and lack the ability to judge whether proffered research is good science, bad science or no science at all'. Some writers go further and argue that the problem is intrinsically related to the expectations the law harbours with respect to science as such. Where the case turns exclusively on expert evidence, the court is presented with a stark choice. Where there is other non-expert evidence, there is a tendency to place disproportionate weight on the factual evidence of non-experts, as opposed to scientific evidence. The result will depend upon the court's understanding of the expert testimony and its ability to select wisely. In turn, much will depend on the quality of the adjudicator. A legal training may not—often does not—suffice to comprehend the scientific material.

14.07 Scientific opinion does not float of its own accord. There has always to be a messenger on hand. And it is the advocate's communicating and interpreting the rival expert opinions to the court that carries the message. The legal mind needs to understand scientific method and its inherent limitations. Lawyers should be able to develop a generic model with which to approach scientific opinion and be able to examine the authority or weight that can be accorded to almost any type of scientific evidence. It is the methodology of scientists, rather than any other attempt to prefer one expert's concluded opinion over another, that could be done only by scientists in the particular field of expertise under scrutiny. And that is not the forensic process, unless we hand the decision-making over to scientists, á la Lord Mansfield, or to an advisory panel of experts á la Judge Learned Hand.

D. Judicial Decision-Making

14.08 In cases where the evidence of expert witnesses is in conflict, a judge (even one who has some, even nodding acquaintance with scientific methods) may not fully comprehend the expert evidence, simply because it is too complex or recondite. The judicial tendency is to decide the case between competing opinions on an artificial basis. Which of the experts was the more qualified? Who explained the scientific issues with greater clarity and simplicity? Whose reasoning was more logically appealing? Or is the fact that the expert gives his services

---

[8] DL Faigman, *Legal Alchemy—The Use and Misuse of Science in the Law* (1999).

free, on the grounds that he supports a pressure group for some social reform, less than independent.[9] Or is there a sound basis for endorsing the prevalent view among the professionals, and querying the radical view? Are judges at fault for using such techniques? It may not be wrong, in terms of judicial decision-making, for a judge to prefer one expert rather than another, because he or she has the more impressive credentials or has a commitment to some social or political cause. But it is highly unsatisfactory, if only because these are factors that do not pronounce on the scientific problems. So what is the answer, if we want courts of law to address directly the scientific issues and display more awareness of scientific material?

E. The Assessor System

One way is to invoke the assessor system more often, whereby an expert **14.09** (or more than one) sits with the judge to advise him, but is not a member of the court, thus preserving the judge as sole decision-maker. A general power to appoint an assessor (or more than one) has long been available to the courts, but has been used very sparingly, and almost exclusively in cases in the Admiralty jurisdiction by the use of nautical assessors drawn from the ranks of the Trinity Brethren, and in high technology patent cases. In *XYZ and Others v Schering Health Care and Others*[10] (a case concerned with the risks involved in the taking of different brands of combined oral contraceptives, to which Professor McPherson's contribution in this case is addressed in Chapter 13 above), Mackay J confessed his knowledge of algebra was at an elementary level, learnt many decades earlier; he was inclined to appoint an assessor. Since the claimants decided not to rely on the evidence of algebraic formulations in connection with a study of the effects of the contraceptive pill, the idea was not pursued. But if the judge's knowledge was so imperfect or basic on one aspect of expert testimony, why did it not prevail for him to order an assessor throughout a three-month trial? This should have been the more compelling, since the expert witnesses were a number of epidemiologists, of whom the judge said: 'The debate was unyielding and almost rancorous in tone', so that their irreconcilable differences could be satisfactorily determined only by a scientific

---

[9] In *McTear v Imperial Tobacco Ltd* [2005] CSOH 69, para 5.18 Lord Nimmo Smith in the Outer House of the Court of Session held that three experts who were called on behalf of the pursuer (the Scottish equivalent to plaintiff or claimant) alleging that smoking had caused lung cancer, also had given their services free on account of their espousal of the campaign against smoking, might have their independence queried. The fact that the experts called on behalf of the tobacco company were paid for their services did not create an a priori assumption that there was any tainting of their evidence.
[10] [2002] EWHC 1420.

expert (not necessarily another epidemiologist, joining no doubt in the maelstrom of the specialty!). It is not a question of transferring the problem from the judge to the assessor, since the latter becomes the interpreter of the scientific issues for the better understanding of the judge, the sole decision-maker. It is designed to provide the judge with unbiased assistance on scientific interpretation.

14.10   The concept of assessors was, on the face of it, given a fillip in April 1999 in new CPR r 35.15. But the modification of the old assessor system, by the assessor reporting to the court, a report which is disclosable to the parties for them to comment on, but *upon which he or she cannot be questioned*, has evoked little judicial encouragement. The one case that has so far come to the Court of Appeal involved a collision of two vessels in the mouth of the Suez Canal,[11] a case in the Admiralty jurisdiction.

14.11   In a postscript to the judgment in *The Bow Spring*,[12] the compatibility of CPR r 35.15 with Article 6 of European Convention on Human Rights was considered. The court was composed of the Master of the Rolls, Lord Philips of Worth Matravers, Clarke LJ, and Sedley LJ. (One suspects that Sedley LJ contributed the postscript.) The European Court of Human Rights in *Ky Ma v Czech Republic*,[13] had ruled that the concept of a fair trial implies the right to adversarial proceedings 'providing the parties' with the opportunity additionally 'to comment on all evidence adduced or observations filed with a view to influencing the court's decision'. Consultations between the assessor and the court should, therefore, take place openly (including disclosure of any answers to questions put by the court to the assessor) as part of the assembling of evidence. The statutory provision in England, that the assessor cannot be 'open to cross-examination or questioning' is arguably remedied, it would appear, by the opportunity for the parties' advocates to comment upon opinion expressed by the assessor. But is that enough to satisfy the precept of Article 6, even if it might be difficult, in practice, to accommodate the questioning?

14.12   Other methods by which courts can be better informed of expert evidence may continue to emerge. In a patent appeal, *Kirin-Amgen Inc v Hoechst Marion Roussel and Others*,[14] the Appellate Committee of the House of Lords was treated to tutorials from the Professor of Biochemistry at Oxford University. The case involved the production of Erythropoietin (EPO)—a hormone made in the

---

[11] Subsequently, Gross J in *The Global Mariner* [2005] EWHC 380, Admiralty, sat with two nautical assessors.

[12] [2004] 1 WLR 144.   [13] App No 35376/97, 3 March 2000, para 40.

[14] [2004] UKHL 46, [2005] RPC 9. Their Lordships had in 1996 the benefit of two expert advisers, about whose assistance Lord Goff of Chieveley described as 'invaluable': *Biogen Inc v Medeva plc* [1997] RPC 1, 31.

kidney which stimulates the production of blood cells—by DNA technology. All five Law Lords warmly welcomed Professor Yudkin's seminars, held in camera with the prior consent of the parties, thus saving an immense amount of time in having to learn about the relevant technology. The Law Lords considered that the practice might usefully be adopted in the future where the technology is 'complex and undisputed'. It is precisely where the expert evidence is in dispute that the courts will need to seek direct assistance, and in these instances the parties' agreement may not be forthcoming, at least not readily. The assessor system, appropriately developed, seems to present the answer. For this to happen, the courts themselves will have to be pro-active—calling for assessors or scientific advisers of their own motion (and without any agreement from the parties) whenever the level of scientific dispute (or even merely understanding) is likely to be high. For parties seldom will ask for an assessor or scientific adviser on their own—the lawyers are too worried about losing control. The court rules should expressly confer a power to appoint an assessor not only to prepare a report,[15] but also merely to assist the court in understanding the technology, in effect, acting as a teacher. Whether the appointment of such an adviser is 'Convention-compliant' perhaps remains to be tested, but given the widespread use of expert advisers to Continental courts, the procedure is likely to be so.

F. Whither the System?

CPR Part 35 has produced a code of expert evidence that, in the traditional pragmatism of the English legal system, does seek to bring—and so far has successfully brought—some order out of the chaotic and expensive system that had prevailed in the pre-1999 expert witness industry. But, as scientific and technical cases become more and more recondite and contentious, and the world is increasingly suffused in technology, the framers of procedural law need to revisit and review the system. As long ago as 1935, Rich J in the High Court of Australia in *Adhesives Pty Ltd v Aktieselskabet Dansk Gaerings-Industri*[16] expressed the view that:

> It is becoming more and more apparent that the courts as now constituted can barely reach such just conclusions when new and complicated scientific facts must be interpreted. Judges, once they have scientific data recorded by experts in the course of the trial *and have them interpreted for them*, will they make the correct decision? The parties will call their experts. The court will look to its advisor for an unbiased, knowingly competent expert, whose advice should not need to be given confidentially or in an intimate capacity. (emphasis supplied)

14.13

---

[15] As the rules now do.   [16] (1935) 55 CLR 523, 580.

14.14 There are times—especially in the world of high technology with society's growing appetite for dispute resolution in the courts—when the ability of judges to understand the true import of expert evidence and reach an informed and well-reasoned judgment will be taxed to the utmost, and even beyond judicial endeavour. There is an anomaly in this situation. If a high-speed train crashes, or a nuclear power station blows up, with a serious loss of life, or if a major scandal erupts in governmental administration or in the financial world, there is likely to be a public inquiry. (The provisions in the Inquiries Act 2005 envisage less reliance on a member of the judiciary to chair public inquiries involving sensitive political issues.) If a judge is appointed to investigate the matter, he would either have experts sitting with him on the panel of inquiry, or he will inform himself by calling expert witnesses of his choosing. Yet where precisely the same issues arise in the course of litigation, the judge would be expected to cope with the problems as best he can on the expert evidence called by the parties in an adversarial, and not an inquisitorial process. (In complex expert issues, that cannot sensibly be provided by a single joint expert.) Why cannot the court use the assessor system under CPR r 35.15? The parties will continue to call their experts, but at least the existence of an assessor sitting alongside the judge will provide assurance that the expertise will be translated forensically.

14.15 Whatever reforms (if any) transpire, the expert must no longer be an outsider or a freak, even if he is brought out of the cold into the hothouse of the courtroom, where his expertise is not misunderstood or misapplied. He must not be treated as a stranger to the process of legal administration. Science and law must find a common language and understanding. Auld LJ, in his impressive Review into the working of the criminal courts of England and Wales, wrote:

> If we expect experts to raise their act in the manner of presentation of their evidence, the least we [the legal profession] can do is complement and assist their task by ensuring a basic level of understanding of what they are talking about.[17]

---

[17] *Review of the Criminal Courts of England and Wales* (September 2001) 582, para 151. Available at <http://www.criminal-courts-review.org.uk>.

APPENDIX 1

CPR Part 35: Experts and Assessors

Contents of this Part

35.1 Duty to restrict expert evidence

Expert evidence shall be restricted to that which is reasonably required to resolve the proceedings.

35.2 Interpretation

A reference to an 'expert' in this Part is a reference to an expert who has been instructed to give or prepare evidence for the purpose of court proceedings.

35.3 Experts—overriding duty to the court

(1) It is the duty of an expert to help the court on the matters within his expertise.
(2) This duty overrides any obligation to the person from whom he has received instructions or by whom he is paid.

35.4 Court's power to restrict expert evidence

(1) No party may call an expert or put in evidence an expert's report without the court's permission.
(2) When a party applies for permission under this rule he must identify—
    (a) the field in which he wishes to rely on expert evidence; and
    (b) where practicable the expert in that field on whose evidence he wishes to rely.
(3) If permission is granted under this rule it shall be in relation only to the expert named or the field identified under paragraph (2).

(4) The court may limit the amount of the expert's fees and expenses that the party who wishes to rely on the expert may recover from any other party.

35.5 General requirement for expert evidence to be given in a written report

(1) Expert evidence is to be given in a written report unless the court directs otherwise.

(2) If a claim is on the fast track, the court will not direct an expert to attend a hearing unless it is necessary to do so in the interests of justice.

35.6 Written questions to experts

(1) A party may put to—
    (a) an expert instructed by another party; or
    (b) a single joint expert appointed under rule 35.7, written questions about his report.

(2) Written questions under paragraph (1)—
    (a) may be put once only;
    (b) must be put within 28 days of service of the expert's report; and
    (c) must be for the purpose only of clarification of the report, unless in any case—
        (i) the court gives permission; or
        (ii) the other party agrees.

(3) An expert's answers to questions put in accordance with paragraph (1) shall be treated as part of the expert's report.

(4) Where—
    (a) a party has put a written question to an expert instructed by another party in accordance with this rule; and
    (b) the expert does not answer that question,
    the court may make one or both of the following orders in relation to the party who instructed the expert—
        (i) that the party may not rely on the evidence of that expert; or
        (ii) that the party may not recover the fees and expenses of that expert from any other party.

35.7 Court's power to direct that evidence is to be given by a single joint expert

(1) Where two or more parties wish to submit expert evidence on a particular issue, the court may direct that the evidence on that issue is to given by one expert only.

(2) The parties wishing to submit the expert evidence are called 'the instructing parties'.

(3) Where the instructing parties cannot agree who should be the expert, the court may—
    (a) select the expert from a list prepared or identified by the instructing parties; or
    (b) direct that the expert be selected in such other manner as the court may direct.

35.8 Instructions to a single joint expert

(1) Where the court gives a direction under rule 35.7 for a single joint expert to be used, each instructing party may give instructions to the expert.

(2) When an instructing party gives instructions to the expert he must, at the same time, send a copy of the instructions to the other instructing parties.

(3) The court may give directions about—
    (a) the payment of the expert's fees and expenses; and
    (b) any inspection, examination or experiments which the expert wishes to carry out.

(4) The court may, before an expert is instructed—
    (a) limit the amount that can be paid by way of fees and expenses to the expert; and
    (b) direct that the instructing parties pay that amount into court.

(5) Unless the court otherwise directs, the instructing parties are jointly and severally liable[GL] for the payment of the expert's fees and expenses.

35.9 Power of court to direct a party to provide information

Where a party has access to information which is not reasonably available to the other party, the court may direct the party who has access to the information to—

(a) prepare and file a document recording the information; and
(b) serve a copy of that document on the other party.

35.10 Contents of report

(1) An expert's report must comply with the requirements set out in the relevant practice direction.
(2) At the end of an expert's report there must be a statement that—
(a) the expert understands his duty to the court; and
(b) he has complied with that duty.
(3) The expert's report must state the substance of all material instructions, whether written or oral, on the basis of which the report was written.
(4) The instructions referred to in paragraph (3) shall not be privileged against disclosure but the court will not, in relation to those instructions—
(a) order disclosure of any specific document; or
(b) permit any questioning in court, other than by the party who instructed the expert, unless it is satisfied that there are reasonable grounds to consider the statement of instructions given under paragraph (3) to be inaccurate or incomplete.

35.11 Use by one party of expert's report disclosed by another

Where a party has disclosed an expert's report, any party may use that expert's report as evidence at the trial.

35.12 Discussions between experts

(1) The court may, at any stage, direct a discussion between experts for the purpose of requiring the experts to—
(a) identify and discuss the expert issues in the proceedings; and
(b) where possible, reach an agreed opinion on those issues.
(2) The court may specify the issues which the experts must discuss.
(3) The court may direct that following a discussion between the experts they must prepare a statement for the court showing—
(a) those issues on which they agree; and
(b) those issues on which they disagree and a summary of their reasons for disagreeing.
(4) The content of the discussion between the experts shall not be referred to at the trial unless the parties agree.
(5) Where experts reach agreement on an issue during their discussions, the agreement shall not bind the parties unless the parties expressly agree to be bound by the agreement.

35.13 Consequence of failure to disclose expert's report

A party who fails to disclose an expert's report may not use the report at the trial or call the expert to give evidence orally unless the court gives permission.

35.14 Expert's right to ask court for directions

(1) An expert may file a written request for directions to assist him in carrying out his function as an expert.
(2) An expert must, unless the court orders otherwise, provide a copy of any proposed request for directions under paragraph (1)—
(a) to the party instructing him, at least 7 days before he files the request; and
(b) to all other parties, at least 4 days before he files it.
(3) The court, when it gives directions, may also direct that a party be served with a copy of the directions.

35.15 Assessors

(1) This rule applies where the court appoints one or more persons (an 'assessor') under section 70 of the Supreme Court Act 1981[1] or section 63 of the County Courts Act 1984.[2]

(2) The assessor shall assist the court in dealing with a matter in which the assessor has skill and experience.

(3) An assessor shall take such part in the proceedings as the court may direct and in particular the court may—

   (a) direct the assessor to prepare a report for the court on any matter at issue in the proceedings; and

   (b) direct the assessor to attend the whole or any part of the trial to advise the court on any such matter.

(4) If the assessor prepares a report for the court before the trial has begun—

   (a) the court will send a copy to each of the parties; and

   (b) the parties may use it at trial.

(5) The remuneration to be paid to the assessor for his services shall be determined by the court and shall form part of the costs of the proceedings.

(6) The court may order any party to deposit in the court office a specified sum in respect of the assessor's fees and, where it does so, the assessor will not be asked to act until the sum has been deposited.

(7) Paragraphs (5) and (6) do not apply where the remuneration of the assessor is to be paid out of money provided by Parliament.

---

[1] 1981 c.54.   [2] 1984 c.28. Section 63 was amended by SI 1998/2940.

APPENDIX 2

Part 35 Practice Direction: Experts and Assessors

This Practice Direction supplements CPR Part 35

Part 35 is intended to limit the use of oral expert evidence to that which is reasonably required. In addition, where possible, matters requiring expert evidence should be dealt with by a single expert. Permission of the court is always required either to call an expert or to put an expert's report in evidence. There is annexed to this Practice Direction a protocol for the instruction of experts to give evidence in civil claims. Experts and those instructing them are expected to have regard to the guidance contained in the protocol.

Expert evidence—general requirements

1.1 It is the duty of an expert to help the court on matters within his own expertise: rule 35.3(1). This duty is paramount and overrides any obligation to the person from whom the expert has received instructions or by whom he is paid: rule 35.3(2).

1.2 Expert evidence should be the independent product of the expert uninfluenced by the pressures of litigation.

1.3 An expert should assist the court by providing objective, unbiased opinion on matters within his expertise, and should not assume the role of an advocate.

1.4 An expert should consider all material facts, including those which might detract from his opinion.

1.5 An expert should make it clear:
   (a) when a question or issue falls outside his expertise; and
   (b) when he is not able to reach a definite opinion, for example because he has insufficient information.

1.6 If, after producing a report, an expert changes his view on any material matter, such change of view should be communicated to all the parties without delay, and when appropriate to the court.

Form and content of expert's reports

2.1 An expert's report should be addressed to the court and not to the party from whom the expert has received his instructions.

2.2 An expert's report must:
   (1) give details of the expert's qualifications;
   (2) give details of any literature or other material which the expert has relied on in making the report;
   (3) contain a statement setting out the substance of all facts and instructions given to the expert which are material to the opinions expressed in the report or upon which those opinions are based;
   (4) make clear which of the facts stated in the report are within the expert's own knowledge;
   (5) say who carried out any examination, measurement, test or experiment which the expert has used for the report, give the qualifications of that person, and say whether or not the test or experiment has been carried out under the expert's supervision;
   (6) where there is a range of opinion on the matters dealt with in the report—

      (a) summarise the range of opinion, and

      (b) give reasons for his own opinion;

   (7) contain a summary of the conclusions reached;

   (8) if the expert is not able to give his opinion without qualification, state the qualification; and

   (9) contain a statement that the expert understands his duty to the court, and has complied and will continue to comply with that duty.

2.3 An expert's report must be verified by a statement of truth as well as containing the statements required in paragraph 2.2(8) and (9) above.

2.4 The form of the statement of truth is as follows:

> I confirm that insofar as the facts stated in my report are within my own knowledge I have made clear which they are and I believe them to be true, and that the opinions I have expressed represent my true and complete professional opinion.

2.5 Attention is drawn to rule 32.14 which sets out the consequences of verifying a document containing a false statement without an honest belief in its truth.

> (For information about statements of truth see Part 22 and the practice direction which supplements it.)

Information

3   Under rule 35.9 the court may direct a party with access to information which is not reasonably available to another party to serve on that other party a document which records the information. The document served must include sufficient details of all the facts, tests, experiments and assumptions which underlie any part of the information to enable the party on whom it is served to make, or to obtain, a proper interpretation of the information and an assessment of its significance.

Instructions

4   The instructions referred to in paragraph 2.2(3) will not be protected by privilege (see rule 35.10(4)). But cross-examination of the expert on the contents of his instructions will not be allowed unless the court permits it (or unless the party who gave the instructions consents to it). Before it gives permission the court must be satisfied that there are reasonable grounds to consider that the statement in the report of the substance of the instructions is inaccurate or incomplete. If the court is so satisfied, it will allow the cross-examination where it appears to be in the interests of justice to do so.

Questions to experts

5.1 Questions asked for the purpose of clarifying the expert's report (see rule 35.6) should be put, in writing, to the expert not later than 28 days after receipt of the expert's report (see paragraphs 1.2 to 1.5 above as to verification).

5.2 Where a party sends a written question or questions direct to an expert, a copy of the questions should, at the same time, be sent to the other party or parties.

5.3 The party or parties instructing the expert must pay any fees charged by that expert for answering questions put under rule 35.6. This does not affect any decision of the court as to the party who is ultimately to bear the expert's costs.

Single expert

6   Where the court has directed that the evidence on a particular issue is to be given by one expert only (rule 35.7) but there are a number of disciplines relevant to that issue, a leading expert in the dominant discipline should be identified as the single expert. He should prepare the general part of the report and be responsible for annexing or incorporating the contents of any reports from experts in other disciplines.

Orders

6A Where an order requires an act to be done by an expert, or otherwise affects an expert, the party instructing that expert must serve a copy of the order on the expert instructed by him. In the case of a jointly instructed expert, the claimant must serve the order.

Assessors

7.1 An assessor may be appointed to assist the court under rule 35.15. Not less than 21 days before making any such appointment, the court will notify each party in writing of the name of the proposed assessor, of the matter in respect of which the assistance of the assessor will be sought and of the qualifications of the assessor to give that assistance.

7.2 Where any person has been proposed for appointment as an assessor, objection to him, either personally or in respect of his qualification, may be taken by any party.

7.3 Any such objection must be made in writing and filed with the court within 7 days of receipt of the notification referred to in paragraph 6.1 and will be taken into account by the court in deciding whether or not to make the appointment (section 63(5) of the County Courts Act 1984).

7.4 Copies of any report prepared by the assessor will be sent to each of the parties but the assessor will not give oral evidence or be open to cross-examination or questioning.

APPENDIX 3

Protocol for the Instruction of Experts to Give Evidence in Civil Claims

Table of Contents*

---

* We are grateful to the Civil Justice Council for granting permission to reproduce this Protocol. The reader's attention is also drawn to the Code of Practice for Experts, which was jointly agreed by the Expert Witness Institute and the Academy of Experts to provide guidance to their members, and which can be obtained from either of these organizations or downloaded from their websites.

18. Discussions between experts
    - Arrangements for discussions between experts
19. Attendance of experts at court

1. Introduction

Expert witnesses perform a vital role in civil litigation. It is essential that both those who instruct experts and experts themselves are given clear guidance as to what they are expected to do in civil proceedings. The purpose of this Protocol is to provide such guidance. It has been drafted by the Civil Justice Council and reflects the rules and practice directions current [in June 2005], replacing the Code of Guidance on Expert Evidence. The authors of the Protocol wish to acknowledge the valuable assistance they obtained by drawing on earlier documents produced by the Academy of Experts and the Expert Witness Institute, as well as suggestions made by the Clinical Dispute Forum. The Protocol has been approved by the Master of the Rolls.

2. Aims of Protocol

2.1 This Protocol offers guidance to experts and to those instructing them in the interpretation of and compliance with Part 35 of the Civil Procedure Rules (CPR 35) and its associated Practice Direction (PD 35) and to further the objectives of the Civil Procedure Rules in general. It is intended to assist in the interpretation of those provisions in the interests of good practice but it does not replace them. It sets out standards for the use of experts and the conduct of experts and those who instruct them. The existence of this Protocol does not remove the need for experts and those who instruct them to be familiar with CPR 35 and PD 35.

2.2 Experts and those who instruct them should also bear in mind para 1.4 of the Practice Direction on Protocols which contains the following objectives, namely to:
    (a) encourage the exchange of early and full information about the expert issues involved in a prospective legal claim;
    (b) enable the parties to avoid or reduce the scope of litigation by agreeing the whole or part of an expert issue before commencement of proceedings; and
    (c) support the efficient management of proceedings where litigation cannot be avoided.

3. Application

3.1 This Protocol applies to any steps taken for the purpose of civil proceedings by experts or those who instruct them on or after 5th September 2005.

3.2 It applies to all experts who are, or who may be, governed by CPR Part 35 and to those who instruct them. Experts are governed by Part 35 if they are or have been instructed to give or prepare evidence for the purpose of civil proceedings in a court in England and Wales (CPR 35.2).

3.3 Experts, and those instructing them, should be aware that some cases may be 'specialist proceedings' (CPR 49) where there are modifications to the Civil Procedure Rules. Proceedings may also be governed by other Protocols. Further, some courts have published their own Guides which supplement the Civil Procedure Rules for proceedings in those courts. They contain provisions affecting expert evidence. Expert witnesses and those instructing them should be familiar with them when they are relevant.

3.4 Courts may take into account any failure to comply with this Protocol when making orders in relation to costs, interest, time limits, the stay of proceedings and whether to order a party to pay a sum of money into court.

3.5 If, as a result of complying with any part of this Protocol, claims would or might be time barred under any provision in the Limitation Act 1980, or any other legislation that imposes a time limit for the bringing an action, claimants may commence proceedings without complying with this Protocol. In such circumstances, claimants who commence proceedings without complying with all, or any part, of this Protocol must apply, giving notice to all other parties, to the court for directions as to the timetable and form of procedure to be adopted, at the same time as they request the court to issue proceedings. The court may consider whether to order a stay of the whole or part of the proceedings pending compliance with this Protocol and may make orders in relation to costs.

4. Duties of experts

4.1 Experts always owe a duty to exercise reasonable skill and care to those instructing them, and to comply with any relevant professional code of ethics. However when they are instructed to give or prepare evidence for the purpose of civil proceedings in England and Wales they have an overriding duty to help the court on matters within their expertise (CPR 35.3). This duty overrides any obligation to the person instructing or paying them. Experts must not serve the exclusive interest of those who retain them.

4.2 Experts should be aware of the overriding objective that courts deal with cases justly. This includes dealing with cases proportionately, expeditiously and fairly (CPR 1.1). Experts are under an obligation to assist the court so as to enable them to deal with cases in accordance with the overriding objective. However the overriding objective does not impose on experts any duty to act as mediators between the parties or require them to trespass on the role of the court in deciding facts.

4.3 Experts should provide opinions which are independent, regardless of the pressures of litigation. In this context, a useful test of 'independence' is that the expert would express the same opinion if given the same instructions by an opposing party. Experts should not take it upon themselves to promote the point of view of the party instructing them or engage in the role of advocates.

4.4 Experts should confine their opinions to matters which are material to the disputes between the parties and provide opinions only in relation to matters which lie within their expertise. Experts should indicate without delay where particular questions or issues fall outside their expertise.

4.5 Experts should take into account all material facts before them at the time that they give their opinion. Their reports should set out those facts and any literature or any other material on which they have relied in forming their opinions. They should indicate if an opinion is provisional, or qualified, or where they consider that further information is required or if, for any other reason, they are not satisfied that an opinion can be expressed finally and without qualification.

4.6 Experts should inform those instructing them without delay of any change in their opinions on any material matter and the reason for it.

4.7 Experts should be aware that any failure by them to comply with the Civil Procedure Rules or court orders or any excessive delay for which they are responsible may result in the parties who instructed them being penalised in costs and even, in extreme cases, being debarred from placing the experts' evidence before the court. In *Phillips v Symes*[1] Peter Smith J held that courts may also make orders for costs (under section 51 of the Supreme Court Act 1981)

---

[1] *Phillips v Symes* [2004] EWHC 2330, ChD.

directly against expert witnesses who by their evidence cause significant expense to be incurred, and do so in flagrant and reckless disregard of their duties to the Court.

5. Conduct of experts instructed only to advise

5.1 Part 35 only applies where experts are instructed to give opinions which are relied on for the purposes of court proceedings. Advice which the parties do not intend to adduce in litigation is likely to be confidential; the Protocol does not apply in these circumstances.[2]

5.2 The same applies where, after the commencement of proceedings, experts are instructed only to advise (e.g. to comment upon a single joint expert's report) and not to give or prepare evidence for use in the proceedings.

5.3 However this Protocol does apply if experts who were formerly instructed only to advise are later instructed to give or prepare evidence for the purpose of civil proceedings.

6. The need for experts

6.1 Those intending to instruct experts to give or prepare evidence for the purpose of civil proceedings should consider whether expert evidence is appropriate, taking account of the principles set out in CPR Parts 1 and 35, and in particular whether:
   (a) it is relevant to a matter which is in dispute between the parties.
   (b) it is reasonably required to resolve the proceedings (CPR 35.1);
   (c) the expert has expertise relevant to the issue on which an opinion is sought;
   (d) the expert has the experience, expertise and training appropriate to the value, complexity and importance of the case; and whether
   (e) these objects can be achieved by the appointment of a single joint expert (see section 17 below).

6.2 Although the court's permission is not generally required to instruct an expert, the court's permission is required before experts can be called to give evidence or their evidence can be put in (CPR 35.4).

7. The appointment of experts

7.1 Before experts are formally instructed or the court's permission to appoint named experts is sought, the following should be established:
   (a) that they have the appropriate expertise and experience;
   (b) that they are familiar with the general duties of an expert;
   (c) that they can produce a report, deal with questions and have discussions with other experts within a reasonable time and at a cost proportionate to the matters in issue;
   (d) a description of the work required;
   (e) whether they are available to attend the trial, if attendance is required; and
   (f) there is no potential conflict of interest.

7.2 Terms of appointment should be agreed at the outset and should normally include:
   (a) the capacity in which the expert is to be appointed (e.g. party appointed expert, single joint expert or expert advisor);
   (b) the services required of the expert (e.g. provision of expert's report, answering questions in writing, attendance at meetings and attendance at court);
   (c) time for delivery of the report;
   (d) the basis of the expert's charges (either daily or hourly rates and an estimate of the time likely to be required, or a total fee for the services);
   (e) travelling expenses and disbursements;
   (f) cancellation charges;

---

[2] *Carlson v Townsend* [2001] 1 WLR 2415; *Jackson v Marley Davenport* [2004] 1 WLR 2926.

(g) any fees for attending court;

(h) time for making the payment; and

(i) whether fees are to be paid by a third party.

(j) if a party is publicly funded, whether or not the expert's charges will be subject to assessment by a costs officer.

7.3 As to the appointment of single joint experts, see section 17 below.

7.4 When necessary, arrangements should be made for dealing with questions to experts and discussions between experts, including any directions given by the court, and provision should be made for the cost of this work.

7.5 Experts should be informed regularly about deadlines for all matters concerning them. Those instructing experts should promptly send them copies of all court orders and directions which may affect the preparation of their reports or any other matters concerning their obligations.

Conditional and contingency fees

7.6 Payments contingent upon the nature of the expert evidence given in legal proceedings, or upon the outcome of a case, must not be offered or accepted. To do so would contravene experts' overriding duty to the court and compromise their duty of independence.

7.7 Agreement to delay payment of experts' fees until after the conclusion of cases is permissible as long as the amount of the fee does not depend on the outcome of the case.

8. Instructions

8.1 Those instructing experts should ensure that they give clear instructions, including the following:

(a) basic information, such as names, addresses, telephone numbers, dates of birth and dates of incidents;

(b) the nature and extent of the expertise which is called for;

(c) the purpose of requesting the advice or report, a description of the matter(s) to be investigated, the principal known issues and the identity of all parties;

(d) the statement(s) of case (if any), those documents which form part of standard disclosure and witness statements which are relevant to the advice or report;

(e) where proceedings have not been started, whether proceedings are being contemplated and, if so, whether the expert is asked only for advice;

(f) an outline programme, consistent with good case management and the expert's availability, for the completion and delivery of each stage of the expert's work; and

(g) where proceedings have been started, the dates of any hearings (including any Case Management Conferences and/or Pre-Trial Reviews), the name of the court, the claim number and the track to which the claim has been allocated.

8.2 Experts who do not receive clear instructions should request clarification and may indicate that they are not prepared to act unless and until such clear instructions are received.

8.3 As to the instruction of single joint experts, see section 17 below.

9. Experts' acceptance of instructions

9.1 Experts should confirm without delay whether or not they accept instructions. They should also inform those instructing them (whether on initial instruction or at any later stage) without delay if:

(a) instructions are not acceptable because, for example, they require work that falls outside their expertise, impose unrealistic deadlines, or are insufficiently clear;

(b) they consider that instructions are or have become insufficient to complete the work;

(c) they become aware that they may not be able to fulfil any of the terms of appointment;

(d) the instructions and/or work have, for any reason, placed them in conflict with their duties as an expert; or

(e) they are not satisfied that they can comply with any orders that have been made.

9.2 Experts must neither express an opinion outside the scope of their field of expertise, nor accept any instructions to do so.

10. Withdrawal

10.1 Where experts' instructions remain incompatible with their duties, whether through incompleteness, a conflict between their duty to the court and their instructions, or for any other substantial and significant reason, they may consider withdrawing from the case. However, experts should not withdraw without first discussing the position fully with those who instruct them and considering carefully whether it would be more appropriate to make a written request for directions from the court. If experts do withdraw, they must give formal written notice to those instructing them.

11. Experts' right to ask court for directions

11.1 Experts may request directions from the court to assist them in carrying out their functions as experts. Experts should normally discuss such matters with those who instruct them before making any such request. Unless the court otherwise orders, any proposed request for directions should be copied to the party instructing the expert at least seven days before filing any request to the court, and to all other parties at least four days before filing it (CPR 35.14).

11.2 Requests to the court for directions should be made by letter, containing.

(a) the title of the claim;

(b) the claim number of the case;

(c) the name of the expert;

(d) full details of why directions are sought; and

(e) copies of any relevant documentation.

12. Power of the court to direct a party to provide information

12.1 If experts consider that those instructing them have not provided information which they require, they may, after discussion with those instructing them and giving notice, write to the court to seek directions (CPR 35.14).

12.2 Experts and those who instruct them should also be aware of CPR 35.9. This provides that where one party has access to information which is not readily available to the other party, the court may direct the party who has access to the information to prepare, file and copy to the other party a document recording the information. If experts require such information which has not been disclosed, they should discuss the position with those instructing them without delay, so that a request for the information can be made, and, if not forthcoming, an application can be made to the court. Unless a document appears to be essential, experts should assess the cost and time involved in the production of a document and whether its provision would be proportionate in the context of the case.

13. Contents of experts' reports

13.1 The content and extent of experts' reports should be governed by the scope of their instructions and general obligations, the contents of CPR 35 and PD 35 and their overriding duty to the court.

13.2 In preparing reports, experts should maintain professional objectivity and impartiality at all times.

13.3 PD 35, para 2 provides that experts' reports should be addressed to the court and gives detailed directions about the form and content of such reports. All experts and those who instruct them should ensure that they are familiar with these requirements.

13.4 Model forms of Experts' Reports are available from bodies such as the Academy of Experts or the Expert Witness Institute.

13.5 Experts' reports must contain statements that they understand their duty to the court and have complied and will continue to comply with that duty (PD 35 para 2.2(9)). They must also be verified by a statement of truth. The form of the statement of truth is as follows:

> I confirm that insofar as the facts stated in my report are within my own knowledge I have made clear which they are and I believe them to be true, and that the opinions I have expressed represent my true and complete professional opinion.

This wording is mandatory and must not be modified.

Qualifications

13.6 The details of experts' qualifications to be given in reports should be commensurate with the nature and complexity of the case. It may be sufficient merely to state academic and professional qualifications. However, where highly specialised expertise is called for, experts should include the detail of particular training and/or experience that qualifies them to provide that highly specialised evidence.

Tests

13.7 Where tests of a scientific or technical nature have been carried out, experts should state:
    (a) the methodology used; and
    (b) by whom the tests were undertaken and under whose supervision, summarising their respective qualifications and experience.

Reliance on the work of others

13.8 Where experts rely in their reports on literature or other material and cite the opinions of others without having verified them, they must give details of those opinions relied on. It is likely to assist the court if the qualifications of the originator(s) are also stated.

Facts

13.9 When addressing questions of fact and opinion, experts should keep the two separate and discrete.

13.10 Experts must state those facts (whether assumed or otherwise) upon which their opinions are based. They must distinguish clearly between those facts which experts know to be true and those facts which they assume.

13.11 Where there are material facts in dispute experts should express separate opinions on each hypothesis put forward. They should not express a view in favour of one or other disputed version of the facts unless, as a result of particular expertise and experience, they consider one set of facts as being improbable or less probable, in which case they may express that view, and should give reasons for holding it.

Range of opinion

13.12 If the mandatory summary of the range of opinion is based on published sources, experts should explain those sources and, where appropriate, state the qualifications of the originator(s) of the opinions from which they differ, particularly if such opinions represent a well-established school of thought.

13.13 Where there is no available source for the range of opinion, experts may need to express opinions on what they believe to be the range which other experts would arrive at if asked.

In those circumstances, experts should make it clear that the range that they summarise is based on their own judgement and explain the basis of that judgement.

Conclusions

13.14 A summary of conclusions is mandatory. The summary should be at the end of the report after all the reasoning. There may be cases, however, where the benefit to the court is heightened by placing a short summary at the beginning of the report whilst giving the full conclusions at the end. For example, it can assist with the comprehension of the analysis and with the absorption of the detailed facts if the court is told at the outset of the direction in which the report's logic will flow in cases involving highly complex matters which fall outside the general knowledge of the court.

Basis of report: material instructions

13.15 The mandatory statement of the substance of all material instructions should not be incomplete or otherwise tend to mislead. The imperative is transparency. The term 'instructions' includes all material which solicitors place in front of experts in order to gain advice. The omission from the statement of 'off-the-record' oral instructions is not permitted. Courts may allow cross-examination about the instructions if there are reasonable grounds to consider that the statement may be inaccurate or incomplete.

14.   **After receipt of experts' reports**

14.1   Following the receipt of experts' reports, those instructing them should advise the experts as soon as reasonably practicable whether, and if so when, the report will be disclosed to other parties; and, if so disclosed, the date of actual disclosure.

14.2   If experts' reports are to be relied upon, and if experts are to give oral evidence, those instructing them should give the experts the opportunity to consider and comment upon other reports within their area of expertise and which deal with relevant issues at the earliest opportunity.

14.3   Those instructing experts should keep experts informed of the progress of cases, including amendments to statements of case relevant to experts' opinion.

14.4   If those instructing experts become aware of material changes in circumstances or that relevant information within their control was not previously provided to experts, they should without delay instruct experts to review, and if necessary, update the contents of their reports.

15.   **Amendment of reports**

15.1   It may become necessary for experts to amend their reports:
       (a) as a result of an exchange of questions and answers;
       (b) following agreements reached at meetings between experts; or
       (c) where further evidence or documentation is disclosed.

15.2   Experts should not be asked to, and should not, amend, expand or alter any parts of reports in a manner which distorts their true opinion, but may be invited to amend or expand reports to ensure accuracy, internal consistency, completeness and relevance to the issues and clarity. Although experts should generally follow the recommendations of solicitors with regard to the form of reports, they should form their own independent views as to the opinions and contents expressed in their reports and exclude any suggestions which do not accord with their views.

15.3   Where experts change their opinion following a meeting of experts, a simple signed and dated addendum or memorandum to that effect is generally sufficient. In some cases, however, the benefit to the court of having an amended report may justify the cost of making the amendment.

15.4 Where experts significantly alter their opinion, as a result of new evidence or because evidence on which they relied has become unreliable, or for any other reason, they should amend their reports to reflect that fact. Amended reports should include reasons for amendments. In such circumstances those instructing experts should inform other parties as soon as possible of any change of opinion.

15.5 When experts intend to amend their reports, they should inform those instructing them without delay and give reasons. They should provide the amended version (or an addendum or memorandum) clearly marked as such as quickly as possible.

16. **Written questions to experts**

16.1 The procedure for putting written questions to experts (CPR 35.6) is intended to facilitate the clarification of opinions and issues after experts' reports have been served. Experts have a duty to provide answers to questions properly put. Where they fail to do so, the court may impose sanctions against the party instructing the expert, and, if, there is continued non-compliance, debar a party from relying on the report. Experts should copy their answers to those instructing them.

16.2 Experts' answers to questions automatically become part of their reports. They are covered by the statement of truth and form part of the expert evidence.

16.3 Where experts believe that questions put are not properly directed to the clarification of the report, or are disproportionate, or have been asked out of time, they should discuss the questions with those instructing them and, if appropriate, those asking the questions. Attempts should be made to resolve such problems without the need for an application to the court for directions.

Written requests for directions in relation to questions

16.4 If those instructing experts do not apply to the court in respect of questions, but experts still believe that questions are improper or out of time, experts may file written requests with the court for directions to assist in carrying out their functions as experts (CPR 35.14). See section 11 above.

17. **Single joint experts**

17.1 CPR 35 and PD 35 deal extensively with the instruction and use of joint experts by the parties and the powers of the court to order their use (see CPR 35.7 and 35.8, PD 35, para 5).

17.2 The Civil Procedure Rules encourage the use of joint experts. Wherever possible a joint report should be obtained. Consideration should therefore be given by all parties to the appointment of single joint experts in all cases where a court might direct such an appointment. Single joint experts are the norm in cases allocated to the small claims track and the fast track.

17.3 Where, in the early stages of a dispute, examinations, investigations, tests, site inspections, experiments, preparation of photographs, plans or other similar preliminary expert tasks are necessary, consideration should be given to the instruction of a single joint expert, especially where such matters are not, at that stage, expected to be contentious as between the parties. The objective of such an appointment should be to agree or to narrow issues.

17.4 Experts who have previously advised a party (whether in the same case or otherwise) should only be proposed as single joint experts if other parties are given all relevant information about the previous involvement.

17.5   The appointment of a single joint expert does not prevent parties from instructing their own experts to advise (but the costs of such expert advisers may not be recoverable in the case).

Joint instructions

17.6   The parties should try to agree joint instructions to single joint experts, but, in default of agreement, each party may give instructions. In particular, all parties should try to agree what documents should be included with instructions and what assumptions single joint experts should make.

17.7   Where the parties fail to agree joint instructions, they should try to agree where the areas of disagreement lie and their instructions should make this clear. If separate instructions are given, they should be copied at the same time to the other instructing parties.

17.8   Where experts are instructed by two or more parties, the terms of appointment should, unless the court has directed otherwise, or the parties have agreed otherwise, include:

(a) a statement that all the instructing parties are jointly and severally liable to pay the experts' fees and, accordingly, that experts' invoices should be sent simultaneously to all instructing parties or their solicitors (as appropriate); and

(b) a statement as to whether any order has been made limiting the amount of experts' fees and expenses (CPR 35.8(4)(a)).

17.9   Where instructions have not been received by the expert from one or more of the instructing parties the expert should give notice (normally at least 7 days) of a deadline to all instructing parties for the receipt by the expert of such instructions. Unless the instructions are received within the deadline the expert may begin work. In the event that instructions are received after the deadline but before the signing off of the report the expert should consider whether it is practicable to comply with those instructions without adversely affecting the timetable set for delivery of the report and in such a manner as to comply with the proportionality principle. An expert who decides to issue a report without taking into account instructions received after the deadline should inform the parties who may apply to the court for directions. In either event the report must show clearly that the expert did not receive instructions within the deadline, or, as the case may be, at all.

Conduct of the single joint expert

17.10   Single joint experts should keep all instructing parties informed of any material steps that they may be taking by, for example, copying all correspondence to those instructing them.

17.11   Single joint experts are Part 35 experts and so have an overriding duty to the court. They are the parties' appointed experts and therefore owe an equal duty to all parties. They should maintain independence, impartiality and transparency at all times.

17.12   Single joint experts should not attend any meeting or conference which is not a joint one, unless all the parties have agreed in writing or the court has directed that such a meeting may be held[3] and who is to pay the experts' fees for the meeting.

17.13   Single joint experts may request directions from the court—see section 11 above.

17.14   Single joint experts should serve their reports simultaneously on all instructing parties. They should provide a single report even though they may have received instructions which contain areas of conflicting fact or allegation. If conflicting instructions lead to different opinions (for example, because the instructions require experts to make different assumptions of fact), reports may need to contain more than one set of opinions on any issue. It is for the court to determine the facts.

---

[3] *Peet v Mid Kent Area Healthcare NHS Trust* [2002] 1 WLR 210.

Cross-examination

17.15 Single joint experts do not normally give oral evidence at trial but if they do, all parties may cross-examine them. In general written questions (CPR 35.6) should be put to single joint experts before requests are made for them to attend court for the purpose of cross-examination.[4]

18.   Discussions between experts

18.1 The court has powers to direct discussions between experts for the purposes set out in the Rules (CPR 35.12). Parties may also agree that discussions take place between their experts.

18.2 Where single joint experts have been instructed but parties have, with the permission of the court, instructed their own additional Part 35 experts, there may, if the court so orders or the parties agree, be discussions between the single joint experts and the additional Part 35 experts. Such discussions should be confined to those matters within the remit of the additional Part 35 experts or as ordered by the court.

18.3 The purpose of discussions between experts should be, wherever possible, to:
   (a) identify and discuss the expert issues in the proceedings;
   (b) reach agreed opinions on those issues, and, if that is not possible, to narrow the issues in the case;
   (c) identify those issues on which they agree and disagree and summarise their reasons for disagreement on any issue; and
   (d) identify what action, if any, may be taken to resolve any of the outstanding issues between the parties.

Arrangements for discussions between experts

18.4 Arrangements for discussions between experts should be proportionate to the value of cases. In small claims and fast-track cases there should not normally be meetings between experts. Where discussion is justified in such cases, telephone discussion or an exchange of letters should, in the interests of proportionality, usually suffice. In multi-track cases, discussion may be face to face, but the practicalities or the proportionality principle may require discussions to be by telephone or video conference.

18.5 The parties, their lawyers and experts should co-operate to produce the agenda for any discussion between experts, although primary responsibility for preparation of the agenda should normally lie with the parties' solicitors.

18.6 The agenda should indicate what matters have been agreed and summarise concisely those which are in issue. It is often helpful for it to include questions to be answered by the experts. If agreement cannot be reached promptly or a party is unrepresented, the court may give directions for the drawing up of the agenda. The agenda should be circulated to experts and those instructing them to allow sufficient time for the experts to prepare for the discussion.

18.7 Those instructing experts must not instruct experts to avoid reaching agreement (or to defer doing so) on any matter within the experts' competence. Experts are not permitted to accept such instructions.

18.8 The parties' lawyers may only be present at discussions between experts if all the parties agree or the court so orders. If lawyers do attend, they should not normally intervene except to answer questions put to them by the experts or to advise about the law.[5]

---

[4] *Daniels v Walker* [2000] 1 WLR 1382.
[5] *Hubbard v Lambeth, Southwark and Lewisham HA* [2001] EWCA 1455.

18.9 The content of discussions between experts should not be referred to at trial unless the parties agree (CPR 35.12(4)). It is good practice for any such agreement to be in writing.

18.10 At the conclusion of any discussion between experts, a statement should be prepared setting out:
  (a) a list of issues that have been agreed, including, in each instance, the basis of agreement;
  (b) a list of issues that have not been agreed, including, in each instance, the basis of disagreement;
  (c) a list of any further issues that have arisen that were not included in the original agenda for discussion;
  (d) a record of further action, if any, to be taken or recommended, including as appropriate the holding of further discussions between experts.

18.11 The statement should be agreed and signed by all the parties to the discussion as soon as may be practicable.

18.12 Agreements between experts during discussions do not bind the parties unless the parties expressly agree to be bound by the agreement (CPR 35.12(5)). However, in view of the overriding objective, parties should give careful consideration before refusing to be bound by such an agreement and be able to explain their refusal should it become relevant to the issue of costs.

19. **Attendance of experts at court**

19.1 Experts instructed in cases have an obligation to attend court if called upon to do so and accordingly should ensure that those instructing them are always aware of their dates to be avoided and take all reasonable steps to be available.

19.2 Those instructing experts should:
  (a) ascertain the availability of experts before trial dates are fixed;
  (b) keep experts updated with timetables (including the dates and times experts are to attend) and the location of the court;
  (c) give consideration, where appropriate, to experts giving evidence via a video-link.
  (d) inform experts immediately if trial dates are vacated.

19.3 Experts should normally attend court without the need for the service of witness summonses, but on occasion they may be served to require attendance (CPR 34). The use of witness summonses does not affect the contractual or other obligations of the parties to pay experts' fees.

INDEX